ATLANTIC SALMON FISHING

Collection of The Sporting Gallery and Bookshop, Inc., New York

PLAYING A BIG ONE—DOWN'S GULCH

FROM A WATER COLOUR PAINTING BY OGDEN M. PLEISSNER

ATLANTIC SALMON FISHING

BY CHARLES PHAIR

FOREWORD BY RICHARD C. HUNT

ILLUSTRATED BY

OGDEN M. PLEISSNER AND ROBERT NISBET, N.A.

THE DERRYDALE PRESS

LANHAM AND NEW YORK

THE DERRYDALE PRESS

Published in the United States of America
by The Derrydale Press
4720 Boston Way, Lanham, Maryland 20706

Distributed by NATIONAL BOOK NETWORK, INC.

Original Derrydale printing 1993
First paperback printing with french folds 1999

™The paper used in this publication meets the minimum requirements of American National Standard for Information Sciences—Permanence of Paper for Printed Library Materials, ANSI/NISO Z39.48-1992.
Manufactured in the United States of America.

THIS BOOK IS DEDICATED TO THE LATE

FRANK GRAY GRISWOLD

A GREAT SPORTSMAN

AND

A GREAT FRIEND

FOREWORD

It is thirteen years since George M. L. La Branche's "The Salmon and the Dry Fly" was published, and fifteen since Edward R. Hewitt's "Secrets of the Salmon" started many an American angler along new ways of fishing for salmon. Since then, the interest in low-water salmon fishing has consistently increased from year to year, and, in addition to the dry fly, greased line fishing of small sparsely-dressed wet flies and the method of fishing hair flies known as "the Patent" have been added to the salmon fisher's older ways.

Charles Phair's "Atlantic Salmon Fishing" is, therefore, a timely book covering as it does not only the old accepted ways but the new methods as well. But the book is more than timely for it is a comprehensive book written by a fisherman of great experience over many years on many rivers. Indeed, I know of no other man who has fished as many of our eastern Canadian rivers, and of not more than one or two who have fished longer or killed more salmon.

Since fishermen are opinionated creatures and I am myself a fisherman, it is perhaps superfluous to say that with all of Mr. Phair's views, I do not agree. For me that has given the book an added interest, and next season I propose to see whether he is not right, as he probably is, and I wrong. Certainly, he has had a far greater experience in salmon fishing.

It is a happy circumstance that this book is not only written by a fine angler and fly dresser, but illustrated by another and published by a third. Ogden M. Pleissner's water colours will, I am sure, carry your memory back to your favorite salmon pool, and Eugene V. Connett III has as always made a beautiful book. Indeed, I suspect that he cannot make a book that is not beautiful.

Richard C. Hunt

September 24, 1937.

TABLE OF CONTENTS

FOREWORD ix
By Richard C. Hunt.

CHAPTER I. I
Salmon Water.

THREE COURSES OPEN TO SALMON FISHERMEN IN SECURING WATER—CLUB MEMBERSHIPS—EXPENSES—LEASING—FREE FISHING—SEASONAL CONSIDERATIONS—LOG DRIVES—PITCH OF WATER—NAMES OF POOLS—ADVISABILITY OF SECURING RELIABLE RECORDS OF RIVER'S FISHING—EFFECTS OF FRESHETS—THE IDEAL SALMON POOL—UNSUCCESSFUL LEASING—A FURTHER CONSIDERATION IN LEASING—DRY FLY WATER—ACCESSIBILITY OF FISHING AND AVAILABLE ACCOMMODATIONS—CAMP COOKS—PRIVATE WATER—EXPENSES—FACILITIES FOR PACKING AND SHIPPING FISH—ADVANCE IN PRICE OF GOOD SALMON WATER—TESTING WATER CONSIDERED FOR LEASING.

CHAPTER II. II
Selection of Guides.

REQUISITES OF A GOOD GUIDE—APPROACHING THE POOL—"DROPS"—TYING ON THE FLY—CASTING, HOOKING, PLAYING, GAFFING AND KILLING—THE STORY OF JACK MACK—JIMMY WATERS AND WAINRIGHT POOL—"A MINUTE TO A POUND" IN LANDING FISH—SULKING FISH—STORING TACKLE FOR THE NIGHT—SMOKING SALMON—THE GUIDE'S KNOWLEDGE OF A POOL IMPORTANT—INADVISABILITY OF CONSPICUOUS CLOTHING—GASPÉ BOATS AND CANOES—THE KILLICK—INDIAN GUIDES—THEIR METHODS OF FISHING—THE AUTHOR'S EARLY EXPERIENCES FISHING WITH CHIEF OF THE MELICETES—THE AUTHOR'S FATHER'S VIEWS ON CONSERVATION—JOE JEFFERSON AT THE SKIFF LAKE CLUB IN CANADA—DUTIES AND PREROGATIVES OF CAMP COOKS AND GUIDES.

CHAPTER III. 19
Tackle.

SELECTION OF A ROD—DIFFERENT RODS FOR DIFFERENT USES—FOLLOWING THE WATER DOWN, AS THE SEASON ADVANCES, WITH LIGHTER TACKLE—TIGHTENING ON A FISH RATHER THAN STRIKING—AVAILABILITY OF THOROUGHLY SEASONED BAMBOO—MASS PRODUCTION METHODS DETRIMENTAL TO QUALITY OF RODS—FAD FOR LIGHTWEIGHT TACKLE CARRIED TOO FAR—THE TOBIQUE REEL—REEL AND LINE SHOULD BALANCE ROD—LINE MUST BE OF RIGHT WEIGHT TO BRING OUT BEST ACTION OF ROD—THE QUESTION OF TAPER, AND ITS EFFECTS UPON CASTING—PROPER TEXTURE AND FINISH FOR LINES—CARE OF LINES—LEADERS—LEVEL AND TAPERED—.010 TAPER AS FINE AS CAN BE FISHED SUCCESSFULLY—CARING FOR AND TESTING LEADERS—A ROD'S FITTINGS AND FINISH—SPECIFICATIONS FOR A COMPLETE OUTFIT, AND ITS COST—A LESS COMPLETE OUTFIT ADEQUATE FOR MOST FISHING—TACKLE FOR GRILSE—ELEVATION OF THE ROD WHILE PLAYING A FISH.

TABLE OF CONTENTS

CHAPTER IV. 29

Flies and Their Uses.

ABOUT THREE HUNDRED AND EIGHTY PATTERNS IN USE IN IRELAND, SCOTLAND, ENGLAND AND CANADA—PROBABLY LESS THAN FIFTY USED ON CANADIAN RIVERS—A LIST OF TWENTY-THREE MOST COMMONLY USED IN CANADA—HISTORY OF THE JOCK SCOTT—FAVORITE FLIES—CHANGING STYLES IN FLIES—THE NIGHT HAWK—PATTERNS WHICH ARE KILLING ON ONE RIVER NOT ALWAYS SUCCESSFUL ON OTHERS—FLIES FOR SPRING FISHING—DOUBLE AND SINGLE HOOKS—PROPER PRESENTATION OF FLY IMPORTANT—"TROUT-FISHING" A SALMON POOL—NUMBER OF RODS ON A RIVER AFFECTS RANGE OF PATTERNS—SALMON OFTEN PARTICULAR ABOUT PATTERN—PATTERNS FOR ALL CONDITIONS OF WATER AND LIGHT—KELSON'S FLIES—FLIES FOR EVENING FISHING—THE GRISWOLD GRAY—THE AUTHOR'S APPROACH TO NEW IDEAS—THE PINK LADY—ADVANTAGES OF EYED HOOKS—ADVANTAGES OF GUT LOOPS—SLIM-BODIED, LIGHTLY-DRESSED FLIES—THE AUTHOR'S EXPERIMENTS WITH NEW PATTERNS—THE BONBRIGHT DRY FLY—NOTHING NEW IN SALMON FISHING EXCEPT THE DRY FLY—NYMPH FISHING—THE AUTHOR'S FAVORITE PATTERNS AND SIZES—PATTERNS INDICATED FOR SPECIAL USES—WHY A FLY IS SUCCESSFUL—OCCASIONS WHEN SALMON SHOW A DECIDED PREFERENCE FOR ONE PATTERN—THE BUMBLE BEE—DIFFERENT FLIES FOR DIFFERENT RIVERS—FIGURE-EIGHT, BLOOD, TURLE AND CAIRNTON KNOTS—WHY A SALMON TAKES A FLY—SALMON DO NOT FEED IN FRESH WATER—CONDITIONS UPON WHICH SIZE AND PATTERN DEPEND—KELSON'S "THE SALMON FLY" AND "TIPS"—HIS SALMON FLIES—DEVELOPMENT OF THE AUTHOR'S FLIES—LOW-WATER FLIES—ALL-HACKLE DRY FLIES—TROUT PATTERNS GENERALLY UNSUCCESSFUL—HAIR FLIES—"THE PATENT."

CHAPTER V. 47

Casting.

REMARKS ON LEARNING TO CAST A FLY—DIFFICULTIES EXAGGERATED—THE ROD DOES THE CASTING—MUST BE HELD FIRMLY—THE OVERHEAD CAST—DEVELOPING ACCURACY—TENDENCY TO OVERLOOK FUNDAMENTALS—MENDING THE CAST—GETTING THE "FEEL" OF THE ROD—DIFFERENCES IN IDENTICAL RODS PALPABLE ONLY IN CASTING LONG LINE—ROD MUST BE FIRMLY HELD, AND BACK CAST HIGH—IMPORTANCE OF FUNDAMENTALS—DISADVANTAGES OF LEARNING ON GRASS—SHOOTING THE COILS—DIFFERENT CASTS INDICATED FOR DIFFERENT USES—THE SWITCH CAST—THE LOOP CAST—THE SPEY CAST—THE WYE CAST—THE GALWAY CAST—THE STORY OF AN ERSTWHILE CHAMPION CASTER—CASTING FOR MOOSE WITH SALMON TACKLE.

CHAPTER VI. 55

Fishing the Wet Fly.

FISHING FROM GASPÉ BOATS AND CANOES—GASPÉ BOATS ON HEAVY WATER—EQUIPMENT, AND METHOD OF FISHING FROM THEM—CANOES—APPROACHING THE POOL—DROPPING THE KILLICK—CASTING—"DROPPING"—PUTTING THE

FLY WITHIN SIGHT OF ALL SPOTS WHERE FISH MIGHT BE LYING—POSSIBLE EXCEPTIONS—WAITING FOR SLEEPY FISH TO FEED—ADVISABILITY OF RESTING POOLS—CHANGING FLIES AND FISHING POOL AGAIN—"SORE SPOTS"—PRESENTING AND MANIPULATING THE FLY—TIMES OF DAY INDICATED FOR FISHING—A DECENT BAG LIMIT—ADVERSE WEATHER CONDITIONS—AT WHAT POINT IS THE FLY MOST ATTRACTIVE?—SIZE AND PRESENTATION MORE IMPORTANT THAN PATTERN—SPEED OF FLY IMPORTANT—HOW SALMON RISE TO FLIES—"FISH SENSE"—WILL NOT TAKE FLY HE DOES NOT WANT—KELSON'S "EXAGGERATION AND MODIFICATION" METHOD—HOWARD FINNEMORE ON LAZY FISH—FISHING FROM THE SHORE, AND WADING—TOWING—RESTING A POOL IN LOW WATER—METHODS OF PRESENTATION—DRY FLY CAST TO DROP LIGHTLY—WET FLY NOT NECESSARILY HANDLED SO DELICATELY—DISTANCE AT WHICH FISH CAN SEE FLY—LARGE FLIES FOR HIGH, MUDDY WATER—FIVE-INCH IRONS—BEGINNER—TENDENCY TO FISH IN STEREOTYPED FASHION—OBSERVATION, EXPERIMENT AND IMPROVEMENT OF CASTING—ENCOURAGEMENT FROM GUIDES—SALMON ABOVE HEAVY RAPIDS—MANZER HOWARD—FISHING WITH BETTER FISHERMEN THAN ONE'S SELF—FRED SHAW AND REGINALD HUGHES—VALUE OF KNOWLEDGE OF THE DIFFERENT WAYS TO PRESENT THE FLY—ACROSS AND DOWN—THE ARTHUR WOOD METHOD—CASTING ACROSS AND DRAWING THE FLY—UNORTHODOX DRY FLY PRACTICE—EFFECT ON SALMON OF CONCUSSION ON THE WATER—KEEPING QUIET IN BOAT—LEAPING SALMON—CHARACTER OF JUMP ALTERS AS SEASON PROGRESSES—EYES OF LEAPING SALMON—THE LATE THOMAS ALLEN—EFFECT PRODUCED ON SURFACE BY SALMON RISING TO THE FLY—BEST METHOD OF HOOKING FISH—EFFECT OF HOOKED SALMON ON OTHERS IN POOL—RUBBING OUT BROKEN HOOKS—TRYING FLY ON SHORT LEADER—SALMON CANNOT BE HELD ON SHORT LINE WHEN FIRST HOOKED—FOUL-HOOKED FISH—CLAUDE KNAPP'S AND HOWARD FINNEMORE'S EXHIBITIONS OF PLAYING SALMON.

CHAPTER VII. 79
Fishing the Dry Fly.

THE GENESIS OF DRY FLY FISHING FOR SALMON—COL. AMBROSE MONELL AND GEORGE LA BRANCHE—EDWARD R. HEWITT'S "SECRETS OF THE SALMON"—TWO-HAND ROD PREFERABLE—DISADVANTAGES OF SINGLE-HAND ROD—SCARCITY OF SUITABLE DRY FLY WATER—FROM CANOE OR GASPÉ BOAT—THE CURVE CAST TO THE LEFT—THE CURVE TO THE RIGHT—SHOOTING THE COILS—FIGHTING FISH HARD—DIFFICULTIES OF CASTING FROM BOAT—CASTING A LOOSE LINE TO SIDE—ROD, LINES, REEL AND LEADERS—FURTHER DISCUSSION OF THE CURVE CASTS—THE CURVE TO THE LEFT DESCRIBED—THE CURVE TO THE RIGHT—AN EXPENSIVE EXPERIENCE WITH THE RIGHT-HAND CURVE—ALTERNATE METHOD OF CASTING—APPEARANCE OF WATER CAN BE VERY DECEIVING—WITH A SINGLE-HAND ROD IMPOSSIBLE TO CAST A LARGE HACKLE FLY IN A CURVE AGAINST THE WIND—VARYING CONDITIONS IN PRACTICE CASTING AND FISHING A POOL—DRY FLY AND WET FLY TECHNIQUE DIFFER—KNOWLEDGE OF CURRENTS AND ABILITY TO JUDGE WATER HELPFUL—CRUISING FISH—IMPORTANCE OF CURRENTS—INSECTS.

TABLE OF CONTENTS

CHAPTER VIII. 87

Greased Line Fishing.

INVENTED ABOUT THIRTY YEARS AGO BY ARTHUR WOOD OF SCOTLAND—BASED ON SOUND PREMISE—FISH WANT FLY EITHER AT OR NEAR SURFACE, OR NEAR BOTTOM—WOOD'S FLIES THEREFORE DRESSED IN TWO DIFFERENT FASHIONS—WITH LA BRANCHE'S DEVELOPMENT OF THE DRY FLY, ONE OF THE GREAT ADVANCES RECENTLY MADE IN SALMON FISHING—GREASING THE LINE—CASTING—WOOD'S THEORY OF THE FISH'S VIEW OF THE FLY—CHANGING DIRECTION AND SPEED OF FLY—HOOKING—PULL OF CURRENT ON SLACK LINE SENDS HOOK HOME—EXPERIMENTING WITH THE GREASED LINE IN VARYING CURRENTS—EARLY-SEASON FISHING WITH SMALL FLIES AND GREASED LINE—FLIES—BLUE CHARM AND SILVER BLUE—FURTHER DISCUSSION OF CASTING—RODS FOR GREASED LINE FISHING—WOOD'S RODS—LOW-WATER FISHING UNPRODUCTIVE BEFORE INCEPTION OF GREASED LINE—AN EARLY INSTANCE OF SUCCESSFUL GREASED LINE FISHING—LOOPING BELLY OF LINE OVER TO COUNTERACT CURRENT—AS SEASON ADVANCES SPEED AT WHICH FLY IS FISHED SHOULD BE INCREASED.

CHAPTER IX. 93

Weather.

TOTALLY DIFFERENT WEATHER CONDITIONS ON EACH OF THREE BEST DAY'S FISHING IN AUTHOR'S EXPERIENCE—FISHING GENERALLY BAD WHEN THERE IS FOG OR MIST ON THE WATER—THUNDER AND LIGHTNING ALSO CAUSE POOR FISHING—REMARKS ON FISHING CALENDARS AND BAROMETERS—TEMPERATURE—EFFECTS OF WATER TEMPERATURE ON POSITION OF FISH—BEST FISHING WEATHER.

CHAPTER X. 97

A Month's Salmon Fishing Trip.

A BEGINNER'S TRIP—SECURING FISHING—EXPENSES—OUTFITTING—ARRIVAL ON RIVER AND PREPARATIONS FOR FISHING—HIGH-WATER WET FLY FISHING—LEARNING TO CAST—DROPPING—THE FIRST SALMON—HOOKING, PLAYING AND GAFFING—LOWER WATER—STRIKING RATHER THAN TIGHTENING—JUMPING FISH—SULKING FISH—LANDING—CLEAR WATER AND SMALLER FLY—SHORT LINE—FISH AT TAIL OF POOL—GOOD WEATHER AND A RUN OF FISH—STORING AND PACKING FISH—FISHING NEIGHBORS' POOLS—COLD WEATHER AND POOR FISHING EARLY IN THE DAY—FOLLOWING WATER DOWN WITH LIGHTER TACKLE—CASTING FROM STANDING POSITION—CONSIDERATIONS OF WEATHER—SMALLER FLIES FOR FISH SWIRLING UNDER FLY—OLD WORN-OUT FLIES—PLAYING FISH ON A SINGLE-HAND ROD—HOOKS—GAFFING FISH BY FIRELIGHT—A "JIGGING" SALMON—GREASED LINE FISHING—TAILING SALMON—CASTING—DRY FLY FISHING—LONGER, FINER LEADERS—ALL-HACKLE DRY FLIES—CURRENTS AND CASTING—SIZE, NOT PATTERN, IMPORTANT FACTOR—GRILSE FISHING—A FRESH RUN OF SALMON—SCORE FOR FIVE WEEKS' FISHING—ARRANGEMENTS FOR FOLLOWING SEASON.

TABLE OF CONTENTS

CHAPTER XI. 123

Life History.

SALMON RETURN TO RIVER WHERE THEY WERE SPAWNED—EXCEPTIONS INSIGNIFICANT—RETURN FOR SPAWNING—OCEAN FEEDING—MIGRATIONS—OBSTACLES TO SAFE RETURN TO SPAWNING GROUNDS—BEHAVIOR OF SPAWNING FISH—THE SPAWNING PROCESS—KELT—MAXIMUM RETURN FROM SPAWNING—PERCENTAGE OF RETURN TO RIVER—INCUBATION PERIOD—ALEVIN, PARR AND SMOLT STAGES—RIVER LIFE AS INDICATED BY SCALES—SPEED AT WHICH SALMON TRAVEL—FACTORS UPON WHICH SPEED IS DEPENDENT—EARLY FISH DO NOT LINGER IN POOLS—AS WATER DROPS, TRAVEL SLOW AND REST IN POOLS—PARR—GRILSE—EXPERIMENT OF TAGGING PARR—EGGS FROM GRILSE ARTIFICIALLY FERTILIZED—FISHING FOR KELT UNSPORTSMANLIKE—FALLACY OF "WELL-MENDED" FISH—FISH RETURNING TO OTHER RIVERS THAN THEIR OWN—FISH ADAPTED TO THEIR OWN RIVERS—LATE-RUN FISH LOATH TO TRAVEL HEAVY WATER—PREDATORY ENEMIES—TABLE OF LOSSES AT VARIOUS STAGES—HATCHERIES AND ARTIFICIAL HATCHING—NATURAL SPAWNING ESSENTIAL—HATCHERY FISH SUFFER GREAT LOSSES AT SEA IN SMOLT STAGE—FURTHER DISCUSSION OF KELT—THEIR VALUE—FISHING FOR THEM QUESTIONABLE PRACTICE—PERCENTAGE OF RETURN OF KELT—OPINION OF J. ARTHUR HUTTON—TABLE OF DIFFERENT STAGES OF SALMON'S LIFE—SPRING FISH—SUMMER FISH—VALUE OF ARTIFICIAL HATCHING QUESTIONABLE—LIFE HISTORY OF SALMON WRITTEN ON ITS SCALES—EQUIPMENT FOR SCALE READING—METHOD OF READING—RIVER LIFE, OCEAN FEEDING, SPAWNING AND AGE INDICATED BY SCALES.

CHAPTER XII. 137

Improving, Protecting and Stocking Salmon Rivers; together with Etiquette and Customs.

HISTORY OF THE RESTIGOUCHE—EARLY COMMERCIAL FISHING—ABOUT 1864 BECAME KNOWN THAT RESTIGOUCHE FISH WOULD TAKE FLY—FISHERIES ACT OF 1869—LEASING OF RIVERS IN 1871—PISCICULTURE STARTED IN 1873—CONTINUED COMMERCIAL FISHING—ARTIFICIAL PROPAGATION—IMPROVEMENT IN SALMON FISHERIES—1886 PRICE OF HOLDINGS OF NETTERS IN RESTIGOUCHE ESTUARY—RENTAL PRICES OF SALMON WATER—RESTIGOUCHE SALMON CLUB INCORPORATED 1880—COST OF PROTECTION OF SALMON RIVERS—RESTIGOUCHE RIPARIAN ASSOCIATION FORMED 1911—FIFTY PER CENT MORE FISH IN RIVER TODAY THAN IN 1897—PROPERTY INVESTMENT AND EXPENSES OF RESTIGOUCHE CLUB—IMPROVING—VERY LITTLE DONE IN CANADA AS COMPARED TO ENGLAND—BLOWING AWAY ROCK TO FLATTEN CURRENT—PLACING ROCKS IN RIVER GENERALLY UNSUCCESSFUL—EXPERIMENT ONLY UPON UNPRODUCTIVE WATER—PROTECTION—POLLUTION—PREDATORS—FISHWAYS—WARDENING SERVICE—POACHING—AN INSTANCE OF GOOD WARDENING—COURTESY TO NATIVES—CARE OF BANKS OF POOLS—STOCKING—EXPENSE—METHODS OF HATCHING AND DISTRIBUTION—ETIQUETTE AND CUSTOMS—CLUB CUSTOMS—CUSTOMS AMONG GUIDES AND CAMP COOKS—MAIL BOAT SERVICE—TIPPING—IMPOSITIONS UPON GUIDES.

TABLE OF CONTENTS

CHAPTER XIII. 149

Salmon Fly Dressing.

CASE TO HOLD MATERIALS—DRESSING FLIES ON THE RIVER—PURCHASING MATERIALS—BRITISH METHODS OF FLY DRESSING—REQUISITE TOOLS AND MATERIALS—COLLECTION OF MATERIALS—LEARNING TO DRESS FLIES—KELSON'S AND PRYCE-TANNATT'S BOOKS—CROSSFIELD'S FLIES—TYING THE FLY—THE TAG—THE TAIL—THE BUTT—BODIES—FUR—HACKLE PALMER-TIED—FLOSS SILK—RIBBING—SILVER BODIES—JOINTED BODIES—DYED GUT—BODY AND THROAT HACKLES—WINGS—WHOLE-FEATHER WINGS—STRIP WINGS—BUILT WINGS—MIXED WINGS—TRANSFERRING WINGS—DRESSING OF SUCCESSFUL LOW-WATER FLY—FEATHERS FOR WINGING SALMON FLIES—ASSEMBLING MATERIALS AND A FISHING LIBRARY—HISTORY OF SALMON FLIES—ALL-HACKLE DRY FLIES—CORRECT DRESSINGS OF FAVORITE FLIES.

CHAPTER XIV. 175

The Atlantic Salmon Rivers of America.

THE SALMON RIVERS OF QUEBEC—THE SALMON RIVERS OF NEW BRUNSWICK—THE SALMON RIVERS OF NOVA SCOTIA—THE SALMON RIVERS OF NEWFOUNDLAND—THE SALMON RIVERS OF LABRADOR—THE SALMON RIVERS OF THE STATE OF MAINE—THE SALMON RIVERS OF ANTICOSTI ISLAND.

LIST OF ILLUSTRATIONS

Playing a Big One—Down's Gulch . . . . *Frontispiece*
Colour plate. From a water colour painting by Ogden M. Pleissner.

Facing page

At Soldier's Gulch 1
Colour plate. From a water colour painting by Ogden M. Pleissner.

Looking Up River on the Restigouche 7

John Phipp's Rock Pool on the Grand Cascapedia 7

Point of Rocks on the Natashquan 8

Third Falls on the Natashquan 8

Canadian Salmon Guides 11

Coming to Gaff 15
From a water colour painting by Ogden M. Pleissner.

June—Devil's Half Acre 19
Colour plate. From a water colour painting by Ogden M. Pleissner.

Playing a Salmon 26

The Author on the Restigouche 29
From an etching by Robert Nisbet, N.A.

Flat Rock Pool on the Nipisiguit 31

The Author Fishing on the Tobique 31

Poling a Gaspé Boat Through Fast Water 31

View of Joseph P. Knapp's Lodge 34

One of Mr. Colgate's Pools 40

Another of Mr. Colgate's Pools 40

Forks Pool on the Tobique 40

Home Pool on the Tobique 40

LIST OF ILLUSTRATIONS

Facing page

Rugged Water on the Natashquan 41

Forks Pool—Tobique 47

Colour plate. From a water colour painting by Ogden M. Pleissner.

Little Chute on the Natashquan 51

The Author Fishing the "Million Dollar Pool" 52

From an etching by Robert Nisbet, N.A.

Fishing from a Gaspé Boat 55

Playing a St. John River Fish 55

Percy Faulding Negotiating Indian Falls 59

James C. Colgate 60

William B. Mershon 60

George D. B. Bonbright 60

Joseph P. Knapp 60

Poling Upstream on the Kedgwick 65

Towing Up River to Camp 65

Noonday Landing 65

Salmon Acrobatics 73

Twenty-Pound Restigouche Salmon 74

Col. Ambrose Monell and George La Branche 79

Arthur Wood's Lodge at Cairnton 87

George La Branche and Arthur Wood 87

New Brunswick Salmon 93

Colour plate. From a water colour painting by Ogden M. Pleissner.

LIST OF ILLUSTRATIONS

Facing page

THE RISE 97
From a painting by Walter M. Brackett.

JOSEPH P. KNAPP'S GUEST LODGE 103

VIEW FROM GUEST LODGE 103

CAMEL'S RUN ON THE RESTIGOUCHE 109

BARN POOL ON THE KEDGWICK 109

JUNCTION POOL 109

SLOW RISE 115

GOING FROM THE BOAT 115

DONE! 115

FINALE 115

NATASHQUAN SALMON 123

FIFTY-FOUR-POUND SALMON 127

SALMON SCALES 135

LEAPING SALMON 137
Colour plate. From a water colour painting by Ogden M. Pleissner.

CASCAPEDIA CLUB LODGES 141

SAGE LODGE 141

LODGE AT TOM'S BROOK 141

JAMES C. COLGATE'S LODGE 141

TOM'S BROOK POOL 144

STEPS FOR SALMON 144

LEAPING SALMON: ICELAND AND 4TH FALLS, NATASHQUAN RIVER . . 145

LIST OF ILLUSTRATIONS

Facing page

The Author's Fly Tying Kit 149

Fly Dressing: Figures 1–8 156

Fly Dressing: Figures 9–16 157

Fly Dressing: Figures 17–22 160

Fly Dressing: Figures 23–28 161

Fly Dressing: Figures 29–34 168

Fly Dressing: Figures 35–40 169

Map: The Atlantic Salmon Rivers of America 175

Map: Anticosti Island 181

ATLANTIC SALMON FISHING

Collection of A. M. Barnes, Esq.

AT SOLDIER'S GULCH

FROM A WATER COLOUR PAINTING BY OGDEN M. PLEISSNER

CHAPTER I.

SALMON WATER

THERE are three courses open to the man who wants to fish salmon. Join a club, rent a stretch of private water, or look up some river where free fishing is allowed.

Americans control most of the best pools on all the salmon rivers in Canada, and there is still other good private fishing to be had. In the first instance, in the case of a club membership, it is a question of deciding first on what river you are desirous of fishing, finding out from the club's secretary if there is a share of stock for sale, and then discovering whether they will consider you as a prospective member. Often one member of a club will hold two shares, one of which he will sell, though only to a person whom the club votes acceptable. He cannot sell simply to anyone he chooses, or at his own price. The club sets the value of the share of stock. Memberships in some of the best clubs are expensive. In one, such as I have in mind, a share is worth $10,000. In addition there are annual dues and assessments, the latter in some years being high, depending on improvements made, such as buying up nets in the tidal waters, building new lodges, purchasing boats and canoes, and the general upkeep of the club property. These yearly expenses, together with the cost of the actual fishing trip, make each fish killed cost a great deal of money. This club in particular is a very old and exclusive one, and has beautiful fishing. From that we graduate down to the small clubs, where a share of stock is worth from $1,000 to $2,500, and where you are more likely to find one available. Available for one of two reasons: a member has sold his share, and has gone to some other river where he can have better fishing, or has given up salmon fishing for some reason of his own. His share is then sold to whom the club sees fit.

The annual dues vary at the different clubs, depending, among other things, on the sort of protection given the river, and the manner in which the club property is kept up. Good warden service, together with restocking, helps insure good fishing.

In renting private fishings, if one is not familiar with the water, reliable information is the first thing to be acquired.

When the pools on salmon rivers were first leased by clubs and individuals, the natives who owned the land on the rivers and had riparian rights, whether they had salmon water or not, claimed that they had and offered it for sale. This was perhaps only natural, after seeing their neighbors just above and below lease or sell their water for good prices. So, in the grand rush which followed a few years later, a great deal of worthless water was purchased or leased. But in some instances, there were settlers who saw what was coming, held on to their water and either sold later for a good figure, or still hold it and lease by the week, month or the entire season. Such fishings as these are easy to get information about, as they have reputations, and are familiar to all old salmon fishermen. I shall later cite some instances of bad leasing on my own part.

For the angler who cannot afford to become a member of a club or to lease private water, there are certain free fishings in Nova Scotia, Newfoundland and Labrador, of which certain of the Newfoundland water is the best. The only expense attached to fishing this water is your transportation, guide and board, a matter of from $6 to $8 a day.

Personally, I am not in favor of free salmon fishing. It generally is poor, for such rivers are overfished; and to give the best results salmon water must be fished with some discretion. Furthermore, such streams are soon depleted, since they do not get as good protection from the Government as they would from private individuals. The Miramichi in New Brunswick and the Margaree in Nova Scotia are examples.

If one intends going to the river early in June for his fishing, it is well nowadays to inquire about the log drive, which often plugs the river for a week at a time. Mr. George Dunn, the largest timberland owner in Maine, was fishing with me once on Nipisiguit when this happened, and for three days we spent our time watching the logs going over Pabineau Falls. Uncle George, as he was called by everyone, was reputed to know every spruce on all his different townships of land, for, as he was a great lover of the woods, he spent most of his time there. The Boss of the drive was standing with us one day when Uncle George, who had a habit of gritting his teeth and being quite profane at times, exclaimed, "There's a damn good spruce going over." To which the Boss replied, "That's not a spruce, Mr. Dunn, that's a princess pine." "It may be a princess pine," said Uncle George, gritting his teeth, "but, by God, it's got spruce bark on it."

The kind of water one leased would depend on the time during the season it was to be fished. If it were to be fished in the spring, when the water in the river was a good pitch, he would want a pool that fished well in high water; if in July or later, it would have to be one that fished best in low water. There are pools that fish well the season through, but there aren't many. All pools, however, fish best at a certain height of water, and there is always some mark on the shore, or a rock in the river, to which guides refer in judging the water.

All pools are named. If there is a barn near-by, it's called the Barn Pool; a large rock in it, the Rock Pool; if it's eight miles up river from somewhere, it's Eight Mile; and so on. But let a man upset the boat and fall in it, and it's Jimmie's or Bill's Hole, as the case may be.

What is known in the salmon world as "riverside information" is not always dependable, and in leasing it is well to get the records of the last three or four years' catches from the owner, and then check up with the men who fished the water during those years. Some pools, especially those with gravel bottom and small rocks, are washed out and ruined when the first good spring freshet comes down, and what might have been a good pool last season is worthless this year. The ideal pool is one that has what is called a salmon ledge along its side, for at least a part of it, and a bottom of rocks and gravel of good size, which will stand ice jams and log jams without washing down river. Each year one finds certain pools changed, and the fish not in the same spots they occupied the year before. This is because the bottom has been disturbed. Salmon have certain places they like to stop in—one of their favorites is a rock just large enough for them to get behind, so that the water runs over their backs. There also seems to be some fascination about flat rocks where there is little current, as fish are often seen lying on the same rock every season. As a rule they like the tail of a pool in high water, and the head of it in low. In high water the current is not so strong at the tail of the pool and it is easier for salmon to rest there. In low water they need oxygen, which they can get at the head of a pool, where the water is broken and full of ripples.

I have gone over certain pools in extremely low water, to find out why some spots so appeal to fish, and have generally found some rock such as I have described. On the Restigouche there is a flat rock opposite Tom's Brook on the island side, where the water is very quiet with very little current. You can get near a fish there and see him plainly. Numerous times I have seen one lying right on it, not simply above it, but with his belly touching it. I showed one of these fish to Jack Wyers one day, and he said there had been fish on that rock for the last thirty years, that he knew of, but that he never could take one. I fished there for three years, and never raised one.

The ideal pool should also have a cold spring brook coming in at the head; in hot weather when the temperature of the water gets high, the fish will lie along the shore in the cooler water for a considerable distance. In these circumstances the fish are lively and take the fly well. There is such a pool at Hartland, New Brunswick, and some good catches are made there, when fish are not taking anywhere else in the river.

A salmon river seems different to me from other rivers. The water is clearer, and the smallest objects can be seen on the bottom at great depths. The current is heavier and has more push. In places one has to be careful in wading even up around the ankles, or he gets swept off his feet. The river runs through hills and mountains covered with woods which look as though they had never seen an axe: there is something grand and magnificent about the whole thing.

Using my own judgment in leasing salmon water, after getting what I considered plenty of information, has not always been entirely successful. There is a certain very famous river in Canada. Books had been written about it, and accounts given of the big catches made there. Many Englishmen had come over and fished it with marked success. Having read all these accounts, I had a great desire to fish it, and being hit by the fishing fever early one year, I started in February to see what could be done about it. A letter in my possession, addressed to the American Consul, brought about an introduction to a gentleman who had three miles of water, which I leased. I liked the man and liked his story. On my way home I stopped off in Campbellton, to see my friends Max Mowat, Guardian of the Restigouche, and his brother, Alex, who was then head of the Fishery Department. Jack Wyers came around and we all had dinner together, and, as you can imagine, we discussed salmon and salmon water till well into the night. As a result, I learned that I had leased as poor salmon water as there was in Canada! The man had told me about the big catches that had been made there, but he neglected to say they had been made years ago. If I had stopped off in Campbellton on my way over instead of on my way back, I would have saved about two thousand dollars, and a great deal of time. I fished the water thirty days and never killed a fish.

One often finds upon leasing a pool that, while the salmon lie on his side of the river, it fishes best from the other side, which may belong to someone else and therefore be unavailable to him. I once leased a pool on the Restigouche under such circumstances; the other side belonged to the Restigouche Salmon Club, though I didn't know of it.

I was fishing from the Club side one day, when Henry De Forest, president of the Club, came upstream, towing up to one of the lodges. Coming ashore he introduced himself and explained the situation, declaring that he was sure I didn't know they owned that side. Before going on he invited me to fish there the rest of the day as his guest, and every morning after that when the mail-boat came down river it brought an invitation from him for the day's fishing. He didn't for one moment let me think I had any right there whatever, but he took that most courteous way of helping me out of a difficult situation.

If the man leasing salmon water wants to do some dry fly fishing, he will find suitable water very difficult to obtain, since this fishing is best done by wading, for boats not only frighten the fish more or less, but are awkward to fish from. Practically all the good dry fly water I know of is either under lease or privately owned. There is some dry fly water in Nova Scotia and Newfoundland, but it is free fishing and gets fished to death. A river such as the Margaree in Nova Scotia is ideal for this style of fishing, but the river seems to be pretty well depleted, probably from overfishing, as it is a free river. There is good dry fly water on some of the rivers of Anticosti Island, and some of the rivers of Labrador, but these involve long, hard trips which few fishermen are willing to take. On the whole Tobique River, which is approximately fifty-five miles in length, there are not more than six of what I would consider good dry fly pools; but of course there are little runs here and there where a fish may occasionally be taken.

It often happens that after hearing a fisherman's account of his catch, you will go to that same water later and hear the guide's version. They don't always agree! I once happened to fish a certain river about which I had heard a great deal from one of our leading politicians, who told me some great stories of the big salmon he had caught there. My guide told me that the nearest he had ever come to a salmon was once when he fell off the scow into the river! One day, in a canoe piled high with baggage, his son was poled up past a pool I was fishing, and my guide remarked that he did not look to be in very good condition to be in a canoe. About five minutes later the river was full of suit cases, rod cases and all sorts of luggage, and we knew they had upset. Poling upstream as fast as we could, we arrived just in time to see the guide dragging him ashore by the feet!

The accessibility of fishing and the available accommodations must be taken into consideration. If, for instance, there is a chance of your being called back home on short notice, you must be where you can get to the railroad quickly; therefore it is not advisable to get too far back in the wilderness. If, on the other hand, there is no such danger, you will find some of the best fishing farther away. Your accommodations depend on how particular you are in regard to food, etc. I have never yet fished where things of this sort were not perfectly all right. You will find that the women of the households along the river are good cooks, and know especially how to cook salmon. If you are taking your own cook, it is a different matter. It is no trouble at all on any of the salmon rivers to hire one whose work will be entirely satisfactory.

Some of the men who cook in the lumber camps during the winter and on the river during the summer will surprise you with what they can put on the table.

As an instance of what can be had in the way of private water for not too much money—and there are any number of places like it on this river and others—I know of a man who owns two pools and a small country hotel, acts as guide and takes fishermen in the summer. One of his pools is especially good, and fishes well in both high and low water. It is one of those pools in which fish will always take well. There is a good current running all the way through it, with a good-sized cold brook running in about half way down. This pool alone, judiciously fished, is good for one hundred salmon each season. About a half mile below, he has another pool, which fishes best early in the season, for here

LOOKING UP RIVER FROM COL. ROGERS' ON THE RESTIGOUCHE

JOHN PHIPPS' ROCK POOL ON THE GRAND CASCAPEDIA

the water is not so heavy and the river is more flattened out. Fish come up along the shore, and are frequently taken here before they are taken anywhere else in the neighborhood. In the summer when the water gets down, you can usually go out on the covered bridge, where some of the boards have been taken off the sides, and, looking down, see fish lying there. There are boards taken off at different places on each side, so that you can look at the fish and watch people fishing. It was currently reported in the village there that one man had worn off both of his ears watching me fish! There is also some water above and some below which is owned by this man's neighbors, and he can always get a day's fishing in some of it if his own should be poor. These people along the river, who own pools at different places, are very generous about exchanging water. You give them a day's fishing in yours, and they will always give you one in theirs. In this way a man really gets a lot of water to fish over.

The food and service at this hotel are both excellent, and the owner and his wife, like everyone else you will find along the salmon rivers, are most hospitable. For the privilege of this fishing, which is private and all yours while you are there, good board, your guide and his board, the cost is $15 a day, and in all my fishing experience, I haven't found a pleasanter place to go.

On another river which is more celebrated, where the fish run larger and there are more of them, the charge is $25 a day for everything, except, of course, your fishing license. In addition to better fishing, you have more water, as here there is fifteen miles of it.

If these prices are beyond the fisherman, there are any number of places where a farmer who does not make a real business of taking fishermen, may have one or two pools, which are not considered particularly good fishing. There is no trouble, however, in taking an occasional fish in such water. His neighbors would also have some water of about the same kind which you would have the privilege of using. Here you would pay $4 for his services as guide, $4 for your board and $2 for his board; and you would live at his house. The food would be excellent here also, and the chances are that there would be a room which had been fixed up especially for some sportsman who might come along.

In other words, one can get good fishing water which is expensive, fair water at a reasonable price, and ordinary water for very little; so there is fishing to fit all pocketbooks. All of the places I have described have ice, and regular fish boxes for shipping fish can be found at a number of places along the river.

These boxes are sawed out at a little mill on the river which makes a regular business of it. You can kill your fish here in the morning, and if you box it and ice it, and put it on the stage which goes down the river and connects with the Boston train it will be in New York the next afternoon at three o'clock.

Free fishing is a different matter. You perhaps just get located on a good-looking piece of water when along come two or three other fishermen. The first thing you know, you are all casting over the same stretch of water. You kill a fish in a certain place in the evening, and, knowing there are more fish in the pool, think you will get back there early in the morning to take another one. But the chances are that when you arrive, someone else will be there. As a rule it is very unsatisfactory fishing; yet four or five of the right sort of fellows can divide up the water and fish in turn, killing in this way quite a number of fish. A great many of the pools can be fished from the bank and so no guide is required; hence your only expense is about $2 or $3 a day for your board.

The advance in price of good salmon water is interesting. One very valuable spot which I know of on one of the best rivers was originally sold by the native who owned it for $4,500. That same water today could not be purchased at any price. The Tom's Brook water on the Restigouche was offered me at $15,000 at one time. Within three years it sold for $28,000. This water has really only two pools. I could have bought a stretch of water, consisting of four pools, on another river for $12,000; it sold within five years for $23,000 or $24,000. Another pool with about seventy-five acres of ordinary farmland, but no buildings at that time, was considered one of the really good pools on the river. It was purchased for $800. This pool was afterwards sold for around $3,000. A friend of mine once got an option on a certain stretch of water on a good river for $60,000, took the first train south, and offered it to a gentleman I know for $110,000. The latter would have taken it, but he knew what the man's option price was, and thought he would be getting too much profit. The man took the next train to New York and sold it right away to the first man he interviewed for $122,000, if I remember correctly. Another friend of mine bought a little stretch of very ordinary water on the river one spring, while we were there fishing, for $800. He sold it the following year for $14,000. A little money judiciously invested in those days would have brought in big returns. If I had spent what money I did buying salmon water instead of leasing and fishing it, I could have made a lot of money.

POINT OF ROCKS, SECOND FALLS ON JOSEPH P. KNAPP'S WATER ON THE NATASHQUAN

Photographs courtesy of Joseph P. Knapp

THIRD FALLS ON THE NATASHQUAN

SALMON WATER

A gentleman once asked me to fish a month on five miles of water he was thinking of leasing. He wanted to know just how the pools fished at different stages of the water. I took the late Percy Faulding, one of the best canoe men and salmon fishing guides in Canada, to handle the boat for me, and put up at a farmhouse on the river which was notorious for never giving people enough to eat. After three weeks' fishing without a rise, and both of us half starved, I managed one morning to hook a good fish well over twenty pounds. I was so hungry for salmon and wanted that fish so badly I was shaking all over. And to make matters worse, every time the fish jumped Percy would say, "Is he still on? My God! don't lose him!" That fish gave us both heart trouble for ten minutes or so, until I brought him in to the gaff. When Percy got him ashore and the hook out of his mouth, he picked him up and started on the run for the house, with me after him. The folks were all away, but in no time at all Percy cooked four or five big slices and we filled up on it. That night I telegraphed the gentleman the water was not worth leasing, and resigned the job. This is the only time I ever thought I would probably keep after salmon until I starved, although some of my friends had always predicted it. My fishing this water cost the gentleman some $500 but it saved him $5,000, which was what the owner wanted for a lease.

NEWELL FRANCIS

REMI WILLETT

MANZER HOWARD

JACK MACK

CANADIAN SALMON GUIDES WHO HAVE GUIDED FOR THE AUTHOR

CHAPTER II.

SELECTION OF GUIDES

THE guide not only must be a good boatman or canoeman, but he must be congenial, if your fishing is to be enjoyable. Remember, he is going to be your companion every day for the entire trip; therefore you want someone who not only knows the duties of a guide but is good company.

Most guides on the different salmon rivers of Canada are good fishermen and fly casters, but there is a great difference in them. Some are extremely anxious that you catch fish and will work hard and give you every opportunity, while others are not quite so painstaking. Perhaps the most important thing is their knowledge of the pools to be fished, such as knowing where fish lie at different stages of the water, and where the "sore spots" are. Good guides want no noise or racket going on in their boat, such as kicking the paddles, knocking the ashes out of your pipe on the side of the boat, or any disturbance that will create a vibration in the water.

The experienced guide is extremely careful in approaching the pool to be fished. In going up river to the head of the pool to commence the fishing, he will keep well in to the shore, so as not to disturb any fish that may be lying there. He usually first drops the killick, which is a lead weighing from twenty to thirty pounds, and which holds the boat in position, well at the head of the pool, a good long cast from where he would expect the fly to go over a fish, and from then on every drop he makes through the pool—i.e., every time he takes up the killick and drops it again to hold the boat in a new position—he does very carefully and with as little disturbance as possible. Then, provided he does it for you, he ties on the fly which you are to use, with the figure-eight knot; and you will notice he leaves about one-eighth of an inch of the end of the leader showing after the knot is tied. This is to prevent any danger of the end pulling through and untying when it tightens on a fish. This extra eighth of an inch of gut lies dead straight with the fly and is tucked in between the wings out of sight.

His eye will never leave the fly from then on. He is watching your back-cast, both on his own account and yours, and the position of the fly on the water while it is being fished. If the fish raises and is not hooked, he can pretty nearly tell you whether he missed the fly or whether you took it away from him. The chances are he has been on this pool for years and knows every rock in it, and is full of stories of happenings there, all of which keep you interested. When you hook a fish, if you struck instead of tightened, he will remind you of it, and probably add that it is a mighty good leader you have on to stand the jerk you gave it. With the fish on, he pulls up the killick and eases the canoe off to one shore or the other, opposite and a little below your fish, so you can make him fight you and the current both. When you bring the fish in to the gaff, there will be no mistakes, such as cutting your leader with the gaff when he makes the stroke. After hitting your salmon a couple of clips on the head with the priest, he puts him in the canoe with plenty of grass under and over him to keep the hot sun off and hurries to set you out in the pool, just where you hooked this one, and is all ready for you to take another.

I had a funny experience in gaffing one season with a guide, Jack Mack, whom I had taken to the camp on the Restigouche. Jack was born on a salmon river, the Miramichi, but as a young man had come over into Maine, where I lived, and had taken up the guiding business. He was one of the most conscientious and willing men I have ever known, and it was said of him that he could carry a heavier pack on his back than any man in that country, and could stand more grief. He had fished and hunted with me in Maine for a great many years, but had never done any guiding for salmon fishermen.

The first salmon he gaffed for me he took across the beach, which was quite wide at that particular place, disappearing in the bushes, and, when I went to get my fly out of the fish's mouth, I found him some fifty yards into the woods. I asked him why he went way off in the woods with the fish, and he said he was afraid the fish would flop off and get back into the river again. I told him that was all right, but not to go so far the next time. But every fish after that, Jack would keep on going until he got into the woods. One day some fishermen stopped at my camp for lunch and I was telling them how Jack, when he gaffed a fish for me, always took him into the woods and up on the second ridge, for fear he would flop back in the river. Jack happened to be standing on the piazza and overheard me, and at four o'clock that afternoon when I went down to the boat to go out for the evening fishing, he walked over to me and said, "Charlie, any time you don't like the way I gaff fish for you, you can get somebody else, but by God, no fish I gaff ain't going to flop back in no river!"

Most all guides are good with the gaff; some are exceptionally so. A number of times I have had them gaff grilse which would take a quick run up river past the stern of their canoe. That is quick work as the grilse is small and very fast.

One season when fishing was especially poor on the Tobique, and club members were taking very few fish in their water, one of my pools was yielding fish every day and I was having great sport all to myself. This, of course, in time became known all up and down the river. Colonel Robert Emmett, president of the club at that time, a fine fisherman and most delightful gentleman, one day invited me to Wainright Lodge for the day's fishing. "You fish Wainright Pool today," he said after breakfast, "and I'll go on down river." Now, Wainright Pool was and is the poorest excuse for a salmon pool on the whole river, and only infrequently is a fish taken there. Jimmy Waters, a well-known Tobique guide, one of the best in my acquaintance, and a grand fellow in every way, was guiding me; and if there is one guide for whom I'll fish hardest and the best I know how, Jimmy is the one. We gave that pool a real overhauling, from top to bottom, and managed to kill two fish. That night the Colonel came back late and reported that he had not seen a fish all day, and when I asked him what water he had fished, he replied, "Yours, at Hayden's." I'll never forget the expression on Jimmy's face when he heard that; he was very well pleased.

If a fish weighs twenty pounds you should be about twenty minutes killing him; for the old saying, "a minute to the pound," is about right, provided, of course, he is not one of those sulky fish that wants to put his nose up behind a rock out in the heavy current and stay there. That being the case, the guide will drop the canoe well down below him to one side and show you how to put a good side strain on and hand line him. This soon pulls his nose around and the current washes him out of there. However, the guide sometimes has to go out with the canoe and frighten some of these fish away from the rock with a pole. After the day's fishing, he sees that your rod is hung up on the pegs, and all the line that is wet is stripped off and crisscrossed back and forth between a couple of these same pegs which your rod rests on, to dry it. These are only a few of the many things your guide will do for you.

If you have your own lodge get a good woods cook, that is, a man who cooks in the lumber camps winters. He not only knows how to cook well, but can do many other things. If you want to smoke some salmon during the summer to take back home, he knows just where to build the little smokehouse on the bank. He will have his fire down below on the shore, so that when the smoke gets to the fish it will be cool. While they are being smoked he takes them out two or three times, and with a brush gives them a good coat of olive oil. This not only helps preserve them but makes them turn a beautiful color. Then they are packed away between sheets of birchbark and put away in a cool place. You can take them home and have smoked salmon all winter. If you want to take some home which will keep fresh indefinitely, he knows how to preserve them and puts them up in glass sealers.

Your guide's knowledge of the pool you fish, very often makes the difference of whether you get fish or not. He knows where to anchor his canoe in the pool so that your fly will fish to the best advantage, because he has probably tried fishing this pool anchored from several different places, and knows from which one it fishes best. He will not be able to give you any scientific reasons or use any technical terms for doing this or that, but he knows the right way from experience.

It is well not to wear any conspicuous clothes, such as a white shirt, for instance. Some color such as green or gray is much better, especially when you are bringing a fish in to the gaff. Once I brought a fish in to the gaff on the shore near a small village, and a great part of the population was standing on the bank watching the proceedings. Just as I had the fish up within about ten feet of the guide, a woman in a white dress rushed down to where he was standing, with the result that the fish made a wild rush across the river, jumped, and got away. The guide used some pretty strong language to her, and I never saw her near the river afterwards.

Collection of Eversley Childs, Jr., Esq.

COMING TO GAFF

FROM A WATER COLOUR PAINTING BY OGDEN M. PLEISSNER

The most particular man about the position of a boat in a pool was Mike Broderick, and it seemed as though the killick had to go down within an inch of where he wanted it, or the stern man got a growl. Mike certainly knew his salmon water.

If you are outfitting your own lodge, whether you should purchase a Gaspé or canoes would depend entirely on whether you were on a big river with heavy water, or a small river which was more quiet. In the first instance you would want a Gaspé boat, as it is not altogether safe to fish big heavy water from canoes. A good Gaspé, twenty-two feet long, costs about $100. On a small river canoes are much better. You can get around easily and quickly with them, and without any danger. A good one, such as a White or Chestnut, built eighteen feet long, would cost about $90.

The killicks which any tinsmith will run for you, should weigh about thirty to forty pounds for a Gaspé. For a canoe, under ordinary circumstances, twenty to twenty-five pounds is heavy enough. The guides will make these for you themselves if they can find some lead, and will use an old tin coffee pot for a mold, setting a swivel in the top when they run it. To this swivel a coil of window cord makes a good line. A killick for a canoe costs about $3; one for a Gaspé, $5.

The Indian guide, until you understand him, is more or less of a puzzle. He has ideas of his own about fishing and no one can change them, but if you treat him well, there is nothing he will not do for you. Three of the Melicete Tribe in Canada, Nick Lola, Newel Francis and Tom Moulton have been with me most of the time for ten years, and are not only good fishermen but faithful men.

The Melicete Tribe reservation is at the mouth of the Tobique salmon river in New Brunswick, and their land fronts on about five miles of the river, and what fishing there is on that water belongs to them. So if you want to fish any of it, you can do so by employing one of them as guide.

Some of them are good fishermen; Newel Francis and Tom Moulton are the best. They anchor the canoe in what they consider the best spot in a pool and fish there all day, always casting the same length of line. Their idea is that the fish must come up past them at some time or other, and will be sure to see their fly; whereas if they dropped, they might go past one. Upon hooking a fish, they lay down the rod, take up the killick, and pole ashore. If the fish is still on, all right; if not, it is all right just the same, and they go back for another. They do not fight their fish very hard, with the result that they have them on a long while and eventually lose a great many. The hook wears a hole and drops out. They fish for days in the same spot, casting the same length of line, and to show that this is not such a bad idea, I will say that in 1934 Tom Moulton, fishing alone, from the bank at one particular place, killed seventy-two salmon. This was especially good fishing considering the tackle he used. They make their own rods, using ash for the butt and generally hornbeam for the second joint and tip; some of these rods cast well. It is quite usual for one of them to fish one fly until it is worn out, that is, if he thinks it is the right one. These men all handle canoes well.

When I was eight or ten years old and wanted to go fishing, which I did most of the time, if I could get an old Indian, known as Newel Bear, to go with me, it was all right with my father, for he had great confidence in him. Newel was in those days Chief of the Melicetes and I had my first experience at salmon fishing with him.

The Aroostook River in northern Maine then had quite a few salmon in, but there was practically no fly fishing done for them. If a man wanted a fish, he went out in a boat at night with a flambeau in the bow and speared himself one. About this time a dam was built across the river at a town called Caribou, and no fishway was put in. It was what was called a roll dam and had an apron. The fish would jump up on the apron and swim up over, provided there was water enough. If not, they would be washed back in the pool below. The first few years this dam was in there, it was a great sight to watch the fish jumping all over it, and some of them were caught by local anglers on a fly. One summer Newel built a bark canoe and he and I, taking a tent, supplies and what trout fishing tackle I had, started down river for this dam twelve miles away. I caught no fish with my trout outfit, but they were jumping all around us and all over the apron. After three or four days and no fish, Newel said he was going to the village and told me to watch the tent. He came back in about two hours with an iron about eight inches long, flat and sharp at one end. He then whittled out a pair of jaws, and lashing the iron on the end of a pole with the jaws on each side of it, was ready for action. That night after dark we went down to the dam and he waded out, as there were only about six inches of water running over the apron, and having caulked shoes on, such as a river driver wears, had no trouble. He only had to wait a little while before a fish jumped up near him, and, driving the spear into him, he brought him ashore. After that we had all the salmon we wanted. The iron of this spear went down through the salmon's back and cut the backbone, the jaws at the same time closing around the fish, springing out as the man strikes, and springing back around the fish and holding him on.

One day a man caught one in a net below us and I bought it to take home. I did not notice that the net marks showed plainly and Newel did not tell me. When I got home I showed the fish to my father, who asked me how I had got it. I told him I caught it at the Caribou Dam, and he turned around and walked off with the remark, "God, how I hate a liar!" He had seen the net marks.

My father was the first conservationist I had ever known, although I did not realize it at the time and did not think very much of his way of fishing. He would not catch enough fish to suit me. He would catch enough for a meal, and then take me home. I wanted him to stay and catch them all. Some nights after supper he would take me up river to where a cold spring brook came in, and one night he caught two trout there that weighed four pounds each. I coaxed him to stay and catch some more, as there were a lot in there, but he said we had enough, so that ended it. The next day I took Newel and we went back there and caught about fifty—all there were. I remember I had to stay in bed all the next day for that, but it did not stop me from wanting to catch all the fish there were, everywhere I went.

When I was twelve I was taken to the Skiff Lake Club in Canada. This club was composed of twenty-five men who controlled the fishing and owned the twenty-seven islands on the lake, which was four miles long and one and a half miles wide. This was landlocked salmon fishing, and the water was protected by wardens. Joe Jefferson, the actor, fished there during those summers, and I remember seeing him being rowed around by Andy, who was considered the best guide there. This was my first really great fishing—the late John Stewart, who was Superintendent of the Canadian Pacific Railroad and also president of the club, used to take me with him. He was considered a grand fly caster in those days, and, as I remember him, he would not look bad in anybody's company today. Lord Northcote of England had been coming over each year for this fishing, and had built a fine lodge, which he presented to Mr. Stewart. Major Howe of New York, another great fly fisherman in his day, also fished there. His wife was shot by some Indians while coming down the Tobique River in a canoe. The guides at this lake were all Irishmen, as this was an Irish settlement, and I remember they were great storytellers. The fishing was all done from rowboats, and when I took an Indian with a canoe there the first time, a lot of the men and women gathered on the shore and coaxed me not to go on the lake in it. They had never seen one before and thought it too frail. I always used a canoe there after that.

When Joe Jefferson came to Skiff Lake he stayed in tents which he pitched on what is now Club Island, which was covered with white birch trees and was a very lovely spot. Each year just before he left he gave a farewell party on the island to all the natives who lived nearby. At one of his parties, after mingling with all of them for a while, he managed to get away in the woods unnoticed, and about the time the party was at its height, a very old man with long white hair and whiskers came hobbling out of the birches on a stick. As he drew near, the natives all became panic-stricken and when one old Irishman hollered, "Holy Jasus!" they rushed to the boats. Then Jefferson took off his Rip Van Winkle outfit.

It is well to let a cook make out a list of food supplies for the lodge himself, as he has probably been doing this sort of thing for a great many years and knows exactly what salmon fishermen like to eat.

If you are running a real up-to-date lodge on a big river where things are done right, the cook will have a helper who gets up the wood and assists him in his work. This man or boy will act as waiter also. Guides, when they come in at lunch time or after dark at night, do not like to have to go out and cut wood and do things like that. Their job is guiding you at salmon fishing and nothing more.

Collection of Mrs. Van S. Merle-Smith

JUNE—DEVIL'S HALF ACRE

FROM A WATER COLOUR PAINTING BY OGDEN M. PLEISSNER

CHAPTER III.

TACKLE

THE selection of a rod for someone else is a difficult proposition. Some anglers desire one with all the backbone possible, in other words a powerful tournament rod; others prefer one with a softer action. One should, of course, select a rod that will afford him the most pleasure in casting; but he should not lose sight of the fact that it must kill fish. Personally I have no use for a rod that is at all soft or whippy, as such a rod is only useful to the man who cannot learn to tighten on his fish, and insists on striking. It will not cast and control a line, especially a long one, and it is too slow. It might be well to explain that what is required of a salmon rod is different from a trout rod. The size of flies to be cast varies from 10, or smaller, to 9/0 and Dee Irons up to four inches long. No one rod will cast all these different flies well. Heavy ones are not right for small flies, neither are light rods right for large flies. With the exception of flies such as the bucktails, and some of the large lake patterns, the trout fisherman's flies are small and light. To illustrate: I carry a thirteen-and-a-half-foot powerful rod, weighing nineteen ounces, for casting the large sizes used in the spring, and when the river is in flood; a thirteen-foot one weighing seventeen ounces, light in the top, for dry fly work and small flies, when I want a lot of distance; a twelve-foot one weighing fourteen ounces, light in the top, for sizes from 6 to 2/0. These are all two-hand rods. Then come two ten-foot rods with detachable butts, one weighing seven-and-one-half ounces, for dry fly, and the other weighing around nine ounces for small wet flies. In other words I follow the water down, by going to lighter rods, lines, leaders and flies. The reels and lines, of course, have to be right for these different rods.

All of these rods are powerful in the butt and second joint, as these are the parts which lift and cast a long line, also the parts which put the strain on a fish. If a man will tighten on his fish, and not strike, and will keep the point of the rod up where it belongs while playing him, he will not break many leaders.

In the last few years a great controversy has been going on among anglers, as to whether bamboo thoroughly seasoned by age was available for rods, or whether that which is used was seasoned by the process called tempering. A few years ago, Mr. Fred Thomas, who manufactures the Thomas rod in Bangor, Maine, showed me bamboo that had been in the racks since Hiram Leonard's time, when the Leonard rod was built by him in Bangor. Mr. Thomas personally supervised the building of eight rods for me from it, and they were without any exception the finest rods I have ever owned. I have an idea that there is some of this long-seasoned wood still left among the old rod-builders.

The trouble with salmon rods in general today is that the old builders are either dead, or because of mass production, cannot supervise the building of each rod as they used to; while the younger generation of rod-makers has not the same interest in the work, or the same knowledge of bamboo and how to work it.

The fad for extra light-weight rods has been carried too far, but that was not the fault of the rod-maker. Some angler would insist on having a certain length rod built an ounce or a fraction of an ounce lighter, but he did not know that after a given weight for a certain length has been reached, if any more weight is taken off, just so much of the backbone is taken out.

One writer stated in a recent article on salmon fishing that regulation equipment—two-hand rods, etc.—is giving way to hip-boots and trout tackle. This statement is very misleading; nothing could be further from the fact. Seven-and-a-half- to nine-ounce single-hand rods with detachable butts are perfectly in order on some pools when the water is down and small flies and fine leaders are necessary, but I think a man would be out of place with such tackle on the Tobique, Restigouche, Cascapedia, Natashquan or any other of the good rivers, in June when there is real water in them, and fishing is fishing, and salmon are salmon.

I had two twelve-foot two-hand rods built, to weigh twelve ounces. I gave one to Mike Broderick, Colonel Rogers' guardian, and kept the other; and they were just as Mr. Thomas said they would be, no good.

The best salmon reel is a multiplier, called The Tobique, which has the handle in the center, with an adjustable drag on the opposite side, so that the tension may be regulated while playing a fish. It is built by Edward Vom Hofe and Son, and can be had in the right sizes for different rods. These reels are all built by hand, and the adjustment of the tension is so fine and smooth that they save a lot of leaders. Salmon running on a jerky reel will break a great many fine tapered leaders. The reel, with the line on, should of course balance the rod correctly.

But let's go back to rods for a minute. Once in a great while you will find one which has an indescribable something: it may be a little kick it gives the line at the finish of a cast, that sends the fly out farther, or it may be the smooth, effortless way it has of doing the whole job. It is hard to describe. To the man who fishes casually, or to whom the killing of fish is all that matters, things like this would not be apparent but he misses one of the many phases of the sport which help make it so attractive.

Lines must be of the right weight to bring out the best action of the rod, and although different makes of lines are numbered the same, their weight varies and this makes it necessary to try different ones till the right one is found. The best lines come from England, and are vacuum dressed. Two of them are Hardy's Filip, and Corona. The Filip is on the order of a tournament line in that it has a heavy belly to carry it out, and a quick back taper to fine line, for shooting. The front taper is short, which I think is an advantage, especially if you are using long leaders. The idea of the line is right, but no line of this type is right for all fishermen. Regardless of the fact that most fish are taken on a comparatively short line, every fisherman likes to be able to cast a long one. A line to give distance must have weight to carry it out, hence the heavy belly in the Filip. Some men, however, can lift more line off the water than others, at the same time keeping the backcast high, and such men would want a heavier belly. If two men are equally proficient, the taller and stronger will cast the longer line, for he can pick up more line off the water, and keep his backcast higher. I used to cut up old lines, and splice them, again and again, till I had a line that was best for a particular rod, and best for me.

A fishing line should be soft and pliable, but with a hard smooth finish to shoot well. The lines I had spliced would not run through the guides well, and I used to send them to a manufacturer, and have new lines made like them. They were expensive, costing from twenty-five to forty dollars. That is a good example of what some fishermen will do, just in order to cast a little farther, and perhaps a little better. I think a fisherman has to be a little crazy on the subject, to be very good at it. Real tournament lines have a long front taper, then some twelve feet of very heavy belly, and taper off quickly to fine line for shooting. Fred Shaw used to call my lines "mineralized hawsers," because of their size, and the powdered graphite with which I polished them, to reduce friction. After you purchase a good line, the important thing is to take care of it. Every time you come in from fishing, all the line that is wet should be stripped off the reel and allowed to dry thoroughly till morning. At the end of the season, it should all be taken off the reel and hung in long coils in a cool place. If this is done, you won't have any "tacky" lines. There are preparations on the market for tacky lines, which help for the time being; but the best thing to do is give such a line away and get a new one. When a line won't shoot well, it has lost its usefulness. The shooting of line to me is the most attractive part of fly casting. I like to hear a good line whistle through the guides.

Leaders are one of the most important parts of the outfit. For large flies such as 4/0, 6/0 and 8/0, the gut must be heavy. Two yards of twisted and one yard of single is sometimes used. There is also what is known as the Joe Welch leader, which is silk covered with a sort of gum preparation. The large single gut leaders are expensive, running from five to six dollars, and most fishermen use a Joe Welch, since they are very strong, and can be purchased for about a dollar.

From this heavy weight, leaders graduate from .018 to the fine ones used in dry fly fishing, which are generally about .010, which is about as fine as can be fished successfully. If fish refuse a fly cast on a leader tapered to .010, I think it is better to improve your casting than to fish finer gut.

It is a good practice always to examine your leader when you reel in while making a drop during your fishing, and if there are any knots in it, which there probably will be if it's windy, take them out, as they will cut the gut with a fish on. Also, after killing a fish, examine the figure eight knot that you have used in tying on the fly, and if it looks at all suspicious, take the fly off and tie it over again, cutting off the end of leader that was used before. Test a leader by pulling it with your hands; if it will stand that it will hold a salmon. Don't pull it on a set of scales, as you will pull the life out of it by so doing; when a leader is once stretched to the limit, it is not much good afterwards. You can feel the leader stretch when you are pulling on a heavy fish, and you get so that you can tell when you are giving it all it will stand.

A salmon outfit is expensive, and every part of it should be well looked after. It's something you can take a lot of pride in owning. Dan Adams, a New York stockbroker, once fished with me on Restigouche. He was as great a crank on tackle as I was, and had just as much. The day he arrived I had ten salmon rods and four trout rods hanging on one end of the Lodge, so Dan hung up the same number of his on the other end. Manzer Howard, one of the guides, looked them all over and said, "Ain't that awful. What that stuff cost would buy the three best farms on the Tobique River!" When I looked at it in that light I thought so too, and didn't buy any more for a while.

A man will be very particular about his leaders. I know of one, for instance, who is continually telling about the brand he uses, declaring that they cast no shadow on the bottom to frighten the fish. At the same time his rod is fitted with bright silver ferrules, and there is a finish on it in which you can see your face, flashing in the sun. I have repeatedly seen a man's rod flashing this way a mile off. For this reason I have the ferrules and reel seats of my rods of oxidized silver, and the varnish done in a dull finish.

I like agate for both the butt-guides and tips, but they break off easily and you have to be careful with them around the boat.

A cork grip should fit the hand, and I like the top part of it to curve up sharply to put my thumb against, as I think it helps stop your rod at the top of the backcast. I used to have a piece of cork set in for my thumb to rest against.

One reason rods often go to pieces is that they are fished too new. The glue has not had time to harden thoroughly, it is well for a rod to stand at least a year before being used. I once had a new fifteen-foot rod built by one of our best builders, and about thirty days afterwards took it to the river. The first fish tore it all apart; it was too green.

I have four rods stored away somewhere that Hiram Leonard built for my father seventy-five or eighty years ago at Bangor, Maine, and the last time I saw them the wood strips were glued apparently as solidly as ever. In my opinion the best rods today are built by Payne.

The powerful thirteen-and-one-half-foot rod in my outfit weighs approximately nineteen ounces, and is suitable for spring fishing on such rivers as the Grand Cascapedia, Restigouche, or on any water where flies as large as 8/0 are required. This rod costs from $80 to $85. The reel is a 3/0 Tobique pattern of multiplier built by Edward Vom Hofe and Son, and cost $70. A No. 3½ Filip line, spliced to 100 yards of stout linen backing will cost about $25. The thirteen-foot dry fly rod weighs a trifle less than eighteen ounces, and costs $70. With this the 3/0 reel, which is used on the thirteen-and-one-half-foot earlier in the season, can be used. By taking off the No. 3½ Filip and substituting a No. 4 Filip spliced to 150 yards of linen backing the one reel answers for both rods. The powerful rod will not be used again until next spring, unless there should happen to be a big freshet during the season, at which time large flies would again be needed. The twelve-foot rod which is light in the top costs $70. A 2/0 Tobique multiplier costs $67.50. On this particular rod of mine I used a Hardy Corona line, the belly of which is eighteen standard wire gauge. This line is spliced to 100 yards of linen backing. The single hand ten-foot dry fly rod, weighing seven and a half ounces, costs $65, with detachable butt. A 1/0 Tobique multiplier costs $65. On this I use a No. 1 Filip trout line spliced to 200 yards of Hardy's silk Solidae No. 0, which tests about eight or nine pounds. The other single-hand ten-foot rod which I use for fishing small wet flies weighs a little under nine ounces, and I use a No. 1 Filip and 200 yards of Hardy's Solidae backing on this also. Two hundred yards of this silk backing with the 30 yards of No. 1 trout line just fills one of these No. 1/0 Tobique reels nicely. The reason for having 200 yards of running line on the thirteen-foot dry fly rod and the two ten-foot rods is that with the fine leaders and small flies you are using, some fish are not easy to stop and they often take out a lot of line. It is better to have too much than not enough.

Care should be taken when the backing and line are wound on the reels that it be spooled on evenly. And in playing a fish, or at any time that you are reeling, care should be taken then that it does not pile on the reel, where it may fall off and tangle up.

I can readily understand how someone not familiar with salmon fishing is going to say right away: "Must I have five rods and the equipment that goes with them to go salmon fishing?" My answer to that question is, "No, not necessarily, as I have no doubt that seventy-five per cent of the salmon caught are taken by men with one rod, which they use for casting all the different types of flies required." The tackle I have listed is that which will best do the work. If I were going to buy only one salmon rod, it would most certainly be a two-hand rod, and thirteen feet in length. And of the three two-hand rods I have listed, I would select the thirteen-foot dry fly rod; thirteen feet because that is large enough for any of the big rivers, and a large wet fly *can* be thrown with it (I do not say cast). It is a little too long to handle well on small rivers fishing from a canoe, but you can get by with it. Also, it will do your dry fly fishing, which is what it was intended for. If I were going to buy two rods, they would both be two-handed, and one would be a thirteen-and-a-half-foot powerful rod, such as I described for casting large flies, and the other the thirteen-foot we just discussed. If it were to be three rods, I would include the twelve-foot two-hand, and the only reason I can give for having single-hand rods at all is that they vary the monotony of continual casting with a two-hand rod. It would be the same with your flies. Where I have specified a half dozen of a certain size and pattern, a great many fishermen buy three. And leaders likewise: where a dozen of one size is specified, buy as many as you think you can get along with. But remember that the fewer you buy of flies and leaders, the better you must fish, because you haven't very many to lose. It makes a great difference in the amount of equipment required whether a man wants to do the different methods of fishing just right and wants the right things to do them with; or whether it doesn't matter so much to him as long as he gets a few fish. It is a question of whether one is going to take his salmon fishing seriously or not. If he is, he wants the best and he wants the right things.

Every fisherman has to go through the stage of buying every good-looking new pattern of fly he sees. My idea is to buy them all the first thing, try them, satisfy yourself as to what you think is good and what is not, and have it over with. You will not take very long to find out that Jock Scott, Black Dose, Silver Grey, and Dusty Miller are the foundation of every salmon fisherman's assortment of flies, and that his collection is all built around them.

When fishing for grilse it is well to take along a fairly heavy trout rod, say four-and-a-half to four-and-three-quarters ounces, with a hundred yards of very fine silk backing, which will test about four or five pounds, spliced to the casting line. It is also well to have a large size trout dip net with a telescoping handle, which is very convenient to have in the canoe, since you can reel a grilse in and dip him from the boat instead of pulling up the killick and going ashore with him; or, if you have gone ashore with the fish, it is possible to use the net instead of taking a chance of losing him in beaching him.

A beginner's greatest trouble when he hooks a salmon is in keeping the tip of his rod up where it belongs. And where it belongs entirely depends on what flies and leaders you are fishing, whether heavy or fine, and what stage of the fight with the fish it is; whether it is while he is running or while he is being brought in to gaff. It is not to be wondered at that the guide has to be continually telling a new fisherman to keep his rod up. The salmon is a heavy fish, and when he makes a run he naturally pulls the rod down; the beginner forgets to put it up again. There is a good deal of discussion as to what is meant by keeping your rod up, and some evidently think that to be up it must be held at the vertical or even past that. I have seen pictures of men holding their rods farther back than perpendicular while bringing fish to gaff. I don't know how a man ever gets fish in at all this way or why more tips aren't broken. The guides certainly must get tired waiting for those fish to be brought in to gaff! I consider a rod well up when it is at 60°, and certainly at 75° it would give a fish plenty of spring to play on without breaking the finest leaders. When a fish commences to show signs of giving up is the time you begin to put the real strain on him, and in my opinion a rod held at 45° is up plenty high enough. At the last end of the fight, when you have the fish reeled in close and are backing up with him on the shore, your rod can be held as low as 30° with safety, provided, if he makes a rush, you let the fish go and do not try to stop him. At 30° he is still getting spring enough from the rod so that he will not get a jerk on the reel. When a rod is held so low that a fish making a run starts off on the reel, it is too low.

In the case of some of the soft whippy rods with which some dry fly men choose to fish: when all the strain they can possibly exert is put upon a fish, the butt is held at an angle of about 60° and the rest of the rod is bent almost directly at the fish. I shouldn't care to fish that kind of rod.

When I look at all the rods and equipment that seem to be needed to fish salmon today, I can't help remembering once when I was going up river and it was not convenient for me to take along a salmon rod. All I could find was a $3 Bristol steel rod. When I reached the last house on the road before going into the woods, I discovered that I had left the leaders and flies behind, but, as

Courtesy of Canadian Pacific Railway

PLAYING A SALMON

ROD UP AS FAR AS IT SHOULD GO

everyone in that community fished salmon, I found one fly and about three feet of an old leader at that house. At another house about a mile below I found two more old flies and about three feet more of leader. The next morning I waked up on a salmon pool with this outfit, caught two salmon over fifteen pounds each, and seven grilse, and I never had more fun fishing in my life!

THE AUTHOR ON THE RESTIGOUCHE

FROM AN ETCHING BY ROBERT NISBET, N.A.

CHAPTER IV.

FLIES AND THEIR USES

THERE are some three hundred and eighty patterns of salmon flies,—Irish, Scotch, English and Canadian. Probably less than fifty are used on Canadian rivers, and I think ten of them dressed in different ways would kill just as many fish as the whole list. The patterns most commonly used are:

Jock Scott
Canadian Black Dose
Silver Grey
Dusty Miller
Night Hawk
Silver Wilkinson
Thunder and Lightning
Brown Fairy
Nipisiguit Grey
Green Drake
Mar Lodge
Griswold Gray
Highlander
Silver Doctor
Causapscal
Black Dog
Ackroyd
Beauly Snow Fly
Lady Caroline
Black Goldfinch
Abe Moon Killer
Mitchel
Bastard Black Dose

The Jock Scott fly, I would say, kills the most fish, as it is fished the most. It has an interesting history: Lord Scott, who was a famous salmon fisherman, had a man who acted as his ghillie, and who had come to him when a boy. All the name he had was Jock, and growing up as he did with Lord Scott, became known as Jock Scott. He became a very skillful fly dresser, a real genius with furs, feathers and silks. On a steamer once, going to Norway for some fishing, he dressed the fly which was named for him, and which has since become famous. It is a great fly in all sizes and all stages of water.

Different rivers have their own favorite flies, such as the Green Drake and Abe Moon Killer on the Miramichi; Dusty Miller on Grand Cascapedia; Night Hawk on Tobique, and so on. A favorite fly is one with which you have been successful at some time or other; and after that you have always fished it more, and fished it better, because you have had confidence in it. One man's favorite fly might perhaps be considered worthless by another.

It is possible to say that styles change in flies. When I first began fishing the Tobique River, the Brown Fairy was said to be the only pattern needed. After that, for some ten years, fish seemed to tire of it, and it was only occasionally you would hear of a fish being killed on it. But three years ago, at a time when fishing was hard and everything was being tried, it was the only fly that would get results. Since then it has again been one of the river's best patterns.

I like a Night Hawk best for early fishing when the water is high, and I came to fish it through Jack Wyers, the owner of Tom's Brook, who was the first "One Fly Man" I had ever met. He would fish nothing else when he could get it, and fished it in all sizes down to a No. 2, in all stages of water. He claimed that fish in this particular water would not take a fly on a hook smaller than a No. 2, and in three years' fishing there I found that they never did, though I tried all manner of patterns in smaller sizes.

It is a peculiar thing, but some patterns that are killing on one river are not successful on certain others. This often applies to different stretches on the same river. The Green Drake kills on the Miramichi, and accounts for some fish on the St. John, but on no other river I know of. I have fished it all over the Tobique without a raise. Standard salmon flies take fish all along the St. John River, except at the Hartland pool, but there trout flies are in order, and such patterns as the Professor, Montreal and Rube Wood kill an average of one hundred fish each season. All silver body flies kill well, and it is possible that they account for the most fish.

For spring fishing, flies should be dressed on heavy hooks, to be fished deep. The water is high and cold, and fish are inclined to hug the bottom. I often wind the shank of the hook with fuse wire to weight it, before dressing the fly. Double hooks, being heavier, fish deeper, and are more inclined to ride heavy water right side up than singles; but they do not hold fish any better, provided the single hook is sent home. They certainly do not cast as well, and I am sure that in the smaller sizes the single hooks will raise the most fish—not because

Courtesy of Charles Nutter

FLAT ROCK POOL AT PABINEAU FALLS ON THE NIPISIGUIT

THE AUTHOR FISHING THE DALLETT WATER ON THE TOBIQUE

Courtesy of Samuel Watts

POLING THROUGH FAST WATER ON THE ST. JOHN IN GASPÉ

the two hooks' showing makes any difference to the fish, but because the single hook can be dressed with a slimmer body, which makes it more deadly.

The way the fly is fished depends on the water it has to cover. For instance, in a pool where the current is heavy fish often stop to rest in pockets along the side of the pool. The fly, therefore, must be presented in such a way that the fish gets a good look at it before it is swept away. Pools that are dead, with not enough current to swing the fly around, have to be "trout-fished," as we call it —that is, must be fished by continual casting and drawing the fly through the water. The whole thing seems to be the proper presentation of the fly, with regard to the water, and the man who understands these things well will take fish that the other fellow will not take. Almost every river has its dead pools, and they are generally named that. It is a tedious job to trout-cast them with a two-hand rod, but it is about the only way to get a fish up. Just below Pabineau Falls on Nipisiguit there is a flat rock you stand upon to cast over the dead water where the fish are. I have trout-fished this place for hours, and it is the only place of the kind I ever enjoyed. Here the water runs down through walls of solid rock, and when you hook a fish you climb the end of the cliff, walk along the top about fifty yards to where you go down the other end, playing your fish from fifty feet up. It is exciting, and you are lucky if your fish is still on when you get to the bottom. This is one of the most sightly places I know of to fish. Edith Wharton had a lodge here; from her porch you could see fish jumping the falls on their way up river, and generally moose feeding in the cove above. The salmon fishing, however, is poor in this river today, and, with the exception of some very good fishing at the foot of the Big Falls, twenty-five miles up, does not amount to much.

The Nipisiguit Grey fly was first tied here, and is the river's favorite pattern. One other effective old-time pattern, the Nicholson, dressed by a fisherman of that name from St. John, New Brunswick, was first used here.

The Abe Moon Killer was tied first by a settler on the Miramichi, who was a salmon fisherman. It is a very plain fly, with a yellow wool body and dark turkey wing, so he did not have to leave his farm to get the materials for it. Which all goes to show that very simply dressed flies, and poorly tied, have killed, and will kill salmon.

The number of patterns needed depends on whether your river is hard fished or not; and the fact that some particular man has killed a big majority of his fish on one pattern in some river, does not mean that he would have been successful in another one. The Grand Cascapedia, for instance, probably does not have over forty rods on it the entire season; whereas the Tobique has around three hundred. In one river the fish see flies occasionally; in the other there are flies going over them all the time. I do not believe the one-fly man would do as well on Tobique as he would on Cascapedia. Fish must get tired of continuously looking at one fly, and want a change.

I was fishing one side of a pool once, while a lady was fishing the other. The pool was full of fish, and they were taking ones, as they were moving around with their back fins showing. The lady on her side was into fish on every cast, while I could not raise one. When she had killed five fish she had her guide pull up, and coming over to my side, insisted that I try where she had been; but I could not raise one there. In all, I must have tried twenty different sizes and patterns; but she killed nine fish on an English Black Dose, and that was one I had not used.

There are patterns of flies for all occasions, such as the Thunder and Lightning for water on the rise. It is a good fly, too. The Candle Stick Maker, for just before dark, is supposed to light the salmon to bed. The Little Inky Boy is for extremely low water. This was one of the first of the lightly-dressed flies, and has very little wing and hackle, with the shank of hook wound with gut dyed black. There are any number of others. Kelson had hundreds of them, and I have tried them all at one time or another. It was fun, but I did not kill many fish with them.

But Kelson tied a beautiful fly and you could tell by looking at one that he was a fisherman. His flies were not overdressed and they had slim bodies. Mr. Marston, Editor of *London Fishing Gazette*, wrote me a number of years ago, and asked me if I would enter into correspondence with General Eagles of Yelverton, South Devon, England, about salmon flies in general, and it was through him that I procured a lot of Kelson's flies. They were my idea of a fishing fly, and I have always tried to tie mine like them. General Eagles was considered an authority over there, and tied a beautiful fly himself.

I always try a few casts the last thing, just before dark, with some large silver-bodied pattern. For instance, if I had been fishing a No. 4 size, I would use 2/0; and Mike Broderick, who was guardian for Colonel Archibald Rogers on Restigouche, had the most successful one of all. Mike called it Fat Mary.

It was a Silver Doctor with a large silver body. I used to tie the body spindle-shaped for him. This fly killed a lot of fish for us.

Mr. Percy Chubb, who had the Ste. Anne des Monts River, was very partial to a Blue Doctor, and wrote me once that he killed about half his fish on it. I found it to be a good fly on the Tobique also.

The Griswold Gray is one of the best flies that have been brought out in recent years. It kills on all rivers, and fishes well in all sizes. It is a quiet fly, and thinking to make it more attractive, I added chatterer cheeks, blue horns, and some other little things to dress it up. But Mr. Griswold did not like it nearly as well. It sold better, however, all of which goes to show fishermen will buy pretty flies, regardless of what the fish think about it.

Mr. Griswold came one summer to fish the Tobique with me and, as always, when you want some particular person to have good fishing, everything was at a standstill. What fish there were had all gone to the top of the river, and there was no rise of water to hurry fish upstream from farther down the river. I brought a Gaspé boat over from the Restigouche for him to fish from, for he had always done his salmon fishing from one; and, as the natives had never seen a boat like it before, it created quite a stir as it was poled up river by his two Indians. He was quite favorably impressed with the way the Indians cast; there are some good fishermen among them. He was especially taken with my own room at the small country hotel where I lived. It was probably the most disorderly place he had ever seen—fishing tackle, boots and clothes strewn everywhere. He gave it one good look and said, "All you need here is a stuffed raven, and Edgar Allen Poe would have nothing on you!" He was the most charming gentleman I have ever met, and a great sportsman.

I became very much disillusioned at one stage of my fishing career, and perhaps it is from that fact that I do not adopt some of the new ideas and call them good or great until I have tried them over a space of time and under different conditions. I have an aversion for the word "scientific," in connection with fly fishing, and I think the word "skillful" is used too promiscuously. You may say that a certain man is artistic with a rod, but I have seen any number of them who could not catch fish.

Some years ago I decided to make a real study of Entomology, and to become familiar with all the insects on which trout feed, so as to be able to identify them at a glance—then I could give the fish my imitation, and my troubles would be over. I accumulated all the books there were on the subject, and for four years devoted myself to that study and to tying imitations of the insects. And here is what happened: Mr. George La Branche produced a very simply tied fly, called the Pink Lady, which would take more trout than all the dry flies I owned, and I had thousands. That fly would take trout anywhere and everywhere, and I have seen a lot of salmon taken with it too, dressed on No. 6 and No. 8 hooks. This experience led me to spend more time with my fly-tying outfit, and with the dressing of that fly in mind, it was no trouble at all to turn out much more killing patterns for salmon. I will tell you later how the Bonbright, the best salmon dry fly of all, happened.

Salmon flies dressed on iron eyed hooks have their advantages. They are cheaper in the end, as they last longer, there being no gut loop to wear out. They can be dressed with slimmer bodies, which is the most essential thing in a killing fly; and last, but not least, when the fly is well chewed up, and ragged looking, with just a few strands of dressing hanging, it can still be used.

But on the other hand, as I have said before, the great majority of salmon fishermen strike when the fish takes a fly, with the result the end of the leader comes up with a bang against the iron eye, and of course breaks. You have lost both your fly and your fish. With a gut loop fly, the chances are you would have saved the fish, as there is just enough give to the gut loop to prevent breaking. If care is taken in tying on and untying the fly, the loop will last a long while. Some fishermen are afraid of the gut loop's pulling out, and no doubt in cheaply tied flies this sometimes happens, but I doubt if it would happen with a well tied one, unless it were very old.

When large sized flies are used, they are almost always dressed on single hooks, although some good fishermen use doubles, because they are more inclined to ride the water right. A fly is not supposed to fish well if it skids or rides on its side. Mr. Ayer always preferred double hooks, even in sizes as large as 6/0 and 8/0, for this reason.

Double hooks are universally used in sizes 2, 4, 6 and 8, and the majority of fishermen think they hold fish better. I do not, and I only use them because they fish deeper. A fly tied on double hooks looks too bulky; and in the smaller sizes for low water fishing, the object of the fly is defeated, because then we want something slim and fine. The fly at that time should be tied on a lighter wire hook and fished nearer the surface.

Courtesy of Joseph P. Knapp

VIEW OF JOSEPH P. KNAPP'S LODGE ON THE NATASHQUAN

It has only been in the last few years that slim-bodied and lightly-dressed flies could be bought at tackle dealers, and it was the fact that I could not get flies of this kind that made me take up salmon fly tying.

I have been fortunate when trying new flies and new methods of fishing, in being able to try them over fish without first having to hunt the fish up. Being on some salmon river or other for the entire season for a great many years, I generally knew of some pool nearby that held fish. The pool I have spoken of, under the railroad bridge at Perth, if it could talk, would probably tell of some queer-looking specimens of the fly tier's art having been floated down over it.

In trying new flies and ways of fishing, I have had the benefit of the experience of Tom Allen and Claude Knapp, who have tried them also, as we have always passed any new information back and forth. The late Col. Lewis Thompson was another good man for me in this work, as he would try anything I sent him; and as he fished the Rogers water on Restigouche, was always over fish. A remark he made to the editor of *The London Field* in England made the Bonbright dry fly famous. He said, "I have tried all the different patterns of dry flies for salmon, by all the different fly tiers, some three hundred in all, and the Bonbright is the best one of all."

With the exception of fishing salmon with the dry fly, we are doing nothing that is new. We have only improved on the old methods. Salmon were being taken on nymphs fifty years ago, and you will find accounts in some of the old salmon books of its being done. Don't they tell you that at times an old fly that has been used and chewed, until it is ragged and there is very little left of it, is the best fly to use? And what is that but a nymph? True, we tie regular nymphs today, and present them better, but it is the old idea. And how often we have had a salmon raise fair opposite us on one side or the other, and have cast the fly over in front of him, and let it float down over him dead, with no motion. This is now the Arthur Wood Method, only we dress the flies on lighter hooks, and with very little dressing, to fish nearer the surface, and we have improved the way of presenting them. All of these improvements have been made by keen and observant fishermen, and have added much to our sport, but they have not discovered a thing that was not known years ago. For a number of years I never gave away an old fly, but always a new one, for I knew there would be a fish that would want just that ragged-looking specimen. No fly dresser has yet been able to produce a fly that looks anything like one that has been chewed by a salmon.

I suppose that I have tried every pattern of wet fly that has ever been put on the market, and all the special patterns that I have ever heard of. I know that when I commence fishing in the spring I have been accumulating flies all winter and have one hundred or more different patterns in most of the different sizes. I am ashamed to tell it, but I have often started my fishing in the spring with 1,500 to 2,000 flies. It gradually commenced to sink into my system, after several years trying this fly and that one, that I was killing almost all my fish on some twelve patterns; so from then on I commenced to cut down and to carry only those that I knew were deadly. These twelve were: Jock Scott, Canadian Black Dose, Silver Grey, Dusty Miller, Night Hawk, Griswold Gray, Thunder and Lightning, Brown Fairy, Mar Lodge, Bastard Dose and, since the Arthur Wood patterns have come out, Silver Blue and Blue Charm; his other patterns have never fished well for me.

The above patterns, with the exception of the Arthur Wood flies, I had dressed on hooks as follows:

Jock Scott Canadian Black Dose Silver Grey Dusty Miller Night Hawk Griswold Gray Thunder and Lightning	Nos. 8/0, 6/0, 4/0, 2/0, 1/0 Single heavy wire hooks Gut loop Also on 4-3½-3-2½ and 2 inch Light wire Dee irons Gut loop
Jock Scott Canadian Black Dose Silver Grey Dusty Miller Night Hawk	Nos. 2, 4, 6, 8 Double heavy wire hooks Gut loop
Griswold Gray Thunder and Lightning Brown Fairy Mar Lodge Bastard Dose	Nos. 2, 4, 6, 8, 10 Single light wire eyed hooks. Very lightly dressed
Blue Charm Silver Blue	Nos. 2, 4, 6, 8 Single light wire eyed hooks. Very little dressing

In addition, if I were going to fish the Miramichi, I would carry the two favorite patterns of that river, which happen to be the Abe Moon Killer and Green Drake. If it were the Nipisiguit I would have some Nipisiguit Greys, which is the favorite fly on that river; or if it were some river with which I was not familiar, I would find out what the favorite patterns were, and would have them. With this lot of flies I should expect to kill my share of fish in any river of Canada.

There are any number of the other patterns which will take fish and I will name some that have been very successful at times.

We used to fish occasionally a fly called the Causapscal, an all yellow fly, and the fact that fish would take it led me to experimenting with all other patterns which had a lot of yellow in them. Out of the whole lot I found that the Torrish was the best among flies of this color. The Black Dog fishes well in high water, also a fly called Ackroyd; and any of a number of the different patterns dressed with the long Spey hackles do well at times. Mr. F. W. Ayer used to kill a lot of fish on Matapedia with the Black Goldfinch. The Silver Wilkinson used to be one of Claude Knapp's favorite flies on Little Main Restigouche; but I don't think he fishes it much now. A Blue Doctor is also a good fly and will kill fish on almost any river. For low water fishing, I used to dress flies to look as nearly as possible like some old fly which would be in the box, which had been all chewed up by salmon, but they were hard flies to imitate. It's fun to tie up a lot of different flies from your own ideas, then go out and see if you can kill a fish with them. Oftentimes the worst looking fly in the lot will prove to be the best. In doing this, however, you will find that, the first thing you know, you will be tying a fly that is pretty nearly a duplicate of some particular pattern you like to fish. It is hard to get a successful fly out of your head and that is why it *is successful.* Every time a fish refuses whatever you have on, the chances are that you will go back to that particular fly. One day, fishing what is known as the Hanson Pool in the St. John River, when the pool was full of fish, which were showing all over it, but would not come to the fly, it occurred to me that these were probably St. John River fish I was over, not Tobique fish on the way up to their river. If that were so, they should take the same fly there—a Green Drake—that was so successful twenty-five miles below in the river. We finally found some in one of the fly boxes and took three fish, one right after the other. A man might fish this fly there under the same circumstances for ten days at a time when fish were showing just as they were then and not take a fish for the reason that he would be fishing over Tobique fish instead of St. John River ones and the Tobique fish won't look at the Green Drake.

I have often thought that perhaps there was something to Kelson's idea that there were "grey rivers" and red ones, and rivers of other colors; that is, that the fish in certain rivers were most susceptible to a fly of a certain color. Flies of a very pronounced color, such as Causapscal and Green Drake, which will kill on the Matapedia, Restigouche, Miramichi and St. John, positively will not take fish on the Tobique; and the Nipisiguit Grey, which is famous on that river and will occasionally take a fish on Tobique, is of no account anywhere else I know of. For very low water I used to dress a very light wire No. 8 hook with black seal's fur body, black wings, black hackle and a few wisps of black hackle for a tail, rib it with silver, add some jungle cock cheeks and kill a lot of fish. There are any number of just such simply dressed flies which will kill salmon at times.

There certainly are times when salmon show a decided preference for some one pattern. One summer on Little Main Restigouche, when the water was very low and it was hard fishing at Mr. Knapp's lodge, the only fly that would take a fish at all was a Bastard Dose No. 8, and any number of fish up to 25 or 28 pounds were killed on it. It has always been a good fly there in low water. It also takes fish in the St. John River, but I have never been able to kill in the Tobique with it. It is the same with dry flies for salmon: one season when I was at the mouth of Kedgwick Colonel Rogers sent Mike Broderick up to see if I could tie an imitation of a Bumble Bee. He and Colonel Thompson had seen a fish come up and take one that was floating down through a pool. I happened to have some yellow and black chenille in my kit for a body and with that and some very transparent feathers from the inside wing of the hen blackbird for wings, I managed to put something together that was a fair imitation. They caught fish with it as fast as they could get it on the water, and for three days I did nothing but tie Bumble Bees for those two men. One day I tied up a couple of dozen of this fly and went up to Mr. Knapp's lodge to see if we could catch fish with it, as he had some good dry fly water. We took Howard Finnemore for a guide and went up river to a pool that held a lot of fish. The fish lay in close to the bank on one side, in water where there was quite a current. Putting Howard up a leaning cedar over the pool, to tell us where our flies were in relation to the fish, we waded out from the other shore and commenced casting. When we were up almost under our arms in the water, we were still a good eighty feet from the fish and there was a high gravel bar behind us, which was just right to catch any low backcasts and break the hooks. In about an hour's time we had broken the hooks off all the flies but had killed two fish and raised a lot more. The mosquitoes had almost devoured Howard and it was a long time before we could get him up another tree. The Bumble Bee has proven to be a very successful fly.

Mr. Roy Atwood, a well-known New York fisherman who fishes Dartmouth River in Gaspé, Quebec, is very partial to a fly dressed with a green body tied spindle-shape with two Plymouth Rock hackles tied on with the fronts back to back. This makes each hackle curve out in opposite directions and consequently the fly is more showy in the water. I have never been able to take a fish with this fly on either the Tobique or St. John River.

Mr. George D. B. Bonbright who fishes the Grand Cascapedia sent me a fly some years ago, designed wholly by himself, dressed with a silver body and Lady Amherst feathers for wings, with which he was having great success. I commercialized this fly and called it Bonbright No. 2, having named one other fly for him, which I called the No. 1. This fly can now be purchased in tackle shops under the name of The Lady Amherst, and is a grand fly on most rivers; fifty per cent of Grand Cascapedia fish are taken on it, though it is very seldom that the Tobique fish will look at it. Instances like these would make one believe that different rivers fish with different ideas in regard to flies.

I am very particular about the hooks on which my flies are tied, and there is a great improvement in hooks today over those used even ten or twelve years ago. The lightly-dressed patterns, of course, together with the dry flies, and the flies for the Arthur Wood Method of fishing, have made it necessary that different patterns of hooks be developed. For wet flies I like hooks slightly out point, such as Hardy's Oval Wire, and I also like them for long Dee irons. For light wire hooks I use Hardy's Low Water doubles and singles, although I would like them better, I think, if they took a little larger bite. The so-called Rational hooks of Price Tannatt are excellent, and good-looking flies can be tied on them. For the bushy-hackled dry flies, a hook with a larger gap is needed, and Hardy makes one with a turn-down eye especially for these flies.

As a rule I do not like long shanked hooks with a small bend. They have never held fish well for me. I think there is too much leverage. But certain patterns of flies must be dressed on them in order to be attractive to the fish.

The points of hooks should be sharp, and they should be watched carefully when fishing, especially if wading, because the least touch on rocks breaks them. Double hooks of today are vastly different from what they used to be, but you will find flies now in some of the tackle shops dressed on the old patterns of hooks, which look stubby and blunt. These hooks not only make a terrible looking fly, no matter how well they are dressed, but they are hard to hook a fish with. They go home so hard that a man could hardly be blamed for striking with hooks of this kind.

The knots used in fishing are so few and simple that one should learn to tie them the first thing. If you cannot figure out the way of tying them from the numerous illustrations in fishing catalogues or books, any guide on the river can show you.

For tying the leader to the wet fly the figure-eight knot is best. It is easily tied and untied, but care should be taken that a little of the gut is left over for the knot to tighten up on when the fish takes the fly. Then there is no danger of the knot's pulling through.

For tying strands of gut together for salmon leaders the water knots and other similar ones will not do, because there is such a heavy strain put on them, and these knots will cut the gut. The best knot is the double blood knot, which, while not a difficult knot to learn, requires some practice in order that the rolls of gut lie nicely side by side, and not on top of one another.

For attaching dry flies with up-turned eyed hooks, the Turle knot is best. For large wet flies with up-turned eyes the Cairnton is best, as it not only holds well but leaves the end of the gut left over, after the knot is tied, to lie in between the wings as in the figure-eight knot.

There have been advanced all sorts of reasons why salmon take a fly: mine, since I happen to be a fly tier, is that my flies are so attractive that salmon cannot help taking them! I really think that the flash of a fly has more to do with it than anything else. A fish is naturally on the lookout for everything coming along in the water, and would naturally make a rush for any strange flashing

Courtesy of James Colgate

ONE OF MR. COLGATE'S POOLS ON THE MIRAMICHI

ANOTHER OF MR. COLGATE'S POOLS

FORKS POOL ON THE TOBIQUE

HOME POOL IN FRONT OF LODGE ON THE TOBIQUE

Courtesy of Joseph P. Knapp

RUGGED WATER ON THE NATASHQUAN

thing. The fly may, however, as some claim, look like something he has fed on in the ocean, or his taking it may result from the habit he formed when he was young and fed on flies in the river. Salmon take trout flies readily in the Miramichi and the St. John; and I know a man in Nova Scotia, with the reputation of taking more salmon there than anyone else, who uses nothing but Rube Wood and White Miller trout flies dressed on double hooks. I have killed fish on a Black Gnat with the body tied with black seal's fur. I am sure that some patterns of flies enrage the salmon, because I have known any number of fish to make vicious drives, with their mouths wide open, at a fly right in front of the boat, where I could see the whole thing. The Durham Ranger pattern they seem to dislike especially. You can see them picking off any of the natural flies on the water at times, and they will also take angleworms; but they evidently eject them, because we never find anything in their stomachs. I did once kill a fish on the Kedgwick River which, when opened, contained what was pronounced, by a doctor who was fishing with me, to be a tapeworm. One thing I know salmon are particular about: that the artificial fly be in proportion. I have never yet seen a successful fly that was not.

The question as to why a salmon takes the fly is generally asked for one of two reasons: first, because information on the subject is really wanted, and second, to start an argument. I have found the latter reason to be the more frequent, and the question is usually asked by someone who has seen salmon take natural insects off the water. But he does not usually add that he has also seen them rise for dead leaves and other things floating downstream. For years it has been known positively that they do not feed in fresh water. I do not see anything peculiar about that, for they come into the river rolling in fat which they have accumulated feeding in the ocean, and they live on that fat until they go back. Bears live all winter on the fat they have accumulated feeding in the summer and there are other instances of the same thing. The greatest evidence of this non-feeding is the fact that there are still trout, chubb and other fish in the salmon rivers. If the salmon were feeding the other fish certainly would not last more than a few days, since fish that are known to have grown fourteen pounds in one season would soon clean out everything in the way of food. A hundred years ago when our rivers were full of salmon, records show there was fine trout fishing too.

Fishermen often ask, "How do you know what size and pattern of fly to use at a given time?" The size depends on the height, condition and temperature of the water. If the river is high and colored, the fly must be large enough for the fish to see, and if the water is cold the fly must be heavy enough to fish near the bottom where the fish are lying. A small fly may be used, however, no matter how cold the water, if the water is clear and the air is warmer than the water. The pattern is governed by the color of the water, and how the light strikes it; and the type of fly depends on whether it is to be fished deep, near the surface, or on it. Guides who are familiar with a pool know that when a certain rock begins to show out of water, or by some other such mark, a certain size is right. This they have found out from experience. But because, we'll say, a No. 6 fly is right for one pool, it will not necessarily be right for some other, because the two pools may be of entirely different kinds of water and the way the light strikes them may be different.

About the third year of my salmon fishing I procured copies of Kelson's books, THE SALMON FLY and TIPS. I studied his methods of fishing all winter, and had every pattern he recommended tied for me in England in nearly all the sizes; and that spring I started out, sure that I would take fish at any time. But I didn't, and the third year afterwards went back to my old patterns and to the way I had learned to fish them from the guides and others who had taught me. I have had a great many disappointments in my salmon fishing but that was the biggest one. Some eight years afterwards General Eagles of Yelverton, England, sent me a lot of flies that had been tied and fished by Kelson, and they were nothing like the flies he had recommended in his books and of which he had shown cuts. These flies had slim bodies and very little dressing, and were beautifully tied.

About then I began to tie salmon flies and copied as nearly as I could the flies General Eagles had sent me for my own fishing. They were more successful than flies I had been buying. When I began to commercialize flies I tied them as nearly like them as I dared to, but fishermen would not buy them at first. They were not as pretty as the old ones we had been using. But it didn't take the guides long to catch on, and through their insistence that sportsmen use them, my flies became quite popular.

It was a long while before I would believe that the flies I tied were at all good, and in spite of the fact that all the guides told me they would take fish, when I went out on the water I always tied on a fly that had come from some fly dresser in England. Manzer Howard, however, who used to guide me in those days, in tying on a fly for me occasionally tied on one of my own, and after we had killed a fish on it would show it to me. But it was not until the guides began to come to me for my flies for their own fishing that I had a great deal of faith in them.

The only one of Kelson's flies with which I ever had any pronounced success was his Little Inky Boy for low-water fishing; and I should have realized then that a black slim body was a good fly in low water. Perhaps if I had done some experimenting with it and had tied on different wings sparsely I might have originated the Blue Charm, which is so successful now. The Inky Boy had a body wound with gut dyed black and with very thin wings. One season on the Restigouche, when we had a long spell of very low water, it was almost the only fly we could fish to kill a salmon; I remember giving some of them to Mr. Henry De Forest, president of the club, and, as I remember, he did well with them. Kelson's Beauly Snow fly would take a fish occasionally in high water, but I never had much success with his other patterns.

The late George Burtis of Worcester, Mass., who could tie a beautiful fly, used to dress the Causapscal fly for me, using mottled yellow feathers for the wings, which were much better than the plain yellow ones. Burtis taught me to tie trout flies, but I regret to say he died before I took up my salmon fly dressing. I fished with him one summer in Maine and he was a fine fisherman. His father, Judge Burtis of St. John, N. B., was a famous salmon fisherman. I have always claimed a man has to be a fisherman to be a good fly tier.

I have tied thousands of different combinations of furs, silks and feathers and have tried them over fish, but the only successful ones were in a way similar to some of our standard patterns. Once I bought a cinnamon turkey in order to get the feathers, which I tied up into every imaginable thing in the way of flies. But I never even raised a fish on any of them until the grilse came in July. Then there was one pattern they went crazy over, and we killed a lot of them with it. There is a great kick in tying a fly yourself and then going out and killing a salmon with it.

I thought Kelson was a great man until I found his stuff wouldn't work, but I do not feel so hard toward him now because lots of other writers have disappointed me since with their advice on rods, leaders, flies, methods and theories. Not too long ago a fisherman wrote at length explaining a certain something he had discovered about fishing; and, because it didn't sound quite right to me, I took his book to a very learned man who was authority on that subject, and asked him to read it and tell me what he thought of it. A few days later I called on him and asked him what he had to say. His answer was, "The best I can say for it is I look on it with sympathy." I hope no fisherman looks on this book that way!

I used to dress some of the all-hackled dry flies with a silver body with the hackles wound over it. I did not use as many hackles on these flies in order to give the silver a chance to show through. Some days they were better than the ordinary patterns. I know that salmon will rise to anything bright like silver, as I have thrown silver cigarette foil over salmon from a bridge, and when it would float down over them they would rise to it repeatedly. I have tied fore-and-aft flies, hackled at the head and tail only, with the middle of silver. Fish always rise well to this pattern, but it will not float high for long. There is not enough hackle to hold it up. The Bonbright dry fly is an enlarged yellow May fly, and Col. Thompson thought that it was the three extra long fibers used in the tail that made it so deadly. He wrote me that he had repeatedly cut them off when fish were taking well, and was not able to raise a fish. But they would immediately take one with the tail fibres left on. This fly does not always land right side up, as it should, when cast. It is inclined to fall over on its side. But when you can get it to float right, it is the best salmon dry fly I know of. I have cut off some of the hackles at the bottom of the fly, which helps make it ride as it should, and then again, I have tied it as a fore-and-aft fly, but the fish evidently do not like that extra hackle in front. It is a very frail fly and goes to pieces easily. I used to dress a fly for George Bonbright which he called the "Cat's Whiskers." It was tied with long soft blue dun hackles fore-and-aft, and would take fish. Mr. Moncure Biddle of Philadelphia once gave me some flies dressed with peacock feathers for hackles which would take fish at times. Trout patterns such as Blue Dun, March Brown, Greenwell's Glory and dozens of others dressed on No. 6 and No. 8 hooks have never been successful for me. But some of them on hooks as small as No. 12 would raise fish.

Hair flies have been fished with conspicuous success by some salmon fishermen, notably Col. Edmund P. Rogers, Walter C. Teagle and the late Lewis Thompson. Col. Thompson, who was probably the first to use them, named this method "the Patent."

Flies tied from red squirrel tail have always been good trout flies. Grey squirrel tail, deer tail, badger and goat's beard make the best ones for salmon. I always use goat's beard when I can get it.

The most successful way of fishing these flies for salmon is to fish them as you would a dry fly or as in greased line fishing, except that the hair fly is not fished on a taut line. The fly is pulled back by the rod before it strikes the water, and allowed to float dead on a loose line. Oftentimes, however, a little motion with the rod, to make the hair open and shut, proves attractive. The best patterns of hair flies for salmon are the Abbey, Grizzly King, Teagle Bee, Silver Bob and Silver Betty.

The origin of hair and streamer flies is uncertain, but I distinctly remember while fishing with my father over fifty years ago, seeing Indians fishing for land-locked salmon on Grand Lake Stream in Maine using not only white bear tail tied on bare hooks, but also white feathers.

Collection of William H. Wheelock, Esq.

FORK'S POOL—TOBIQUE

FROM A WATER COLOUR PAINTING BY OGDEN M. PLEISSNER

CHAPTER V.

CASTING

IT is a well-known fact that casting a fly is not learned from books. Even if it could be, the reader would often be discouraged at the very beginning, by being told, as by one writer in a recent book: "You have a long hard row to hoe." I do not see how such a row could possibly be hard to hoe, when you are having fun all the time you are learning. It seems to be universal among writers, in describing a cast, to make it appear as difficult as possible; and some of them devote pages no end to telling how to do a simple little thing, for example, the overhead cast.

On one fishing trip I was the guest of a man who was an especially good caster. His wife was an experienced surf caster; for six months he had been trying to teach her to cast a fly on their lawn at home. She had a chance to cast on water now, but was getting nowhere. Another gentleman, whose fishing lodge was nearby, had also tried to teach her, with no success. Remember, both of these men were not only good casters, but were writers on the subject as well. The day I arrived, they were both on the wharf with her, and were telling her so many things to do, and not to do, that she was nearly frantic. She turned to me and asked if I thought she could ever learn. I told her that of course she could. She then asked me if I would try to teach her, and I told her I would be delighted, on the one condition that she send those two lunatics away! In less than half an hour she was casting seventy to eighty feet of line as nicely as you would care to see. Her head had been filled with so many things that must be done, that her mind was on too many things at once, and it all seemed too much for her. All that was necessary to do was to show her what a simple thing it was, and to let her think of one thing instead of forty.

The beginner should first be made to understand that it is the rod that does the casting, and that in order to make the rod do the work, he must hold it firmly. If possible, do the first casting on a good current of water, as this will hold the line up instead of burying it. Do not stand squarely facing the object at which you are going to cast, but just enough sideways so that you can glance over your shoulder and watch the backcast without craning your neck around. You will be just as accurate in this position, and you avoid the danger of the line or fly fouling the rod tip.

You cast back and forth, off the point of the shoulder, not over it. You are using now a two-hand rod of perhaps twelve feet. Pull off twenty or twenty-five feet of line from the reel and let it float off in front of you on the current, which will hold it up. Now lower the point of the rod to within say a foot of the water. Be sure that the line is fully extended and with no bags in it. If there are, pull in enough line to straighten it. The object in having the line straightened out is that the action of the rod in making the backcast may pull all the line off the water in one continuous motion. Now, by whipping it up and stopping it as near the vertical as possible, make the rod pull the line off the water and throw it well up in the air behind you. Then just glance over your shoulder, and when the line has straightened out, whip the rod forward, which will throw the line out in front of you on the water. Do not hurry either the back cast or the forward one. Take your time. Be sure you are not moving in a jerky manner, and in a short while, with practice, you will begin to develop a rhythm that will be quite noticeable.

If you wish to develop accuracy always cast at some particular spot on the water. Do not cast out promiscuously, anywhere. I do not like the expression "pushing the line out." The rod, if handled right, drives the line out, and in order to make the drive more pronounced, I like to strike down, as Fred Shaw used to express it. Also, by making the forward cast in this manner, you can defeat any wind that may come up. Remember, it is a salmon fly we are casting, which is generally of good size and has some weight, not a light trout fly, which can be flipped about, here and there, at will.

Very few fishermen ever learn the fundamentals of casting. They make a bad cast, then get someone to show them how to do it right. But they never learn why their cast is bad in one instance and good in the other. An illustration of this sometimes occurs in casting a wet fly from a boat. When the cast swings around in front of us, we pick it up and cast off to either the right or left. And when the line lands on the water, we see a bag in it. Therefore, we have to "mend" that cast, or pick it up and do it over again. When a cast falls so that the line lies in a curve downstream, instead of straight, it may be mended by "looping" the line in such a manner that the downstream bag or curve is thrown upstream without pulling the fly from the water. Why was there a bag in that cast? Because we took the line out of the plane it was in and put it in another. It is poor judgment ever to let a bad cast swing around, since you never know at what second a salmon may take the fly. It is a great deal better to take it off the water lightly, with as little disturbance as possible, and cast over again.

The pull of the line when the cast has straightened out behind you is not noticeable to the beginner, and will not become so until he has done a lot of casting. That is why it is well to stand a trifle side-to, so you can watch the backcast. One has to fish over a considerable period of time before he really gets the feel of the rod and of other things having to do with fishing. It is no exaggeration at all to say that you can feel the hook go home when you hook a fish, or that you can tell exactly when you have reached the limit your leader will stand in pulling on a fish. A number of times I have had two rods exactly alike in length, weight and action. You could not tell one from the other in casting up to a certain distance. But from there on, one would loaf on the job, while you could feel the other give the line a kick at the end of the cast. One of those rods was game, but the other was yellow. When one can detect things like that, he knows what the feel of a rod is.

If one holds the rod lightly, he is more inclined to cast in a lackadaisical sort of way and not get the idea that the rod must do the work. So once more, let me repeat, grasp the rod firmly, as though you intended to make it work for you. Do not be afraid of it just because it is a light, delicate affair. Concentrate on keeping the backcast high and letting it straighten out well before making the forward cast. If you take care to do this, the forward cast will take care of itself. Casting is like the golf swing: if some certain part is done right, other parts just naturally follow.

A well-known teacher of fly casting once told me that he had been told, by a gentleman who said he had never cast on water, that from reading his book he had learned to do on grass all the different casts described in it. The gentleman asked him to come and watch him do them on water, to see if he were doing them correctly. The instructor watched him for an hour, and told me that he had done every cast perfectly. I never quite believed it, but I have no doubt he had learned the fundamentals, which was a good beginning. I believe in casting anywhere for practice; but casting on grass is not very satisfactory, as it exerts too little pull on the line to bring out the action of the rod. The best practice I know of, on a lawn, is to walk around keeping the line alive in the air, lengthening and shortening it as you do it. If there are trees about, all the better; and do not forget to shoot the line under every rosebush you see. Strip off some of the line, and carry it in coils in the left hand. Practice shooting one or more coils at a time. This is good for your dry fly fishing with a one-hand rod, when you get to it.

In salmon fishing from a canoe or a Gaspé boat the overhead cast is the only one used, except in a downstream wind, when the switch cast is useful. You never can tell what a downstream wind will do to a backcast, as, for instance, blowing it around so that you hook your guide or yourself when you make the forward cast.

The switch cast is made by raising the rod to get all of the line in motion and by dragging the line back with the rod held near the horizontal at the side; then, when the tip has gone a trifle back of you or as far as the bushes, or whatever the obstruction may be behind you, will allow (in case you may be fishing from the shore), the line is looped over and out, with a finish of the cast on the upward side: this permits shooting the line.

The line may be shot with the loop, switch or Spey cast, provided the finish of the cast is made out instead of down. In fishing these casts this way, the line does not roll in the nice round loop that it would have if there was a more downward finish to the rod, but you can get more distance because you can shoot line.

The loop cast is done in the same way, only the line is dragged back with the rod at the perpendicular, or just off the point of your shoulder. When the loose line passes your elbow in a big belly, make the forward cast down and out, with the tip of the rod finishing slightly up. This keeps the cast off the water until some line has been shot.

The Spey cast is used when the current has brought the fly around and it

Courtesy of Joseph P. Knapp

LITTLE CHUTE, FIRST FALLS ON JOSEPH P. KNAPP'S WATER ON THE NATASHQUAN RIVER

The salmon happened to jump—though not for the fly—just as this picture was "snapped" lies below you on your side of the river, and you wish to cast it opposite you across the current. The first movement is to raise the rod, lifting all the line possible off the water and getting it moving. Then, as in the switch cast, with the rod at nearly the horizontal, except that this time the line is not dragged back, the line is snatched back so decidedly that it leaves the water and deposits the fly and leader (also part of your line, too, unless you are quite expert) on the water again just above you; the tip of the rod in the meantime has described a part circle around and out, which throws the line and fly across the river. This is all done with one continuous motion of the rod.

The first motion in all three of these casts is to raise the rod, bringing as much line as possible to the surface and getting it all moving.

It is difficult to acquire the timing of the Spey cast; hence it requires a great deal of practice. When the fly is lying below you on your side of the river, you face the river, or across it toward your objective; and after the side swing back with the rod, which snatches everything off the water, the fly and leader are left on the water just above you. You get the swing of your body and your shoulder into the cast, making it easier to snatch the line off the water, especially if you have a long line out. There are three things to remember in doing this cast and they will all seem appropriate after you have become a little familiar with them: lift, swing, throw. For instance, lift line; turn and snatch it off the water sideways; throw it across the river. That is, as nearly as I can tell you, what the Spey cast is. It is a hard cast to make intelligible on paper.

The Wye cast is simply an easier way of taking the fly out of one place and putting it in another. If the fly is at a certain spot and you want to cast at a spot in another direction, turn, before you make your backcast, and face that spot to which you wish to cast. I never thought this cast accomplished much and would always rather pick up the first cast as soon as it landed and do it over again. In other words, mend or doctor it.

The Galway is a lot of fun if you want to cast more line than someone else, but is little used in fishing except when you want to make a long cast and there happens to be an opening in the woods or bushes for your backcast. With this cast you eliminate the danger of being hung up on the backcast, because you are turned around facing it and can see just where to place it. It is all in placing your feet correctly when you turn around, since in this cast you must turn completely around.

The line is extended out in front of you and you hold the slack that is to be shot coiled in your hand. Stand, turned to the left about one-quarter way around, looking over your shoulder at the fly and line. Have the left toe pointed straight back and the right foot square across, turn the rod over in your hand with the reel turned somewhat toward the top, and make your backcast as you would a forward cast; as you turn, face the opening you have chosen for the fly. Now get your feet in place to make a complete turn which consists of again turning one-quarter way around and placing the feet as before, make your forward cast, stepping all the way forward with your right foot. If you make this backcast as you do a forward one, you can get a lot of power into it and get it high, and you are in a good position to make a good forward cast and shoot a lot of line. One can get much more distance this way than by using the straight overhead cast. A friend of mine who was a fine caster, but who had never done any tournament casting and was not familiar with the tackle or methods used, once attended a tournament in which each competitor had a man kneeling at his feet to keep the slack line nicely coiled and see that it did not foul or tangle up when it was shot. In other words, each man had a helper. My friend did not know anything about it, but he did know the Galway cast. When the tournament was over he was invited by the winner to try his outfit, to see how he liked the game; which he did. By using the Galway cast he beat this man's longest cast by some feet. They all immediately called it a foul cast and said it could not be allowed. My friend's only comment was, "Well, it may be foul, but I didn't have to have anyone help me do it." In less than fifteen minutes every man there was practicing the Galway.

A man who claimed to be a champion caster once came to a camp where I was fishing. As we had been killing a lot of fish, more or less Scotch whiskey was being drunk, as was the custom in those days. This man carried his liquor none too well, and before long was about ready to pass out of the picture. We were on the verandah of the camp, guides and all, and just as this man had finished telling of a certain long cast he had made, what I judged to be about a thirty-pound salmon jumped in the home pool right in front of us. He didn't see the fish but heard him, and shouted for the guide to bring his rod. We all tried to discourage him from going out in the canoe, but he was determined, and his guide helped him to it and eased him in. He immediately began stripping line off the reel, casting and, as he supposed, shooting line. After two or

THE AUTHOR FISHING THE "MILLION DOLLAR POOL"
ON RESTIGOUCHE

FROM AN ETCHING BY ROBERT NISBET, N.A.

three minutes of this he had about thirty feet of line wound all around the rod, and as he stripped it off the line now was tangling around his feet. After each cast he would ask the guide if he had reached the fish yet, and the guide would tell him, "No, it will take a longer cast than that to reach that fish." Finally he said, "I think I'll stand up. I can throw a longer line that way." When he stood up the guide was ready for him and caught him as he fell over backwards, and in some way kept the canoe from upsetting. When he was brought ashore we untangled him and put him to bed, and left his rod with about a peck of line and backing just as he brought it in. The next morning when he saw it he was quite indignant and wanted to know how it got in that condition. To which the owner of the camp replied, "Some of your long casts didn't go out quite as well as they might have last night, I guess." We heard no more about his long distance casting after that!

Once, while I was fishing a pool on the Miramichi River with Jack Mack as guide, we saw a cow moose downstream, in water up to her shoulders. She was feeding on the roots of lily pads, and each time she brought her head up, she flopped her big ears to keep off the flies. Her back was turned to us, and Jack was able to let the canoe drift to within sixty feet of her. "Now," he said, "hook her in the ear. You've caught everything but a moose—perhaps you can land her."

Every time she put her head down, I stripped off some line, and when she brought it up, I cast at her ears. Finally the fly either dropped on one of them, or very near it, for when she twitched it, she hooked herself. When that moose felt the steel and looked around and saw us, there was action aplenty. It didn't take her long to get out of the muddy water and onto hard ground, and all the while I was trying to break the leader and save my line, which I did just as she was disappearing into the woods. Since then I haven't tried to land any more moose on salmon tackle.

SHOWING METHOD OF FISHING FROM A GASPÉ BOAT—ST. JOHN RIVER

Photographs courtesy of Samuel Watts

PLAYING A ST. JOHN RIVER FISH—THE ROD IS AT THE PROPER ELEVATION

CHAPTER VI.

FISHING THE WET FLY

IN Canada salmon fishing is done almost entirely from Gaspé boats and canoes, as there are very few rivers suitable for wading, although there are some wadable rivers in Nova Scotia. On large rivers where the water is heavy, Gaspé boats are used, because they are safer and more comfortable to fish from. Some of them are built very elaborately, with mahogany gunwales, and are equipped with a swivel chair, and a large umbrella for wet weather and hot sun. They have two men, the bow man and the stern man, the former having complete charge. The bow man is supposed to have a thorough knowledge of the water to be fished, and tells the stern man when and where to drop the killick.

If the fishing happens to be poor, the fisherman often lets the bow man do the casting, while he sits under the umbrella and reads; but if a fish is hooked, the umbrella is lowered and he takes the rod and plays the fish. I could never quite understand this, except in the case of one not strong enough for continuous casting, as one thereby misses what seems to me the best part of the sport—the casting and hooking of the fish.

Some of the guides who do a lot of casting for their men are known as fishermen, and they consider it quite an honor. If a guide is a good man, he will guide the same sportsman year after year, and in some instances they become very much attached to each other. Many a mortgage has been paid off, and a horse and cow bought for a guide when he needed assistance, and the doctor's bill also taken care of.

Gaspé boats are very light for their size, and get their name from the fact they are built on the Gaspé coast in Quebec. They run easily in the water, and two good men will pole one many miles in a day, if they understand each other. The boats are usually twenty to twenty-two feet in length, with pointed ends.

On the smaller rivers, where there is little heavy water and few bad rapids, canoes are the proper thing, for with a canoe you can get over the river with very little disturbance; and, if necessary, they can be carried around pools and other places. They are light, and the guides simply throw them on their shoulders and walk off. They are eighteen to twenty feet in length, and weigh from seventy to ninety pounds, although for trout streams they are built much shorter and lighter.

To one not used to canoes, they seem frail and unsafe, but in the hands of a good man they will ride a heavy swell. You can't knock around in one as you can in a Gaspé, and it is pretty necessary to keep your weight in the center. The Chestnut canoe, built in Fredericton, New Brunswick, and the White, built in Bangor, Maine, are the two best.

Let's go on the water now and see if we can kill a fish. The guides pole us a mile up river to the head of the pool we are to fish, being careful as they pole by it, to keep close to the shore and not disturb the fish. Some two hundred yards or more before reaching the pool, they had reversed ends of the pole, and have been poling up with the wooden end. The other end, shod with an iron pick, would make too much noise on the rocks, and fish could hear it at a great distance.

The killick is now dropped well above the head of the pool, and we begin casting. The orthodox way is to cast well off to one side and let the fly swing around in front of you; then pick the cast up and do the same on the other side. After doing this, we strip about three feet, or the length of a salmon, off the reel, and cast as before, and we keep repeating this until we have reached the limit of our casting ability. The first cast is made with the line and leader the length of the rod. The bow man having watched carefully where your fly was swinging around on the last cast, orders the killick up, and we make what is known as a drop, downstream to a point where your first cast will not be beyond where your fly had been fished before. In this manner we fish down through the pool; and by using this method, we put our fly within sight of all the spots in which fish might be lying.

In making the cast to right or left, care must be taken that there be no bag in the line as it swings around. If there is, the cast should be mended, or picked up and done over. If there is a bag in the line when a fish hits the fly, you aren't as sure of hooking him as you would be if the line were straight, and he has a chance to spit out the fly before you can tighten on him.

We just made the statement that a fly fished down the pool in the orthodox way, would have to be seen by fish. What we intended to say was that it would be seen if the salmon were not asleep. I have no doubt that they are asleep many times when we fish over them; and why not? They do most of their traveling at night, and it is quite natural they would want to sleep and rest at some time during the day.

I remember a pot hole in what is known as the Jam Pool on the Kedgwick River. It is in close to the bank, and usually, before fishing it, I walked up to have a look and see if there were any fish there. Numerous times there have been two or three fish in it for days that I was unable to move with either wet or dry flies. Believing that fish move about at some time during the day, I commenced going to the pool in the morning with the rod and a book, to sit on the bank and read and watch the fish. Some days they would not move till four or five in the afternoon; other days it would be ten in the morning, and in some instances not till just before dark. With the rod right there, I could wade out above them and get a fly over them while they were swimming around, with the result that I often killed one or two of them. In watching those fish I couldn't help observing the spot at which they had chosen to lie; it was always where very little effort was required to hold them against the current. A gentle waving of the tail kept them in position, which was done just as you would imagine a sleepy fish would do it.

I have watched them behave the same way just below Pabineau Falls on the Nipisiguit, and on the island side opposite Tom's Brook on the Restigouche. I believe that leaving them alone and not fishing over them until they do start to move insures a much better chance of taking them.

I firmly believe in resting pools; and the fact that Mondays are almost always good fishing days, conditions being favorable, is because they have not been fished over the day before. Sunday fishing is not allowed. During high water, however, since fish travel then, one should fish all the time.

I think the reason that salmon will often take readily in a pool after it has been rocked is because they were asleep. Throwing a lot of big rocks in among them wakes them up.

We have fished down through the pool now without raising a fish, fishing the particular pattern and size of fly which seemed suitable to the water and weather conditions, and which is also one of this river's favorites. We feel certain, though, that we have gone over fish, as this pool always holds fish at this stage of the water. So let's go back carefully to the head, and begin over, this time using a fly totally different from the one used before. If the other fly was a dark one, say a Black Dosc, we shall try a Silver Grey now, and reduce the size. In changing flies, it is well to try a smaller size, and also a larger one occasionally, than looks right for the water. For a fish that has raised, it is customary on most rivers to reduce the size. On the Grand Cascapedia, however, the size is customarily increased; but the fish there are very large.

In fishing down this time, we are going to fish only the "sore spots," or the particular places where fish always lie, if there are any in the pool. We are doing this, because another gentleman is to fish the same water this afternoon, and it would not be entirely fair to him if we gave it too much of a going over. Fish your water thoroughly, but don't flog it to death. Even if you are over a fish that refuses, don't keep at him too long. Go try somewhere else, and come back to him later. I have heard a gentleman, who enjoys some reputation as a salmon fisherman, say, "Show me a fish and I'll take him;" and I have known him to take a fish after casting over him for two hours. To me this signifies only one thing—that the fish was finally in a mood to take. It does not mean that the angler had finally outwitted him, or taken him by an especially good cast, or some particular manipulation of the fly.

There are different ways of presenting and manipulating the fly, which make it especially attractive to fish in certain spots and currents of water; and they will take the fly presented in one of these ways when they won't look at it presented in any other. But not always, and there is no rule to follow. What salmon do today has nothing to do with how they may perform tomorrow, even under the same conditions. I think it is better after giving the fish a chance to take the fly presented in several different ways, to leave him alone, if he has refused, instead of trying to tire him out.

Salmon fishermen generally begin their day's fishing around nine in the morning, fishing until lunch time at one o'clock, and later go out again at four

PERCY FAULDING, ONE OF THE GREAT CANADIAN CANOE MEN, NEGOTIATING INDIAN FALLS ON THE NIPISIGUIT and fish till dark. In the early spring, of course, or when the river is in flood, one should fish all day, because fish are running then and not stopping long in the pools. Later on, when the water is down, and they are in the pools, they need resting for the best results. I have known a man to take his lunch with him in the morning, and stay on a pool till the man who had that water for the afternoon fishing arrived, and, of course, the latter had no fishing whatever. Such men don't last long. And in connection with this I would like to add that it is only occasionally now that you hear of a salmon fisherman who wants to see "the boats run blood." A couple of fish in the morning and two or three more in the evening is called good fishing. The limit in New Brunswick, for instance, is thirty fish a week, with no Sunday fishing.

We have fished the pool through twice now, and have a good idea of how a wet fly is cast with a two-hand rod from a boat. But as we have not raised a fish, some excuse is now in order. Fog or mist may have been on the water, or hanging on the hills. An east wind may have been blowing; or we may just have had a big rise of water. Perhaps there has been thunder during the day; or any one of a number of other conditions which are supposed to be bad for salmon fishing may have existed. But nevertheless, fish are taken at times under just such adverse conditions. So there is only one thing to do, and that is to keep on fishing. These are good times to improve your casting.

The question has often been raised as to the particular point when the fly is most attractive to salmon while being fished in this orthodox manner—whether while it is swinging around, or when it comes to rest in front of you. Some claim it is when the fly stops. The fish has been following it, and suddenly seeing it dead still, grabs it. This has not been my experience. The fly seems to me more deadly when it makes the fish think it is being taken away from him. To illustrate: one very successful method is to cast and draw, that is, to make your cast, and, while the fly is swinging around, to keep drawing in the line. This slack will all be shot on your next cast. The only bad feature of this way is that a salmon may rise for the fly just as you draw, with the result that you take the fly right out of his mouth. In any event, it often brings them up, which is seventy-five per cent of the fun. The casting is the other twenty-five per cent. Anyone who enjoys playing fish can have my rod anytime. I haven't always felt like that, however.

Oftentimes when your fly has come to rest in front of you, and you begin to reel in, a salmon will take it. He had seen the fly stop in front of him while you were casting, and it did not appeal to him. But on seeing it suddenly come over his head, and apparently being taken away from him, he rushed and took it. I believe, as Mr. William B. Mershon does, that a salmon is like a dog: you run, and he chases you; you stop, and he stops.

The size and presentation of the fly seems to me to be everything, while the pattern matters least of all. There are many ways of presenting the fly, and one of the best I know, for a pool that you have fished down through with no result, is to let your guide pole you up along the side slowly, while you keep casting straight across and drawing the fly past the noses of the fish. A fish I once hooked in this way in the Meadows Pool on Kedgwick kept me and Murray Howard, my guide, there half of one afternoon. He was a big hook-bill, and all he knew how to do was to bore away out in the middle of the heavy water. I hooked him on a light single-hand rod, and he played us both out. Murray would fight him a while, and then I would. I think we would have been there yet, if a boat had not come down river and frightened him out, so that we finally were able to kill him.

The speed at which the fly is fished is very important. In high water a slow fly seems best, but in low water a fast one gets the best results. You will notice that most salmon fishermen give their fly motion by moving the point of the rod up and down. It becomes a habit after a while and we do it unconsciously. But half the time we are giving the fly no motion whatever. On a short line we do, but when there is any length of line out, the motion is all taken up in the line before it ever reaches the fly. Then there must be a decided lift to the line in order to affect the fly. If a salmon comes to the fly and misses while you are working it, when you cast back at him, let the fly swing around with no motion, and you will probably hook him. You took it away from him before. There are a lot of little tricks like this, and if your guide is an old fisherman, you will learn many of the ones he knows. If you watch your fishing carefully, you will see fish take the fly in a number of different ways, which should suggest to you different methods of taking them. Be inventive, and you will find ways of taking salmon—plenty of them.

An instance of resourcefulness in salmon fishing is the way Mr. Joseph Knapp of New York takes fish in a certain pool on the Natashquan. He sings to them. He has discovered that the fish in this particular pool rise best when a

JAMES C. COLGATE

WILLIAM B. MERSHON

GEORGE D. B. BONBRIGHT

JOSEPH P. KNAPP

FOUR OUTSTANDING AMERICAN SPORTSMEN AND SALMON FISHERMEN

fly is cast beyond them and then dragged over them; and as he drags the fly over them, he sings to them. He once had two guests at his lodge who made a wager as to which of them would catch more fish the next day. Giving them two of his best pools the next morning, Mr. Knapp went on up river. When he came down that evening, he found that the gentleman fishing the upper of the two pools had taken only two fish all day. Going on down to the pool where the salmon must be sung to, he found his other guest, who had also killed only two fish. Mr. Knapp asked him why he hadn't killed more. "There are lots of fish here," he replied, "but I can't raise them."

"Did you sing to them?" asked Mr. Knapp.

"Sing, hell. Don't be silly."

"All right, give me a rod," said Mr. Knapp. And taking it, he cast out beyond where the fish lay. As he dragged the fly in over them, he sang at the top of his lungs, and just as he was singing loudest, a big salmon rose and took the fly. Mr. Knapp killed him and passed the rod back to his guest. "Now," he said, "you sing to them. I want you to catch one and win your bet." The gentleman took the rod, burst into song, hooked and killed a twenty-three-pound salmon, and won the money.

Mr. Knapp, incidentally, in twenty-two years of fishing on seven different rivers—though mostly on the Natashquan—has killed seven thousand and fifty-four salmon. He is a very fine fisherman indeed and knows all the wrinkles of the game.

Oftentimes they come up lazily and simply suck the fly in. Then again they make those vicious drives at it, with mouths wide open, which lead you to believe that the fly has made them mad and that they are trying to kill it. I have known certain patterns of flies to have this effect, particularly a Durham Ranger, which is a very bright, gaudy fly. There will be times during the season when for a week or more all along the river the fish will come short, and just nip the feathers. You can fool these fish by using short dressed flies, as for instance, a No. 6 dressing on a No. 4 hook.

A fisherman becomes familiar with all these things, from constant fishing year after year. When he sees a fish in a certain place and has taken into consideration the different conditions, he quite naturally presents the fly in a way that should attract the fish. This is fish sense, and fishermen who don't have it are not very successful when the fishing is hard. It differs in a way from that sense which the trout fisherman has, inasmuch as the trout fisherman can look over the water and tell at a glance the fishy looking spots, whereas the salmon man fishes all the water, there being no telling where a salmon may be. But that does not prevent the salmon fisherman from manipulating his fly in a way to show it off best in different currents, or, for instance, from making his fly fish well in a spot from which the current tends to wash it away the instant it is cast. There is no fish sense required in fishing the orthodox way, but a man does not have to fish that way entirely, simply because it is universal, or because he happens to be in a boat. He can fish in any place and in any way that looks good to him. Any number of times I have known a man who never fished salmon before to be top rod for the day; but it was only because he was over fish and they were in a taking mood. That same man under hard conditions would not get many. The water would all look alike to him, and he would fish his fly in the same way, all through the pool.

When a salmon wants the fly, he nearly always gets it; and it is no uncommon thing to watch some fisherman's line, leader and fly all land on the water in a bundle, and then to see a salmon come up and pick the fly out of the mess. A number of times I have had a fish take the fly when I was trying it beside the boat, to see whether it was riding the water right before I cast it.

There is no doubt but that a good fisherman will take fish when the ordinary man can't. But there are times when he or no other man can take them. I have seen that proved too often. It is all very fine to think we have fooled a fish, and perhaps have taken him by a certain manoeuvring of the fly, or, in other words, have made him take the fly when he did not want it. This adds to our sport, but we haven't fooled the salmon at all. He wanted the fly in just that way, or he would not have come for it.

I shall cite a few instances which would perhaps make us think we had fooled a fish by a certain manner of presenting the fly; and, in doing this, I am going to introduce you to a man who is without any doubt the finest wet fly fisherman in Canada, Claude Knapp of Andover, New Brunswick. I say that, not because he has been my fishing and shooting companion for more than thirty years, but because he kills fish consistently, not only on his own water on Little Main Restigouche, but on any other water he fishes. He knows salmon, and has fish sense developed to an amazing degree, which, combined with good casting ability and over forty years' experience in fishing the whole of each season, makes invaluable any information he gives you. If I should tell him that any salmon could be made to take the fly by some particular method of presenting it, I know exactly what he would say: "Don't be a silly ass!" Mr. Knapp is an Englishman.

On his water is a pool called Eight Mile, which has a good current running down through it, and in which your fly swings around well. But the orthodox way of fishing is not successful there. The way to fish this pool best is to walk up the left shore, casting straight across and drawing. When there are fish there, you can almost always take some of them. But not always. I have fished there with Mr. Knapp for a whole day, when there were salmon in the pool, and we couldn't catch one. The next day, perhaps, they would all take.

I have seen Col. Archibald Rogers, and Col. Lewis Thompson, fish for days in Col. Rogers' water on Restigouche, and not raise even one, with probably three or four thousand fish there.

I found a fish well over thirty pounds in one of my pools on the Kedgwick one morning, and worked all day over him with wet and dry flies without moving him. The next morning he was still there, and while I was fishing him, Claude came along and tried him also with no success. Two days of as good fishing as we knew failed to raise him, and I remember wishing that a certain well-known dry fly man had been there to try him. I thought he would get him up. But today I don't think so: I have seen too many fish just like him. The next morning the fish had gone on up river.

I do think that if you can get a fish at all interested in your fly, and then make him think it is being taken away from him, you stand a good chance of catching him. The "Exaggeration and Modification" as fished by Kelson, which is an example of this, is often successful. It is done in this manner: we will suppose that a fish comes in a lazy sort of way to the fly, turns and goes back; after resting him a few minutes, you offer him the same fly again, with the same result. After that he refuses to rise at all to anything you offer. If you were fishing a No. 4 dark fly, for example, now change to a much larger and brighter pattern, such as Durham Ranger No. 2/0, or any one of a number of loud patterns. You cast this new fly to the left side, using the same length of line you had when he rose, but you shouldn't allow it to swing over him. Pick it up and cast to the other side, and again take it away before it goes over him. After showing him this pattern two or three times, change again to another pattern of a brilliant fly, and let him have a few looks at this, never allowing the fly to get near enough to him so that he might rise to it. Now go back to the fly he rose to, or some other similar fly in that size, and when you cast this time, allow the fly to swing over him. If he takes that, I have to admit I think you have fooled him. The idea was, he was a lazy fish, and something had to be done to wake him up. Showing him the bright patterns and taking them right away, stimulated him enough to make him take the fly with which he was only playing before. This might perhaps be called brain stimulation.

I can't think of anything better on the subject of fish that refuse to rise than to quote Howard Finnemore, the dean of all Tobique guides, who used to say to me when we happened to find such a fish: "There must be some way to take that fish, but we don't know; and by God, Charlie, there don't any other damn man." Howard is still right.

Fishing from the bank, or wading along the shore, is very little done on Canadian rivers—certainly not to the extent it is done in England and Scotland. Our rivers are not so adaptable, on account of their much larger size, and because the banks are heavily wooded. In fishing from the shore it is customary to keep casting pretty much the same length of line, taking one step for each cast, and allowing the fly to swing as in fishing from a boat. Some pools fish much better from the shore, as, for instance, a pool where the fish lie in close on one side or the other, and the river is narrow. You can't fish such a pool from the salmon's side, as the fly would not go over them in a way to attract them; and from a boat you are too much on top of the fish. Pools out in the middle of our rivers can't be reached by fishing from the shore, and in high water after a freshet it is impossible to do anything without a boat. I much prefer fishing on my feet from a canoe, although a Gaspé boat is much better, because you can stand up in it and fish comfortably. It is probably that old desire to get into a trout stream up to my neck that makes me want to fish my salmon wading! Fishy-looking places on a salmon river differ from those on a trout stream, only in the fact that there are more of them and that the water seems more oily. You can smell fish plainly in some of them, particularly in the Rock Pool on Grand Cascapedia.

If you have fished a pool, two or three miles down river, from a Gaspé boat, it is customary to have a man on horseback there, to tow you back to the lodge. It is an ordinary thing to see a horse coming up the Restigouche, towing

POLING UPSTREAM ON THE KEDGWICK

TOWING UP RIVER TO CAMP

Photographs courtesy of Richard C. Hunt

NOONDAY LANDING

three or four Gaspés with their fishermen, and the umbrellas all up. A horse and a man to ride him are part of your equipment on some rivers.

Many of the lodges on salmon rivers are to be reached only by towing upstream in scows, which are hauled by horses on shore. The scows are from twenty to thirty feet long, in many cases flat-bottomed and square at both ends, with a small deck-house in which to put the dunnage in case of wet weather. There is a man at the bow and another in the stern, whose job it is to keep the boat off the shore and rocks, and to head it right on the way up through rapids. These trips are always enjoyable, for you are continually passing fishermen out in the pools, see a great many salmon during the day, and have plenty of time to enjoy the grand scenery which borders most salmon rivers.

I was once taking my brother up to a lodge I had on a certain river. He always carried fifteen or twenty boxes of Seidlitz powders with him, and this trip was no exception. Going through some heavy rapids, we shipped about fifty barrels of water over the bow, the bow man not being on the job, and it rushed in one door of the deck-house and out the other, washing dunnage and everything else into the river. "Save the cat!" one of the men shouted, as a cat we were taking up to camp was washed overboard. "To hell with the cat," shouted my brother. "Save the Seidlitz powders!"

I once had an interesting experience in resting a pool. One season at Tom's Brook, from the first of July till the first of August, the Restigouche was extremely low, and it was said to be the driest summer the river had ever known. The mail boat men could just get up and down in their light Gaspés; they had to pick rocks out of the river at different places to make a channel. The fish in the river were all congregated in the cold spring holes and at the mouths of brooks. What fish there were in my water were strung along the shore below the mouth of Tom's Brook and were taking badly. It was only occasionally we could get a fish. One Monday night, returning to the camp just before dark, after fishing trout all day up the brook, I had one of the men set me across on the island, thinking I would try a few casts for salmon. On the first cast, one took the fly and started off down river, and it was long after dark before we killed him. After that I did no fishing on that water till about fifteen minutes before dark each night, and we always took one fish. After about a week of this, I tried early in the morning, and at five in the afternoon, with no result. Nor could I get one as usual the last thing at night. My daytime fishing had evidently ruined my chance of taking that one sure fish. From then on I left them alone during the day, and we again began taking our one fish at night, as we had before.

There are many ways of presenting the fly. One which is used a great deal in fishing the dry fly, is to use more force than necessary in the forward cast. This will make the fly kick back and drop lightly when the end of the slack line, as it shoots out, hits the reel. But I am not so sure that a wet fly should be dropped lightly if it is to interest a salmon. A fly striking the water with a pronounced spat often attracts a fish from quite a distance, certainly from farther than he could see it. Once, fishing the tail of a pool, where there was not over eighteen inches of water, I saw a fish come all of fifty feet for a fly. The water was so shallow that we could see his wake as he came, and it seemed as though he would never reach it. He was an enormous fish, and I was using less than thirty feet of line, so we had a good look at him when he rose. In all the excitement of watching him come and the big splash he made, I took the fly right away from him. I saw him open his mouth to take it, but I couldn't wait, and tightened before he had it. I don't believe he saw the fly from such a distance in that shoal water, but, rather, the explosion of light caused when it hit the water. How far fish can see a wet fly I don't know. At times it certainly seems as if they were far sighted; and at others, it appears to be necessary to drop the fly right on their noses, or they don't see it at all. This is probably because it does not excite their curiosity at a distance, or, as one writer claims, because they don't get brain stimulus enough.

But when the river is in flood, and running so full of mud that it would not seem possible for a fish to see the fly, what then? Such was the case the first year I had Tom's Brook. Wanting to be reasonably sure of some fishing that year, I had leased water on two different rivers, the Bogan Water, consisting of about five miles on the Nipisiguit, and Tom's Brook on the Restigouche, consisting of about a mile. I was on my way home from the Nipisiguit to spend Fourth of July, but on going through Campbellton I met Jack Wyers, the owner of Tom's Brook. "We've had a big raise of water," he said, "and the Restigouche is boiling, but it has dropped an inch today. If you are there day after tomorrow, you will get great fishing." I forgot all about Fourth of July, and taking Wyers with me, I went to Matapedia that night. The next morning he had a scow ready, with horses and men, and we towed the thirty miles up river to the lodge, arriving late that night. How those horses got up that river along the banks I don't know, for in places the water was running over the banks and into the woods. But they had been there before and knew their business. The river was full of old trees, stumps and snags coming downstream, and did not look to me as though it would be in condition to fish for a week. The next morning Wyers asked me how large the largest flies were which I happened to have along; and when I told him that they were 5/0 he said they were not half large enough, but that we would try them. On going over my flies, however, I found two 8/0 Night Hawks, which I gave him. We started out with only one man each in our Gaspés, as two of the men had failed to show up at Matapedia; which made it bad in that high water. He went down river to the lower pool, and I fished the upper one. As fish in this kind of water run up close to the shore we began fishing there, but it didn't make any difference where we fished. There were fish everywhere all over the river, and we took just as many on the outside cast as we did on the inside one. Wyers came back to the lodge for lunch and in the afternoon we exchanged pools. That night we had twenty-eight fish. I had eighteen and he had ten, but here is the interesting thing: he had all the big fish. While my largest was twenty-five, his was thirty-six, and his ten weighed within forty-eight pounds of my eighteen. He said that if he had had larger flies, he would have taken still larger fish. They could see my 5/0 fly, and I must have fished over some of those big fish, but the fly was not big enough for them. That was one Fourth of July I missed, but the fish I sent home supplied fifty-four families with all the salmon they could eat. Those fish certainly could not have seen the fly at any distance in that water, and the only way I can account for their seeing it at all is that they must have been swimming near the surface. Since that day I have believed in big flies for big fish, and I always carry them as large as five-inch irons. Jack Wyers was born at Patamajaw on the Restigouche, and, having lumbered and fished on it all his life, probably knew the river as well as any living man. He always said that a salmon could see anything it wanted to.

There is probably no water in any salmon river as dirty as that in the Tobique up around Riley Brook when there has been a big rain up Little Tobique, which is one of the branches, for the water that comes down there is just plain ordinary red mud. Once when there had been a four-foot rise of water and the water was in that muddy condition, Austie Howard, who was guiding me, coaxed me to go out and try under the covered bridge. So, more to please him than anything else, we went out, and he set me in just above the point where he wanted me to cast. After fishing a few minutes, I felt something hit the fly and start the reel, and thought, of course, that it was a piece of driftwood, of which there was a lot coming downstream. But Austie said no, that it was a salmon, and told me to change the fly to one a size smaller. It was all a joke to me, as we were then fishing a No. 2, when the water seemed to indicate a 6/0. Anyhow, to keep peace in the canoe, I put on a No. 4 in the same pattern and on the first cast an eighteen-pound fish took it. I would say that the water was all of twelve feet deep where he took that fly, and full of mud. I have been told that a fish's eye at rest is focussed for close vision, but that he has the ability to lengthen the focus when something, such as a salmon fly, is called to his attention.

A fly dressed on a five-inch iron, while used only occasionally in high water, on a river that holds large fish, will kill today just as it did fifty years ago on some of the rivers in Scotland and England. When Mr. William Mershon was fishing one of the last ones I dressed for him a few years ago, a fish made a vicious rush at it and missed. He wrote me that he didn't offer it to the fish again, since he wanted to have it mounted and did not wish to have the feathers messed up. He was sure that it would have been taken on the next cast.

A great many new fishermen have been making their appearance on some of our salmon rivers in the last few years, and I am wondering just how many of them will take their fishing seriously. If they do their first fishing on water that holds plenty of fish, which happen to be in the taking mood, they are apt to make a lot of false assumptions about the sport. Under conditions like these it requires no skill whatever to take fish, and the fly presented in any way at all seems good enough. I have seen a man take a large fly in his hand and throw it out on the water, and catch a fish. But what will this man do when the blank days come, and he fishes day after day without seeing a fish? Will he keep on fishing the old stereotyped way, if the fishing is poor, and go back home and tell his friends at the club that the river was too high or too low, and that the fish did not come into the river this year as they always have before, or offer another of the many other excuses too easy to make? Or will he admit that there were fish there, but, since he had only one style of fishing in his repertoire, he could not take them? The trouble was that he had not been observant, and, also, that his guide had been satisfied to just set him out in the pool and let him thrash away. There are such guides, you know. If he had spent his time experimenting with flies and different tackle, improving his casting, and observing what some other man, who was taking a fish now and then, was doing, he would have had a lot more fun and would have been more successful.

It is when you get discouraged and begin to lose interest that a good guide does his stuff. He tells you of some man he has guided on this same water, who took fish under these conditions, and describes his tackle and his procedure. Some guides are past masters at this sort of thing. Lindsey Vanderbeck, a Tobique guide, once had a man who was a terrible caster, but with Lindsey's encouragement, finally became quite good. Lindsey's way of doing it worked out well for him, too. This man's casts were all landing on the water in a bundle at first. Finally one day he managed to get out about thirty feet fairly well, and Lindsey said, "That's a good cast, Colonel." The man said, "Thank you, Lindsey, have a cigar." After Lindsey had smoked that, he watched the Colonel very closely, and the next time a cast went out fairly well he said, "That's a damn good cast, Colonel," and the Colonel said, "Thank you, Lindsey. Have two cigars!" A little encouragement from your guide once in a while helps a lot.

If a man was interested in everything that was going on during his first fishing, the chances are that the next season he will go better equipped and keener to take some of those fish that he could not interest the year before.

Lindsey taught the Colonel to cast, and I'll tell you how Octave taught me to look for fish just above the head of certain rapids. Octave was a French Canadian who guided for Mr. F. W. Ayer, at Matapedia; he was a native on the river and knew where to look for salmon. As I was going through Matapedia one day to tow up to my camp, Mr. Ayer invited me to stop over and fish his water, which, by the way, was some of the best on the river, and was afterwards sold at a large price. He gave me Octave for my bow man in the Gaspé. The first day was a blank until about five in the afternoon, but had been interesting, what with Octave's accounts of Mr. Ayer's fishing, and so forth. I suggested we go to the lodge and have a drink, and then come out at seven for the night fishing, but Octave said we would kill a fish the next drop. The killick came up and we started. That was the longest drop I have ever seen, because we dropped two miles down river before the killick went overboard again. We had stopped about a hundred feet from some very heavy rapids, and, because I could see nothing that looked to me like a pool, I remarked that it did not look like good water. At that time I had about seventy feet of line out, and Octave said, "You'll take him the next cast." So, stripping off about three feet of line, I let it go. As the fly was swinging around, I noticed a smooth glassy spot about ten feet across, over which the fly would pass; and at the instant it did, twenty-seven pounds of salmon grabbed it. Octave said afterwards that fish were tired after coming up through heavy water, and would stop to rest at the first good place. This was one of those places and I have found several others since. I forgot to add that I had wagered a new leather jacket I was wearing with Octave against his day's work on that one cast. That night Mr. Ayer advised me to go on up river in the morning, or Octave would have the rest of my clothes! He said he knew too much salmon for me. Mr. Ayer was considered the best caster on the Restigouche, and was the first to advocate getting below your fish and make him fight you and the current both. Octave and I became good friends, and we killed many a fish together on the river.

Manzer Howard, a Tobique guide, was a beautiful caster with a two-hand rod. I doubt if I have ever seen anyone do the overhead cast as well, and it was a joy to watch him handle a rod. He was with me eight seasons, and I learned a great deal about salmon and salmon fishing from him. His backcast was always high, where it belonged, and well straightened out before he let it go. His timing was perfect. He knew every rock in the river, and behind which ones there were salmon. He was full of fishing stories—things that had happened on the river—and there was never a dull moment in his canoe. But it cost a lot of money to fish with him, for we were always making bets about fish and Manzer always won! He was full of suggestions, watched your fishing closely, and let no bad casts get by him without some remark, such as, "Nice bag we've got in our line this morning. Guess I'll have to get me a new sport this afternoon. The one I got now can't seem to fish much." A man will fish better and kill more fish, have more fun, and learn more about the game with that sort of guide in his boat.

I have always made it a point to fish with men who fish better than I do, and I have never had much trouble in finding them. It is a good idea, and gets one away from thinking he is a little better fisherman than he actually is.

The first time I fished a dry fly for salmon with Fred Shaw, I thought I could take about as many fish with my way of casting as any other man, but I soon found out the contrary. My idea was right, but my technique was wrong. I did a lot better after a month's fishing with him. A head wind always bothered me, made me mad and I'd start to fight the rod, because the fly would not go out the way it should. But one day on a little pond in one of the King's Parks, just outside of Kew Gardens in England, Reginald Hughes showed me how to keep the loop of line close and low on the water. Shaw and Hughes had both been champion casters of England. I think Mr. Hughes is the best caster I have ever seen, all styles of casting, including distance-casting, considered.

A good place to demonstrate that a knowledge of different ways of presenting the fly is valuable is a spot between two piers of a railroad bridge over the St. John River at Perth, New Brunswick. The salmon come up river to this place and stop to rest, and you can stand on the bridge and look down on them. It appears at first to be an ideal place to fish them from above, but I was told that no one had ever taken a fish there, although all the good fishermen around had tried for years. One of the best-known guides there, Percy Faulding, lived at the little hotel where I did, and we often discussed possible ways of taking them. Some of my suggestions Faulding thought might work, for he said they had never been shown a fly in those ways. The result was our starting a real campaign against those particular fish.

We tried the old way, anchored above them, letting the fly swing around over them. After trying some twenty patterns in different sizes, I hooked a fish that came half-heartedly at the fly, and we killed him. But we never got another that way. Then, after that, I tried standing at the foot of the pier, casting across and letting the fly swing around over some fish which were farther down under the bridge in more broken water, but not a rise; nor would they take a fly offered in the Arthur Wood manner of fishing, using lightly dressed flies, and letting them float down just under the surface at various speeds. But on casting straight across and drawing the fly back fast in front of their noses, they would chase it, and then it was only a question of fishing the fly at the right speed to catch some of them.

The most exciting way to take a fish there, though, was with a dry fly; which was very interesting, because they wanted the fly presented in a manner not according to Hoyle. Casting a curve up and across, and letting the fly come down over them with no drag, would only occasionally start a fish a foot or so from the bottom; once in a great while he would come half-way to the fly.

Every pattern of fly was tried with no result. Finally one day, having made my last cast, I let the line swing down river, and the fly was dragged across the broken water. A salmon chased it for about twenty feet, but the fly was going so fast he could not get it. After that, by slowing up the speed of the fly as it dragged across this broken water, we killed several. It was a great sight to see them chase a fly that was bouncing around that way, as they were in full view, and going at top speed on the surface. I always kept a man on the bridge while I was fishing, to tell me where the fly was in relation to the fish; and some days, when fish were coming well, half the town would be there looking on.

This was an especially good place for observing the effect on salmon of concussion on the water, as we could stand on the bridge and watch them as a train was passing. The trains had to cross the main street in the town before they reached the bridge, and always gave a number of long sharp whistles there. This was within about a hundred yards of the fish. The whistles had no effect on them, but the instant an engine touched the bridge, every salmon darted off up river. In about an hour's time, however, they would settle back again where they had been. So we had to schedule our fishing on railroad time.

All of this would seem to mean: to keep quiet around your boat when fishing, and not to knock the ashes out of your pipe on the side or kick the paddles around. It also means not to be discouraged if you cannot do the curve cast well, for plenty of salmon are caught on a dragging fly and on a fly cast in a straight line.

It is amusing to watch a confirmed trout fisherman when he first begins to fish salmon. He wants to fish in every bogan, the mouths of all the brooks, and any place that looks like a trout hole. He will coax his guide, until finally the guide, to show him that salmon do not stop in such places, sets him into one, and lets him fish away until he is tired. One of these men came to me one year with a friend who was an old fisherman. I sent them up river, and arranged for one of the best guides there to go with him. In five days they came down; the old fisherman had sixteen fish, the new man not any. I saw the guide in a few days and asked him why the new man had not taken any fish, and he said he had not been able to keep him in a salmon pool, for he wanted to fish in all the bogans.

If a new man can kill a fish the first thing, everything is fine. He will fish where he should with all the patience in the world; and for that reason we

SALMON ACROBATICS

FROM PHOTOGRAPHS BY DR. A. B. FLETT, EDINBURGH

always try to place such a man on a pool that holds plenty of fish. But if he goes five or six days without raising fish or seeing them, he is inclined to think "the game is not worth the candle."

About half a mile from the mouth of the Tobique River, where it empties into the St. John, there is a big pool. After the first of July it always has a lot of fish in it. They do not take well because they are fished over so much, since it is not an uncommon sight to see dozens of canoes in the pool. But how they do jump! There is a fish in the air all the time, and it is a great place to put a beginner, because he expects a fish to take his fly any minute. I have known men to fish there two weeks without a rise, but they had a wonderful time, and always came back the next year with new ideas about taking them. Those fish were known as my trained salmon.

This pool is a good instance of over-fished water. The first year this pool was ever really fished, there were only five men on it, and never more than one or two at a time. That year it gave up around four hundred fish. After that men came from everywhere to fish it.

As the season progresses there is a great difference in the way fish jump. In June their leap is full of life, and they seem to enjoy themselves hugely as they play around in a pool, some going straight up and landing with a big splash, others making long, curving leaps. At these times there is no question but that they are enjoying themselves, and jumping because they like it. When the hot weather comes on in July, their leaps have lost some of the fire they had the month before; and while they do a lot of it at this time, it is not nearly as brilliant an exhibition. In August they have slowed up still more, and what they do is done in a lazy sort of way. But in September it is a different story. They are getting heavy with spawn, and it seems to be an effort for them to get themselves out of the water. One authority says the spawn is becoming ripe now and adhesions are forming, and that they jump to break them, which I think is reasonable.

I have had salmon jump within a few feet of me on numerous occasions, and have had a good look at their eyes. Nothing I know of can register more emotion than they can. One day, near the middle of September, I had waded out into a pool that held about fifty fish, and was trying to raise one to a dry fly. They were apparently all jumping and the air was full of them. A number of them jumped within a few feet of me, and finally one jumped so close that I could have reached out and touched him. I could look right into that fish's eyes, and they looked tired and lifeless. On the other hand, I have seen fish jump in June whose eyes plainly registered fright; and I have a picture of one jumping near the boat that shows it to a marked degree.

There is another pool twenty-five miles farther down, at Hartland, on which it is not an uncommon sight to see a dozen rods at a time. This is an exceptionally good piece of water, as a cold stream of good size comes in at the head of it, and the fish lie along the shore for three hundred yards below in hot weather. Three-quarters of the fish here are taken on trout flies.

Another stretch of water like this is the Harts Island Pool at Fredericton, New Brunswick. There are large numbers of fish there every year, but the water is so lathered up by continuous casting over them that they do not take well. The St. John would be a grand salmon river with the nets taken out, and some protection.

As a rule, the old salmon fishermen have stuck pretty close to the one way of presenting the fly, the orthodox method which we have described. But there were, and are, a few notable exceptions: one of them was the late Thomas Allen, who for thirty-three years was superintendent and guardian of the Tobique River. He looked on the river as his private property; it, and the fish in it, belonged to him. And why not? He knew he was responsible for most of them being there, for the river had been poor fishing when he had first taken charge. He was a good salmon man, and a grand wet fly fisherman. He kept up to date with his tackle, was a connoisseur of salmon flies, and knew every little trick in presenting them to the fish. The only new thing in connection with the game which he would not give a thorough trial was the dry fly, claiming that the salmon of the Tobique did not want it.

He had the reputation of being able to take fish when no one else could; he could do so because he had the right tackle for whatever occasion arose, and knew how to use it. Another man on the same river, who has fished it for forty years or more, and has the right tackle too, is still fishing exactly as he did when he first started, with the result that Allen would kill about five fish to his one. You cannot fish salmon haphazardly and be very successful.

I wonder why it is that every writer of salmon stories who kills his fish on a wet fly, always illustrates his articles with pictures of fish taking the fly with a big splash and making a lot of commotion on the surface? It makes a very

Photo by Dr. H. C. Fleming

TWENTY-POUND RESTIGOUCHE SALMON

TAKEN BY THE LATE LOUIS CLARK

lovely picture, but salmon very seldom take wet flies that way. I doubt if I have ever seen a dozen fish do it. What they do is to come up and take the fly, turn, and go off with it; and in turning they make a big swirl. It is the swirl we see. Occasionally a fish will take the fly, turn, and stop where he is, sometimes for as much as thirty seconds or more, and then make his rush off. He is evidently thinking things over, as that quick jab of the hook has surprised him so he does not know what to make of it. I have never seen a good picture of a salmon swirling at the fly. It would be a hard picture to get. But whether it is swirl or splash, it is a tough time for the novice, especially if he is a trout fisherman, because he will strike or tighten—strike, probably—the minute he sees a sign of anything near his fly, with the result that he will take the fly right out of the salmon's mouth. One of my guides had a fisherman do this one day with a very large fish; that night he asked the man why he did not leave the fly there and let the fish have it. The reply was, "Hell, I gave Charlie Phair two dollars for that fly, and I didn't propose to have him go off with it."

The best way I know to be sure of hooking your fish is, first make your cast, then turn and talk to your guide, or look at the scenery along the river—do anything but watch where your fly is. You'll hook him every time.

I often wondered what effect a hooked salmon had on the others in the pool, until one day I led a fish into a small piece of water behind an island, to net him. There was a mud bottom in there, and only about a foot-and-a-half of water. With the sun in its particular position, we could see everything plainly. As that fish came in, he was followed by nine of the craziest salmon I have ever seen. They kept swimming around him, bumping him with their noses, and doing all sorts of things. They didn't know what to make of it. The question then was, would they go back into the pool, and could we take any more of them? It was soon answered, for in the next two hours we killed three more out of that pool.

After that experience I always looked for such a place to lead a fish into, to see whether any more would follow. Three years afterwards I had the chance, and six fish followed the one I had hooked. While I was playing my fish and we were watching the others perform, I remarked to my guide that those other fish were as good as in the boat, as I knew they would all go back in the pool, and would all take. We killed my fish, set out in the pool again, and fished three hours without a rise.

I used to think that salmon acted differently depending on what part of the mouth they were hooked in. The first couple of fish I killed that had apparently jumped themselves to death—that is, had made one jump after another until they were tired out—were hooked in the tongue, and I thought the hook must hurt or frighten them more there. But I afterwards killed fish that acted the same way hooked in other places. A hook's best hold on a fish is in the corner of the mouth.

Some fishermen claim that salmon do not try to rub out hooks which have been broken off in their mouths. I think they do. We often take a fish with a raw spot on the jaw, which is much larger than could have been caused by a hook but where a hook has been. Then again, we kill fish where this raw spot has all healed over but has left a big scar, which is much too large for the hook itself to have made.

When I tie on a fly I always try it in the water beside the boat with a short piece of the leader in my hand. One has to watch out, however, for a salmon is apt to take it then. A friend of mine who owns some salmon water and is a notoriously poor fisherman, was out on a pool one day which was full of taking fish. He is a very nervous man and wears glasses for distance, although he sees all right close to. He hooks a lot of fish, has them on for a while, but they always get away. This day he hooked five fish and lost them all, the last one taking his leader and fly. Taking off his glasses he tied a new leader and fly on and cast it out, laying the rod in the bow of the boat; while he was putting his glasses on a fish took the fly, and in his hurry to get the rod he knocked the glasses overboard into the river. When he finally got the rod the fish had gone. That was six fish lost. After tying on his last leader he tried the fly on a piece of short leader in his hand at the side of the boat and a big salmon took it. He held on, and, of course, the fish broke away. He gave up then and went home. I know for a fact that this man had hooked fifty salmon in the last two years, and, to my knowledge, had not landed one. The answer is that he does not hook his fish well, because, barring accidents, anyone can land a fish, since that part of the fishing requires the least skill of all. I know any number of fine salmon fishermen who will not bother to land their fish if there is someone around to take the rod.

It has been pretty generally conceded by guides that a man could not hold a salmon on a short line when first hooked: that the fish would either tear the hook out or break the tackle. I once had a twelve-foot rod, with more than the ordinary amount of backbone in it, which I thought would be about right to try for this; so one day, when the fishing was good in a pool on the Kedgwick River, I tied a 6/0 fly on a heavy Joe Welch leader and began casting. In a few minutes a fish of about twenty-five pounds took the fly and, driving the hook well home, I held on. For about five seconds, I suppose, I held him right on the surface, and it was the greatest exhibition of lathering on the water I have ever seen. But by then he was tired of being held on top of the water, and with a mighty surge pointed his nose at the bottom and broke the rod about three inches above where my hands were holding the cork grip. I think that fish would have dragged me in right then and there if the rod had not broken. Only one other time did I ever get such an overhauling as that. A man I shall call Murray was guiding me. Just above the lodge was a big fish that had lain in the same spot at the tail of a pool for a week, and which no one had been able to raise. Coming down river one day to the point where he lay, Murray held the canoe off about thirty feet to one side of him and asked me if I would like to have him on. I said, "Fine." He then untied the fly I had been using and tied on a 4/0 double hook with the body and feathers cut off, and, taking the rod, cast about six feet over the salmon's back and let the hook sink. When it touched something, Murray gave it a great yank. It hooked the fish in the side. Taking the rod, I started to work on him, and for a good half hour he was the wildest salmon I have ever seen. He towed us, canoe and all, for short distances at times, and we were over an hour bringing him to gaff.

The best exhibitions of playing salmon I have ever seen were given by Claude Knapp, with the late Howard Finnemore handling the canoe. There is a bogan at Eight Mile on Little Main Restigouche, full of old logs, stumps and snags, into which salmon sometimes run to lie in the cold spring water. A fish hooked there has to be led out into the river from among the snags and stumps before he can be killed, and Mr. Knapp and Howard had a way all their own of doing it. It was great fun to watch them and to hear Howard's remarks, especially if it happened to be a sulky fish that didn't want to come out. Howard could talk to a mean salmon as could no other guide of my acquaintance, although George Green, one of the old-time guides on the river, didn't do a bad job.

Courtesy of G. M. L. La Branche

COL. AMBROSE MONELL AND GEORGE LA BRANCHE

CHAPTER VII.

FISHING THE DRY FLY

IN 1913 George La Branche was discussing with Col. Ambrose Monell the possibility of taking salmon on a dry fly. La Branche had introduced Col. Monell to dry fly fishing for trout, and the latter's interest in the method was great at that time. Col. Monell told La Branche that he was sure salmon would take a dry fly, inasmuch as he had put a dry trout fly over a fish and the fish had taken it and broken the leader.

Col. Monell was very much interested in the problem and invited La Branche to visit him the next summer (1914) and make a definite attempt to take salmon on a dry fly. La Branche designed the Monell, the Pink Lady and the Mole flies, basing them on trout flies which had been successful and rode high on their hackles. The results of this trip have been told in detail in La Branche's SALMON AND THE DRY FLY (1924). From this beginning dry fly fishing for salmon has become a widely recognized and successful method.

Edward R. Hewitt's well known book SECRETS OF THE SALMON (1922) later played an important part in popularizing dry fly fishing for salmon and had a marked influence in increasing interest in the use of light tackle.

I much prefer a two-hand rod for dry fly fishing, using a single-hand one only when no considerable distance is required in fishing a pool, and to vary the monotony of continuous casting with a two-hand rod.

With a single-hand rod it has always been difficult for me to get any great distance in casting the dry fly, and, to be frank, I think I use more force than necessary with it in making the casts. I suppose this comes from driving wet flies out for so long, from the opening of the season until the water gets low enough so that you can wade the pools and fish dry.

Considering the length of salmon rivers and the number of pools on them, it is surprising the few places there are which are suitable for dry fly fishing. It is impossible to get within casting distance of a great majority of the pools, and it is very unsatisfactory to try to fish a dry fly properly from a canoe. It is not quite so bad from a Gaspé boat; but a Gaspé disturbs the fish too much.

There is no difficulty in casting the curve to the left and, with practice, in becoming accurate with it; but a curve to the right is something else again. It all consists in the timing and when you release the slack line. I like to carry the slack line coils in the left hand, as Mr. La Branche has described in his writings; this is much better than letting it drag around in the water or, if you are fishing from a canoe, having it at your feet, where it is likely to get tangled up. I learned the knack of doing this from Mr. F. W. Ayer, who was undoubtedly one of the greatest salmon fishermen in this country, and at one time owned valuable fishings on the Matapedia. Mr. Ayer, by the way, was the first man ever to take a salmon on a fly at the celebrated Bangor pool, and was responsible for making the pool famous. It was through him that Mr. Archibald Mitchell, a great salmon fisherman in the early days, first happened to fish there.

Mr. Ayer was describing a fish he saw rise a very long cast away, and I remember well his saying: "I shot about half the coils I had in my hand the first cast, and picked it right up and shot the rest of them the next one;" which, as he explained, got the fly over the fish quickly and raised him. He then showed me how he held the coils in his left hand. With practice one can learn to shoot one coil or as many as he likes at a cast, and not tangle them up. If the slack does get tangled up with a salmon on, it is all the more exciting, what with trying to keep your rod up and untangle the line at the same time. Things like that wake up the boat, and make you and the guide hustle for a few minutes. Mr. Ayer used to say he could kill any salmon in the Restigouche in twenty minutes. I have seen him kill a lot of them, and I don't remember that he ever had one on as long as that. His idea was to fight them hard: if a fish is lightly hooked, you lose him at once and can get back after another; furthermore, the longer one has the fish on, the larger a hole the hook makes in the fish's mouth from constant pulling and the more chance there is of its dropping out.

In fishing the dry fly from a canoe, I sometimes have tried taking the killick up in the bow of the canoe with me and anchoring it from my end, so that I was facing upstream and could cast up and across. But as the fly came down I had to keep turning, with the result that when it came time to pick up the fly, I was all twisted out of shape. With the canoe anchored from the stern, to stand facing your guide and to cast up and across is still worse, as your guide is down in your end of the boat with you in order to keep it lying straight in the current; so besides all your other troubles you have him in your way. The best way I have found is to cast to either side, using more line than necessary, and, just before the fly alights, to pull it back, which leaves more or less slack lying on the water. Then as the fly drifts down, keep shaking more slack off the tip of the rod. In this way you can sometimes get a fly to float quite a distance without drag. One can cast down river to either side and, if not at too great an angle, you can make a fly ride a long distance without dragging by shaking off slack line with the tip of the rod. At times fish will take it when it is dragging across the current. I have a large yellow bass dry fly tied with hackles all around the shank of the hook, which Mr. Griswold gave me; he had killed a very large fish, well over 30 pounds, on it, by casting it just as we would a wet fly, off to one side, and by letting it drag across on the surface of the current. But, as there is a right and a wrong way in everything, so there is in fishing a dry fly.

For this fishing I use the thirteen-foot rod described in the chapter on tackle, and which is light in the top and with which it is safe to fish fine leaders. The line is a No. 4 Filip; but if the water is very low and the weather very hot and bright, I sometimes change to a No. 1 Filip trout line, which is smaller and lighter. The reel is the 3/0 Tobique, and the tension is so smooth that there is no danger when fish are running or jigging the fly, as there is with coarse-running reels.

The leader is a twelve-foot one, tapered from .014 at the heavy end to .010 which is about as fine as one can fish safely, although I often do tie a more finely tapered nine-foot trout leader to odd pieces of leaders I may have, if it is a day when my casting is especially bad. I raise more fish, but I do not land many of them.

The curve casts used and advocated by Mr. George La Branche must certainly be acquired if one is to be successful at this style of fishing, for casting the dry fly any other way results in only an occasional fish being taken. I would advise reading the description he gives in his book, SALMON AND THE DRY FLY, as it is all put in a few words and is therefore very intelligible. My description of the curve casts will be very meager by comparison; nevertheless, here it is:

We will take the curve to the left first, since it is much easier. In learning this cast I think it is well to begin with the rod near the horizontal, as you will be able to do a curve at once, which will be encouraging. With just a fair amount of line out for the length of rod you may be using, and with the rod near the horizontal, do some false casting to accustom yourself to doing it with the rod in this position. Then, when it is working to your satisfaction, make a forward cast using more force than you know is necessary to straighten out the line. You will see, as the result, a big, wide curve lying on the water, and what at first seemed to you to be difficult will now seem very easy. But in making this cast you did not shoot any line; so strip off about three feet and cast as before, using more force than necessary. This time let the line shoot as you would in any other cast, and you will find the result to be another big curve, since the fly, leader and part of the line are all kicked around in a wide curve when the slack line brings up against the reel. Now try doing these same things with the rod brought up a little toward the vertical; you will immediately see that the curve has grown smaller, but you will also see that you are more accurate with it. It is not as easy to place the fly in front of the fish by casting a curve with the rod at the horizontal, as it is with the rod more toward the vertical, which throws the curve in more of a V shape. If the fisherman is good at judging distances in casting his wet fly, he will soon be able to judge how much line and force to use with the dry fly. In this style of fishing you are helped by being able to make a number of false casts over the water near the spot to which you intend to cast. These false casts are of assistance in making your real cast go just where you want it. If I can get near a fish, say, within forty or fifty feet of him, I like to throw a big, wide curve, because at that distance one can with practice be very accurate. And I go on the principle that if you are going to throw a curve, throw one. This sometimes works badly for me if the fish is farther off, since I sacrifice both accuracy and distance just for the sake of seeing a nice big curve lying on the water; which, of course, produces no fish.

The curve to the right is a different proposition entirely, and in the beginning one fails for two reasons: first, that he does not use the right force, but either too much or too little; and secondly, that he does not release the slack at the proper moment, which in the case of this cast is sooner than in the ordinary way of shooting line. Just as you began throwing the curve to the left with the rod at or near the horizontal, it is not a bad plan to begin practising the curve to the right in the same way. In this case, however, there is just one thing to bear in mind, and that is that you are going to throw a good belly of line upstream, without any regard whatever to where your fly, leader or end of line may land. Keep doing this until you really can throw a belly of line upstream without the end of the line, leader and fly straightening out with the cast. This means that you must experiment with the amount of force used, and must discover when to shoot the slack, how much of it to shoot, and at what angle the rod should be held to do it best. Also, since more line is required than in doing the curve to the left, because of the belly you are throwing upstream, more slack should be carried in the left hand.

I once had a funny but rather expensive experience with this curve cast to the right:

There is a pool I used to fish where the salmon all lay within about five feet of a gravel bar. I always fished from the opposite side of the river casting a curve to the left. But one day I was on the same side as the fish, with no guide or boat to get me over on the other side; so I cast a curve to the right, which left a lot of the line lying on the gravel, and of course the fly could only travel a few feet before the line would catch up on a rock, and I would have to pick it up and begin all over. Finally, I got the fly over a fish that took it and started down river. For a few seconds the air was full of gravel, he was dragging the line so fast; but it finally caught on a sharp rock and he went off with some forty feet of line together with the fly and leader.

When these two curve casts don't go out to suit me, which is pretty frequent, I go back to the old way I have always had of fishing a dry fly, and which works very well provided there is not too strong a current between you and the fish; even then you can often make a fly float far enough to do the trick. It is done something like this: stand opposite and just above your fish and cast a fly in a straight line about three or four feet in front of his nose, then keep shaking slack line off the tip of your rod. It does not sound like much, but it will catch fish just the same.

Water which at first glance looks perfectly suited for dry fly fishing can be very deceiving. I have two pools in mind, about three miles apart, both of which look to be ideal dry fly water. But when fished they both have their drawbacks. One is just above and between two piers of a bridge and requires a curve cast to the left; the other is fished from a beach, on the opposite side from where the fish lie, and a curve to the right must be cast. There is a smooth current of water running through the pool at the bridge, until the tail is reached, and since most of the fish lie in this smooth water and can be seen by a guide located above them while the fishing is being done, everything has the appearance of being perfect until the casting is begun. Although the day may be perfectly still, with no sign of a breeze whatever, between the piers of a bridge there is always a breeze, or perhaps I should say a draft, which has just enough force to blow a dry hackle-fly out of control. It would be only natural to suppose that this draft would be up river at times and then again down, but it doesn't work that way at all; it's always up river, or at least always seems to me to be, and blows the fly upstream to be immediately dragged by the line below. Having fished this pool pretty continuously for about eight seasons I will venture that during that time there were not over a dozen times when the draft was not in the wrong direction, to blow my fly around and down. When a fisherman using these large hackle-flies can get a light down river breeze he is right in clover and need have no worries about his ability to do curve casts, as the breeze will take care of that nicely for him and will probably do a much better curve than he would. This very same pool, which looked at first so suited to the dry fly, has one other disadvantage. The smooth even flow of water that looks to be traveling about a mile per hour is really doing not less than four, and is what is known as heavy water, which of course floats our line down ahead in a hurry and drags the fly.

The other pool up river is about one hundred and fifty yards long, with a good beach on the left shore and the fish lying in a fast current on the opposite one, where the water is broken in places and will drown the fly if care is not taken as to where it is cast. It is impossible to see the fish in this fast water, and since they lie everywhere for its entire length, every foot of it from head to tail must be covered with the fly. In other words, beginning at the tail each cast must make the fly travel down in a new lane, not more than a foot from the previous one. I say a foot, because I have never seen a salmon come for a dry fly that was placed much farther away from him than that. It does not matter with grilse; they will come from twenty or thirty feet off. When I fish this pool, beginning at the tail, I lay it off in my mind in sections, casting over these sections systematically; it takes me a good four hours to cover the hundred and fifty yards of it, and I am not a lazy fisherman. Continuous systematic casting over a pool in this manner accustoms one to judge distance so accurately that two or three false casts over the water are all that are needed to drop the fly at just the desired spot.

With a single-hand rod it is impossible to cast one of the large hackle-flies around in a curve against the wind. One cannot give enough force to the line to drive it around. But with a two-hand rod of about thirteen feet, the pressure can be put on, and unless it is a distinctly windy day the fly must behave.

A fisherman who can do curve casts in practice on a quiet piece of water is all upset when he first begins the actual fishing of a pool. For instance, there may be a breeze blowing the wrong way which bothers him, or a faster or slower current between him and the fly, or bushes may interfere with his back-cast; any number of other things can happen. While in fishing a wet fly he had simply taken a rod and slammed it out, here he finds that there is not only a certain technique which must be acquired, but that he must learn to judge the different currents of water on which his fly and line will travel down river. If the current is such that the line will ride a lot faster than the fly, he must perceive it at once and allow for it. It is good practice to take the rod and walk along the shore looking for different currents, casting the fly into them and watching what happens; this teaches one to judge a piece of water accurately and quickly. It is not tiresome work doing this; it is a lot of fun because you cannot help noticing improvement.

All the salmon I have ever seen taking natural flies were cruising fish, which were swimming around near the surface with their back fins out. I have never seen one salmon keep rising in the same place for flies as trout do. I am quite sure they do, nevertheless, because some of my friends have seen them. Even when the surface is covered with flies, these cruising fish pick off only an occasional one, and they certainly do not appear to be feeding on them. Cruising fish can be seen plainly at times in some still water pools such as bogans and the quiet-water side of certain pools. One place where I have seen a great many such fish is in a bogan at the head of Eight Mile on Little Main Restigouche; and another is the quiet-water side of Five Finger Pool on the same river. I once hooked a cruising fish at Five Finger and was backing up with him on the beach to bring him in to be gaffed by Murray Howard, who was guiding me, when I backed into a hole left by the spring freshet. It was about ten feet deep, with about two feet of mud and water in the bottom. Murray said that just as he reached for the fish with the gaff the line all went slack and the fish ran off into the river. Looking around to see what was the matter with me, all he could see was the tip of the rod sticking out of the hole. He had to come and get me out.

I don't believe I would do a great deal of looking for grooves or strips in the current with the idea of casting the fly in them simply because natural insects were being carried down in them; if I did cast in one of them purposely, it would be because I thought that groove or strip was running over a natural resting place for a fish.

ARTHUR WOOD'S LODGE AT CAIRNTON ON THE ABERDEENSHIRE DEE

GEORGE LA BRANCHE AND ARTHUR WOOD

Photographs courtesy of G. M. L. La Branche

CHAPTER VIII.

GREASED LINE FISHING

IT was about thirty years ago that Mr. Arthur Wood of Scotland discovered a way of fishing wet flies with a greased line, which has now become very popular. But it has only been within the last few years that we have known very much about it. The method is based on sound ideas, one of which is that a fly can best be controlled by a floating line; since you certainly cannot manipulate a fly properly if you cannot control the line, it is quite reasonable. Believing as he did that salmon either want the fly at, or very near the surface, or else near the bottom, he naturally had flies dressed to fish in these two different ways. For the surface fishing, the flies were dressed on light wire hooks with a minimum of materials.

This is a very attractive way of fishing and, with Mr. George La Branche's method of fishing the dry fly, is one of the two greatest advances made in salmon fishing in my time.

For fishing this way, about thirty-five feet of the line, or whatever you expect to have lying on the water, is greased. It is well when doing this to wipe off all the surplus grease, which not only gums up the guides on the rod, making it difficult to shoot line, but which, if there is too much of it near the end of the line, is sure to get down on the leader, which is undesirable. It is better to grease the line oftener than to get too much on at once. It is well, however, every once in a while to grease the entire line, or as much of it as you can cast; one never knows just how much he will have to cast on occasion.

The fly is cast straight across the current, and drag is prevented by lifting the line and looping it over upstream, which with practice can be done without affecting the movement of the fly. Mr. Wood's idea was that the fly is most attractive to the fish when presented side-to, which is reasonable, as the fish certainly gets a better view of it in that position. Furthermore, with the line on the surface, by looping it over, it is possible to change the direction and speed of the fly, the latter being all important. With your line floating on the surface, any number of different ways of working the fly may be used, as, for instance, holding back the line with your rod tip and preventing its traveling as fast as the current. In fishing this way, there is, of course, more or less slack line on the water all the while, and you are not in quick contact with your fish as you are in the old way of fishing the wet fly. In that instance, we wanted to feel the fish the minute he had the fly in his mouth and to send the hook home before he had a chance to spit it out; this way we do not want to make contact at all, for the reason that the tackle is fine and the pull of the line being dragged in the water is sufficient, when the fish takes the fly, to send home the fine wire hooks on which these flies are dressed.

Some funny things will happen when there is a lot of slack line out and fish hook themselves. I once had a salmon take a fly on a long cast and, not having paid very strict attention to what I was doing, without knowing it I had allowed a big belly of the line to drift down with the current ahead of the fly. I saw a fish take the fly about opposite me and I began to reel in some of the slack, which I noticed reeled in very hard. Thinking that it was the fish I felt and that he had gone downstream where my line was pointed, I simply stood there holding the rod well up. All at once a salmon jumped away above me, and seeing the leader hanging from his mouth, I knew he must be my fish. The pull of the current on the line was so strong that I had to go down below and reel upstream in order to get in touch with him; all of which shows how a hook will be driven home when there is a good current pulling on the slack.

This style of fishing gives one a chance to display his knowledge of different currents of water and of what effect they have on a line. By experimenting with different ways of handling the greased line on the surface it is possible to make a fly ride anywhere and in any way you wish. A man can really become a great inventor of methods of fishing a fly—even if he is not one, he often thinks he is, which adds to his sport. This style of fishing keeps one constantly interested in his fly and particularly his line; he must take care that the line does not have an undesirable effect upon the fly. Greased line fishing with small flies fished at or near the surface, proves that the salmon want the fly there when the air is warmer than the water, because Mr. Wood was successful as early in the year as February, when perhaps there was still snow on the hills. If the water is clear enough to permit the fish to see these small flies, and the air is warmer than the water, you are likely to be successful with them. In Canada, of course, we cannot fish as early as that, for the rivers are frozen over and there is likely to be five or ten feet of snow in the woods. The early fishing we have in June often corresponds, if it happens to be a season when the ice was late in leaving the river. If the water is high and cold, as it almost always is, conditions then most nearly correspond to Mr. Wood's February fishing. Fishing this way, I have caught salmon with about a No. 2 fly, which was his customary size.

Of his patterns, the Blue Charm and the Silver Blue are much the best, with the Blue Charm the best fly of all. It is really a great fly in low water fished any way at all. My experience in weighting the shanks of hooks differently before I dressed them, so that they fish at different depths, has shown me that a fish wants the fly either near the bottom or near the surface, and that fishing at intermediate depths does not amount to much. For years I have leaded flies this way, and they have proved very successful. For early fishing when the water is high and cold, a cast may be mended or doctored by using the greased line method of fishing the wet fly; whereas, fishing in the old way, you usually have to pick the line up and cast it over again. In describing the lifting of the line and the looping it over upstream to prevent a fly from dragging, perhaps it would have been more lucid to say that it is the *belly of line*, carried downstream by the current, which is lifted and rolled upstream. What you really do with the rod is to *roll the loop over*. This looping of the line over and upstream is great for casting at a fish which may be lying in quiet water across the current, or in some of the eddies or pockets which are found at the side of some pools; it permits the fly to remain there long enough for a fish to take it if he wants to, before it is swept away. It has the same result as casting a dry fly with a curved cast in such spots. I generally use the same thirteen-foot rod for this fishing that I use for dry fly fishing; but if it is early spring, and I am using large, heavy flies, I use the thirteen-and-a-half-foot rod I have described in my outfit. With a single-hand rod I cannot get sufficient distance, nor can I roll the loop over upstream as well as I can with the two-hand rod. Mr. Wood used twelve-foot single-hand rods weighing eleven to fourteen ounces, but there are very few fly casters who could use single-hand rods of this weight. They would be entirely too heavy. I understand that Mr. Wood was a very powerful man and fished continuously throughout the season.

Looking back to when I first began salmon fishing makes this greased line method, and that of the dry fly as fished today, all the more impressive, because then, when the water got low and warm in summer and the salmon would not take our wet flies, except perhaps an occasional one, we used to sit around the camp and pray for rain, and thought that was our only salvation. Today at such times, with these two new and different ways of fishing, we go out and have good sport.

I believe in giving full credit to a man who introduces some new way of fishing or improves upon one of the methods we have been using; and I think most fishermen feel the same way about it. I know of one, however, who does not feel at all that way about it; and no matter what comes up, he has known all about it long before. I had a lot of fun humoring him one season.

During the year when the greased line way of fishing was first being talked of in this country, he came to the river I happened to be fishing. A friend of his, who really knew what it was all about, had described it to him the winter before; so when he landed on the river he was full of greased line and Arthur Wood, and that was all we heard from daylight to dark. I had some pretty good information on it myself, but as I could not fish that way well enough to care to have anyone see me at it, I was keeping pretty quiet. One day this gentleman was fishing a pool and I was sitting on the bank watching him. There was a ledge running through part of one side of the pool, and that was the sore spot, for, when there were fish in the pool, it was there that we found them. He fished down over it without raising anything; but his guide, looking over along this ledge, saw a number of salmon lying there, just opposite the bow of the canoe. The guide told him about them; he cast straight across in front of them and let the fly float down without any motion. A salmon took it immediately, and he came ashore, killed it, and went right back and did the same thing with another fish. When it was all over, he exclaimed: "There! That is the first chance I have had to show you what the Arthur Wood method would do. What do you think of it?" It was hard fishing all along the river about then and, with no one taking any fish to speak of, they were all coming to me for low water flies and fine leaders. I would tell them that Mr. So-and-so was catching plenty of fish using a new greased line method, and that, if they went to see him, he would show them how it was done; which they all did. I must have sent about every man, woman and child on the river to him, so I had some fun, too.

In fishing a fly in a strong current where there is a much slower one between the fly and the rod, the fly travels faster, leaving the line with an upstream belly; this should be looped over as before, but, in this case, downstream.

The rolling over of the line is accomplished by throwing the rod tip over and out, up- or downstream, whichever the case may be. Care must be taken that too much force is not used; otherwise the force applied to the line during the operation carries right on through the line and rolls leader and fly off the water at the finish.

The beginner must not be surprised if he sees his fly make a ten or twenty-foot leap in the air up or down river when he puts too much snap in the roll. When I first began rolling a line over, I concentrated on trying to put what I thought was a good-looking roll in the line, and forgot all about the fly; when I watched to see what the fly was doing, I found that it was making all sorts of wild jumps up river. By giving the rod point a snap at the finish of the stroke in the operation, one gets more speed to the roll than he realizes until he sees the fly go. And as its position should not be changed in this manner, it is well to watch it closely and to see just what the line is doing to it. I did a fine roll but raised the dickens with the fly at first.

This is the most fascinating way of fishing that I know of. There are so many things one can do to make the fly fish differently.

Early in the season, when the water is cold and fish hug the bottom, they will best come to the surface for a fly if it is fished slow; as the season advances, the speed at which the fly is fished should be increased.

Collection of Martin J. Keogh, Jr., Esq.

NEW BRUNSWICK SALMON

FROM A WATER COLOUR PAINTING BY OGDEN M. PLEISSNER

CHAPTER IX.

WEATHER

THE best three days' fishing I have ever had presented totally different weather conditions each day, with the exception that it rained on two of them. One of these days the water was very high and dirty, and, while there was no fog or mist in the air, it was cold and damp, and looked and felt as though it would rain any minute. One other day the sun was bright, and it was very hot, but it was raining as hard as I have ever seen it. It came down in great big drops which, upon hitting the water, seemed to explode and fly in every direction. It rained so hard that it was impossible to tell where the leader and fly were at the end of twelve feet of line. I fished that length of line for over two hours, and a salmon took the fly on the first cast every time. I simply cast and waited for the big tug which was sure to come in a few seconds. The third day was late in the season when the water was low after a long spell of hot weather, just before the water began to rise in the river after about six hours of heavy rain and hail. For about two hours and a half it was like trout fishing: we took a fish on every cast.

I have only once seen salmon caught when fog was on the water, and that was on the St. John River about five o'clock one morning. In extremely hot weather in the summer, when the water was down low, I would walk up to the Indian Reservation at the mouth of the Tobique, to meet my guide, Newel Francis, who lived there. There was a very heavy fog on the river this particular morning, so thick that when I shouted for Francis, though he was only about a hundred feet out, I could not see him. He called back: "I can't come for you now. I have a fish on." He finally came ashore farther down and killed a nice twenty pounder. After that I got into the canoe, he poled me back to the pool, and I killed another. You could not see thirty feet in the fog that morning. I have tried since on every occasion when conditions were similar, but I have never been able to take a fish. All old guides and fishermen will tell you that fishing is bad when fog and mist are hanging on the water.

Thunder and lightning are also bad for salmon. I have taken them, however, when you could hear thunder rumbling a long way off, but never when it was very pronounced. I had read in some old salmon book of a man's taking a fish when the thunder was very heavy and there was lightning all around him. I intended to try it the first good chance I had; and, as I was on the Restigouche at the time, I did not have long to wait, for that river is noted for just that very thing. I had with me a guide named Jack Mack from the Miramichi, and one day when we heard the thunder coming down river and getting nearer, we dropped down to a pool which we knew held a lot of fish. I suppose I had fished ten minutes, with the lightning playing all around us, when it got too hot for Jack, and he pulled up the killick and poled ashore as fast as he could. When we got out of the canoe, he threw my rod and steel gaff as far as he could in the bushes, turned the canoe over, and said: "Get under quick!" About that time came the biggest crash of all, and I thought surely it had struck the boat, but it missed us by about fifty feet, and hit an old tree on the bank. That cured me; but every time it started to thunder after that Jack would say: "Let's go try for a fish. It looks like your kind of weather coming!" He always declared that he saw fire fly off my reel while I was fishing that day.

That the weather plays a great part in our fishing there can be no reasonable doubt. I have fished by the barometer, the thermometer, and by a very fine fishing calendar, made by a man who claimed to know the days in each week when fish would take. But they all went back on me sooner or later, and today, if the water is right, and the weather clear with a good clean smell in the air, I look forward to taking fish if there are any about.

The fishing calendar was very elaborate and most artistically done. I had it tacked on the verandah of the small country inn where I was staying that season, and all the guides on the river came to consult it. The days in each week when fish might be expected to take were marked. For about five weeks I could not take a fish on those days, and my guide tore it up in disgust one morning. That ended fishing by calendar.

The barometer did better, however. It lasted a full season, but when fishing time came the next spring I left it with a man who managed a farm for me, so that he could do his haying by it. I explained it to him, and told him that, if he would watch it, he could tell when it was going to rain and could get in what hay there was in the fields before it got wet. When I came home at the end of the season I asked him if he had had good luck with his haying. He said that he had, except when he went by the machine I had left. When I asked him where it was, he told me he didn't know, because he had thrown it away somewhere! It had cost seventy-five dollars; and that is all the barometer fishing I did!

It is interesting to keep a record of the temperature of the water, especially on those days when you have had good fishing. In the spring when the water is very cold, fish seem to hug the bottom; and when it is hot, they are up near the surface. Therefore a fly fished deep is most successful in the first instance, and a dry fly on the surface in the latter one.

The best fishing days, I think, are ones such as we have in early June, when the nights are still cool, with the sun coming out warm in the morning. The water is cold, but the surface soon gets warmed up, which seems to make salmon want to come to the top. The water is on the drop then, too, and getting clear after the spring rains. Everything is washed clean and the air has a good smell. If I can have a day like that, I don't care if the barometer, the thermometer and all the theories in the world are contrary. I know fish will take then if they are in the river. If I could only have one good condition, however, with all the others bad, I'd choose a day when the water was on the drop.

Photo by J. W. Black, from the original painting by Walter M. Brackett

THE RISE

CHAPTER X.

A MONTH'S SALMON FISHING TRIP

THIRTY-FIVE years of salmon fishing from the beginning of the season until its close each year have shown me pretty well how I would begin if I had it to do all over again. In fancy let me take you on a month's trip to the place where I would go if I were a beginner, and let me show you my reasons for going there. I shall write of the trip as though it had really happened, as indeed much of it has.

In the winter, well before the season opened, I wrote to engage a month's fishing with a man I had been told of, who owns a country inn and two salmon pools on a small river in Canada and who guides for his guests. I did not select this place in hopes of having any big fishing or of killing any big fish—quite the contrary. Knowing nothing whatever about the game, I wanted to fish where the salmon run smaller, averaging about twelve pounds, and where, though it is not "big fishing," the fishing is good. Another reason for going to this particular place was that the sole topic of conversation there is salmon; old and young talk salmon day and night, all of them have fished and most of them have guided all their lives. It seemed a good place to learn.

In time I got a letter back from my host, whose name happens to be Jim, saying that he would be delighted to take me from June 5th, which is about the time when salmon get up the river to his water, until July 5th, for $15 a day, which would include boarding at his inn, his guiding and the privilege of fishing his water. Such incidentals as trips in his car up or down river to fish some of his neighbors' pools, the boxing and icing of fish I might want to ship out to friends, and my government license, which would cost about $25, would comprise practically my only extra expenses.

I now had my water, so I next set out to assemble my equipment (which consisted of the rods, reels, lines, leaders and flies described in the chapter on Tackle). The five Payne rods cost about $350. The five reels were multipliers, called the Tobique, built by Edward Vom Hofe and Son, and cost about $290. I bought multiplying reels because when a fish makes a long run and there is a lot of slack to be reeled in, it can be taken up much faster on a multiplier than on a reel of the old single-action type. The five lines were Hardy's Filip, and, with the backing and running line spliced on each one, cost about $125. My leaders were nine feet in length; I got six heavy, twelve medium and twelve light, which cost about $100. The heavy ones were about .018 in diameter, the medium .015 or .016 and the light .012; they were all level leaders. I took also a dozen twelve-foot leaders tapered from about .014 or .015 to .010. These were for dry fly fishing and were about as long and fine as can be fished successfully; they cost $27.

My flies were the patterns and sizes suggested in the chapter on Flies and Their Uses. For the early high-water fishing I chose Jock Scott, Canadian Black Dose, Silver Grey and Night Hawk in sizes 8/0, 6/0, 4/0, 2/0 and 1/0; two of each pattern in each size cost about $60. To these same patterns in sizes 2, 4, 6 and 8, dressed on heavy wire double hooks, I added Dusty Miller, Griswold Gray, Thunder and Lightning, Brown Fairy, Mar Lodge and Bastard Dose, and bought six each, which cost $240 altogether. I also bought six each of the same patterns in sizes 2, 4, 6 and 8 on very light wire eyed double hooks, which cost $240, six each of the same ten patterns very lightly dressed on Nos. 4, 6, 8 and 10 very light wire eyed single hooks, which cost $180, and six each of Blue Charm and Silver Blue lightly dressed on sizes 2, 4, 6 and 8 eyed single hooks, which cost $29.50. For dry flies I bought six each Colonel Monell, Mole Palmer and Pink Lady Palmer in sizes 4, 6 and 8, and four dozen Bonbrights in sizes 4 and 6, which cost $29.50. I got two dozen in each size of the last pattern because it has an elongated cork body which lasts for only one fish and often goes to pieces in casting.

Fly boxes, a leather chamois-lined case for leaders and a large leader box to keep them moist, cost about $100. Because Jim, like all other guides, has gaffs and nets, I did not buy any except an aluminum gaff to serve in the event I might want to gaff a fish myself. It was about three feet long when extended, telescoping to about fourteen inches and attaching to the waders. My fishing clothes were from Burberry of London, who makes the best. In the light weight, which I chose, they cost about $60. For waders I selected the feather-weight ones with boots attached, costing about $20. Waders of heavy-weight material are quite uncomfortable in hot weather, and it is a nuisance putting on and taking off the brogues and the stockings worn under them.

I now had what may seem to you a good deal of money invested, but I had the best of everything; with the exception of the flies, leaders, lines, waders and clothes, such equipment should last a lifetime if taken care of. I was equipped not only for the small river I was planning to fish, but for any river, such as the Cascapedia or the Restigouche, where larger and heavier tackle is required.

Starting from New York June 4th I arrived at a little station at the end of a certain railroad in Canada at six o'clock the next evening. Jim met me there with his car and drove me up river to his home in about an hour.

Upon arriving I saw on the verandah four or five husky, good-natured-looking fellows who turned out to be guides. Preparations for fishing began that instant. My rods were taken from their cases and put together, and lines were run on the reels. While Jim and the boys were doing this I hurried upstairs with the dunnage bag that held my fishing clothes. When I came down the rods were all ready, hanging on pegs on one side of the verandah. Jim had chosen the thirteen-and-a-half-foot heavy rod, because the water was pretty high and dirty and consequently I would have to show the fish a large fly. We went down to the river just back of his house. The canoe was there, all rigged out for fishing, with killick, line, gaff and pole.

On the way up river through about half a mile of pretty heavy water, Jim advised me to put on the heaviest leader I had. Tying it on, I stripped all the casting line off the reel and trailed it behind the canoe to take all the kinks out of the new line and to soak the leader. When Jim swung the canoe around at the head of the pool and dropped the killick, he explained that he was setting in pretty high up so that we could cover the whole pool because the water was high and the fish might be running almost anywhere. I now reeled in the line and leader to the length of the rod and tied on a Night Hawk, which is a favorite pattern on that river for early fishing, on a 4/0 single hook, which Jim told me was about the right size for that stage of the water. He showed me how to tie the leader to the gut loop on the fly with a figure-eight knot, which is generally used for flies with either gut loops or turned-down eyes.

As the method of casting to one side of the canoe and then the other and letting the fly swing downstream was explained to me, I realized that I was casting a really good-sized fly and had a real honest-to-goodness rod in my hands—not the light trout rod and the delicate flies I was accustomed to using. It was awkward at first handling a two-hand rod, especially sitting in the bow of a canoe, but I soon acquired the knack, and the habit of keeping my weight in the center of the canoe, and when I did, I had the chair raised so that I could sit higher and cast more easily.

At first Jim left me pretty much alone to become accustomed to the rod, but as we dropped down into the part of the pool where he expected fish, he suggested things like mending my cast when it had a bag in it, and casting at more of an angle downstream to keep the line and leader straight. I learned then that casting squarely across to the left or right, as shown in the diagrams in salmon books I had read the winter before, keeps you mending your casts to eliminate the bag; in so doing you shorten the line, and the fly does not cover as much water as it should.

After fishing four drops this way, I began to get the feel of the rod and to wait for the line and leader to straighten out well behind me before making the forward cast. If the cast is made too soon in fishing a large fly, it will buckle back on the leader. As Jim put the killick over for our next drop, he pointed out a little stretch of quiet water on one side where the current was not as strong, and said, "If we are going to get a fish in this pool tonight, he should be lying right there; so keep your finger over the line to be sure to drive the fly home if he takes it."

Meanwhile the guides we had seen at the inn had walked up the shore to watch us, and one of them called over to us, "You fellows should take a fish on that drop sure."

At just that instant a fish did take my fly and was off down river. It all happened so quickly that I don't know whether I had my finger over the line or not. I had turned around and was talking to Jim, and didn't even see my fish when he rose; but the tension had been set on the reel and, taking out line, he hooked himself. Jim got the killick up and we dropped down to the beach just below, which was a good place to land the fish, though it was hard to tell what would happen in the strong current. After taking out all of my casting line and thirty or forty yards of the running line, he stopped and began to work upstream, but not so fast that I couldn't take up the slack on my multiplying reel and keep tension on him. He made several runs fifty or sixty yards across and up river; but though he had been on about ten minutes, he had not yet jumped. "I wouldn't be surprised," Jim remarked, "if that was a pretty good fish. It's a sign of a big one when they don't show."

But just at that instant he made another race across the river and leaped about two feet out of water, and we had a good look at him. Jim estimated that he weighed about twenty pounds, but of course I thought he would weigh a lot more. After five minutes more, his rushes were shorter and weaker, and Jim said, "You'd better give him plenty of butt now and reel him in. I think he'll come all right."

With my rod held vertical I began reeling in. When Jim saw where I was holding it, he advised me not to hold the rod so high, but to lower it to put some strain on the fish. Lowering it to an angle of 45° or 50°, which I have found out since is right, I soon had him up where Jim could reach him with the gaff. He was a beautiful fish weighing eighteen pounds.

About six the next morning, after finishing breakfast, I took the line off the pegs, where it had been hung to dry during the night, wound it back on the reel and was ready to start fishing. But when I asked Jim how soon we were going out, he laughed and said, "We'll go out about half past eight or nine. Salmon don't take well early in the morning, except later in the season when the water gets low and the weather very hot. Then, sometimes, we can take a fish in the early morning."

About nine o'clock we got in the canoe and started up river to where we had been the evening before. During the night the water had dropped six inches and had cleared considerably, so Jim advised a smaller fly. He set us in above a couple of rocks in a slow current, and I cast across and down so that the fly swung over them. On about the fourth cast a fish rose. This time I was paying attention and saw the big swirl he made, but, like all trout fishermen fishing salmon for the first time, I leaned back on the rod and struck, with the result that I took away the fly before he had it. Jim told me to strip in my line and wait a moment before casting over him again. "But don't wait too long," he said, "because at this time of year, and in this pitch of water, he may go right along up river."

After about a minute I cast out to the side again, shooting all the slack I had stripped in, so that the fly would swing around on the same length of line as when I had first raised him. Jim told me not to move the rod until I could feel him on, and then to give it to him. When he rose again and I felt him on, I gave him such a jerk that the leader broke. After that I got some good sound advice, expressed in such plain language that I thoroughly understood that that was not the way to hook a salmon; instead, I must simply raise the tip of the rod and tighten on him, with the line under my finger. I soon found out that this is not so easy to do, especially if the fish makes a big splash when he takes the fly. A beginner is very likely to strike then and either take the fly away from the fish or snap the leader. Jim told me of one green fisherman he remembered, fishing a pool farther up river when the salmon were taking well, who lost nine leaders on fish in less than two hours.

After fishing one more drop there, we went on up to the big pool where we had been the evening before, because, as Jim told me, we had a better chance of getting a fish there, and there were many things salmon could show me that he couldn't. He set us in lower in the pool than he had before, since there was only an hour before lunch time and we had decided to fish only the best spot. Putting on a heavy leader and tying on a Night Hawk, I made the first cast to the left; this time I remembered not to cast too far to the side, but more downstream, and there was no sign of a bag in the line. I was just congratulating myself on having done so well, when a fish took the fly. Instead of racing off downstream as the other one had done, this fish stayed put, and I thought I must have hooked a snag. But after ten or fifteen seconds, which seemed an hour, he made up his mind and off he went, right past the canoe and on up river a hundred yards, jumping twice on the way. "That will take some of the fight out of him," Jim observed. "They're pretty strong, but they can't fight your rod and the current and do much jumping without getting played out."

We dropped down to the beach and got out of the canoe, and Jim allowed that my fish would be back downstream before long. Jim suggested that I take some of the tension off the reel to encourage the fish to run, and told me that

JOSEPH P. KNAPP'S GUEST LODGE ON NATASHQUAN; MAIN LODGE BEYOND

Courtesy of Joseph P. Knapp

VIEW FROM GUEST LODGE

the time to fight him and make him work was when he stopped to rest. After two or three more sharp runs up and across, I found that I could reel him back slowly, and in a few minutes we had him back in front of us in the middle of the river, where he stopped. "Let's walk down the beach, get below him and pull him out of there," said Jim. "He's resting now, and we don't want him to do that."

I found that by holding the rod nearly horizontal and pulling in the line carefully with my left hand, I could get him started. Jim told me to be very careful, because the fish might make a quick rush and I must be prepared for it. The side strain pulled his nose around and the current washed him out from wherever he was lying. He made one more short run up river, and when we saw his tail come out of water we knew he was pretty tired. When a fish sticks his tail up he is about done.

When I had reeled him in within forty feet of us, Jim said, "You'd better back up with him now. Keep your rod just high enough so that if he started he'd get some of the spring. When you start back, don't stop unless he makes a run. Keep him coming every second."

So, looking around to make sure that I wouldn't stumble over anything, I found that it was much easier to bring him to gaff this way than it had been to reel in my fish the night before. After Jim had gaffed him, I asked whether it was always best to back up with a fish that way if you are on a beach or a bank where it can be done. He replied that he believed it was the best way to bring a fish to gaff, but that you must watch him every second and let him go if he makes a run.

We hurried back to the pool and set in at about the same spot, but we raised nothing there, or on the next three drops, so we went back home to lunch.

"I guess we'd better go right out now," said Jim when we had finished lunch. "That will give us a good long time until dark. Fish aren't very plentiful in the river yet, and it looks as though we'd have to work for what we get for a few days—until more of the run get here. I called up a neighbor of mine who lives about a mile below here, and asked him if he was going to fish his pool this afternoon. He said no, and for us to come down and give it a try. It's a pretty good pool, and perhaps we'll meet some of the run coming."

On the way down I noticed that the water was much clearer than it had been the day before; in places we could see bottom. "This river comes up very quickly and goes down very quickly," said Jim in reply to my observation. "The water has dropped a foot since last night. If there are any fish in the pool tomorrow, we should have some great fishing. All salmon water is best when the water is dropping after a raise."

For fishing the first two drops at the head of the pool, where the water was pretty clear and not very deep, I tied on a No. 4 Jock Scott. Jim told me that after that, until we got to the lower end where the pool flattened out, I would have to use a larger fly, because there was fifteen feet of water through the middle of it. When I commenced casting I found I could get out a very fair line, and Jim was not making his drops as often as he had at first. I asked him how much line he could cast. He laughed and said that he didn't know, but that distance was no object in casting a wet fly at that time of year in high water, since most fish were taken then on a short line, of fifty to seventy feet. "You can hook a fish better on a short line because you have more control of it, and it's easier to keep the bags out of a short line than a long one. I never like to see a man try to cast more line than he can handle easily and well."

When we had fished down to the tail of the pool, and I had changed back to the No. 4 Jock Scott from the large fly with which I had fished the deep water, Jim announced, "From here down is where I expect we'll get a fish. In high water the fishing is most always better at the tail of a pool than anywhere else. They run up the river and rest there before going up through the pool. When they once start in high water they generally keep on going, and that's why it's not a good plan to rest a fish very long, if at all, in this stage of water."

I fished the first drop without raising anything. When we made the next one, I passed the rod to Jim and asked him to fish while I filled my pipe. Standing behind me in the canoe, he commenced casting. It was the first casting with a two-handed rod I had ever seen done, and it was fine the way he sent that line out, down and across the river. There were no bags in his line, and from watching him I learned more about how it should be done than from all the books I had read the winter before. "We won't get anything here," he declared, when he had out about ninety feet of line and the fly had swung around in front of the canoe. "This is the last drop there is in this water." And he began to reel in the fly. He could not have reeled in more than twenty feet when I saw a big swirl and heard Jim exclaim, "I've got him! Take the rod, quick." Passing the rod to me, he pulled up the killick, and we were off down the river again.

This fish jumped the instant he took the fly, and we saw that he was a good one. Jim allowed he'd go over twenty pounds and said that we would have to take him down river a way before we could go ashore with him. We drifted along on one side with the fish on the other, and soon got below him, since he did not make the usual run downstream. He jumped three or four times, and, except for hanging back a little at first, he let himself be led right along to where we went ashore below. Once out on a little beach, I soon got him into some quiet water at one side and, reeling him up short on about thirty feet of line, started backing up with him. But as I got him pretty close to Jim, who was ready with the gaff, the fish changed his mind and made a long run across river and jumped twice. But that run and those two leaps finished him, for I had no trouble getting him back into the quiet water, where Jim gaffed him.

On the porch of the lodge that evening, when I told the guides about smashing a leader on a fish that morning, Manzer recalled a fisherman he had guided one season. They had fished a week without a rise or without even seeing a fish, and the gentleman was getting pretty well discouraged, even going so far as to say he did not believe there were any salmon in that part of the river. He had become lazy with his casting, and was not taking many pains with it. Finally, one day, after letting the fly swing around in front of the canoe, he challenged desperately, "Take it, take it, damn you, I dare you to take it!" He had no sooner got the words out of his mouth when, Manzer said, the biggest salmon he had ever seen in that river jumped on the fly. The gentleman leaned back on his rod, striking as hard as he could, the leader parted and he tumbled over backwards right into Manzer's lap, almost upsetting the canoe. After he had been helped back onto the board which was serving as a chair in the bow of the canoe, he turned around and said, "He did take it, didn't he, Manzer?"

The following morning was bright and warm; the water was clear and still dropping. We poled upstream to the pool where I had killed my first fish; the killick wasn't down before we saw three fish jump and Jim exclaimed, "I thought they'd be here this morning!" I was pretty much excited, of course, but after failing to raise anything on the first drop I quieted down and was really in better condition to fish. I think that if a salmon had taken the fly on the first drop I would have smashed another leader on him. Just as I was picking up a bad cast to do it over again, a small fish took the fly and started off. He ran across the river and jumped as many as eight or nine times while we were getting the canoe pulled up on the beach. I found then that I could reel him right in. I could not have had him on more than four or five minutes, though he weighed about ten pounds. Jim said he thought he had jumped himself to death, for he had often caught fish that acted the same way.

From then on until lunch time it only required a few casts to hook a fish. The pool seemed to be full of salmon and, as Jim said, they were in the mood. When we had five good big ones in the canoe, one weighing twenty-two pounds, I told Jim I thought we had enough for one forenoon. But he answered that we had better take another anyway, because it might be some time before we would find them coming so well again, and there would be a lot of lean days before I left the river.

We killed one more, a fish of about fourteen pounds, and went to lunch. That afternoon we nailed together some salmon boxes and got them ready to be packed the following morning, to be sent down by the stage to connect with the New York train at noon. Jim had a good icehouse, part of which was especially arranged for storing salmon.

At four o'clock we went back to the pool and killed four more fish, which were all under ten pounds. There seemed to be a number of fish left from the run of small ones which had been in the river when I had arrived.

The next morning Jim told me that he had called up two or three of his neighbors down river; they had all reported a big run of fish and had invited us to come down if we wanted to fish their water, since they were not going to use it. As they would probably have some sportsmen fishing it a few days later, Jim said we had better go at once. Taking a lunch, we started off down river. Jim's pool, which we fished first, did not yield anything, so we went on down and fished Tom's home pool, as well as two pools belonging to a neighbor of his, killing two fish in all. There seemed to be plenty of fish in all the pools, but they were not taking. We had heard thunder rumbling in the distance all day, and Jim said that was the reason. He had occasionally taken fish when there was thunder far away, but never when it was close by. That night there was very sharp lightning and heavy thunder. We could hear it coming from a distance up river; it followed the river right down to us, and passed by.

The next morning was again bright and clear, but very cold, which Jim thought might hurt our fishing. We did nothing that forenoon, but about two o'clock in the afternoon it warmed up, taking the chill off the water, and by four o'clock I had killed two, one a very fair fish of eighteen pounds. I killed this fish on a No. 6 fly; it was the first time I had used such a small one. Jim told me that until we had a run or a rise of water I should have to do most of my fishing with a No. 6, using a No. 4 only where the water was deep and heavy.

Before we started out the following morning Jim told me I could put away the thirteen-and-a-half-foot rod, for unless we had a rain and a big rise of water I would not need it again during my stay on the river; and that from then on my twelve-foot rod was the one for what fishing I would do with a two-hand rod. He explained that the other rod was altogether too powerful for the light leaders and small flies I would now use, and said that its line was so large and heavy that in clear water it would probably put down a lot of fish. I had noticed Jim trying the twelve-foot rod at the landing where we pulled up the canoes, and I thought he rather liked to cast with it, so I asked him about it. He said it was the ideal rod for that river, and that it would handle flies as large as 2/0 very nicely. He also said that I would enjoy using this rod much more from the bow of the canoe, because the cork grips were not as long as on the other one, and it was more in proportion to what I could do from that position. He told me, too, that after I had become a bit more accustomed to fishing from the canoe, I might try casting from a standing position, because it would often be necessary to get all the distance possible. At his suggestion I changed from my heavy boots to a pair of moccasins, which I found more comfortable in the canoe. When we went ashore Jim beached the canoe before I got out, so I had no occasion to wear anything to keep my feet dry.

On the way up to the pool, I had noticed that Jim kept looking at a place up in the hills. When he had turned the canoe around and put the killick out, I asked him what he saw up there that interested him so much. "Do you see that gap between those mountains?" he replied. "Well, whenever there is any fog or mist up there you never kill very many salmon; it seems to make the fishing just as bad as mist or fog on the water does. I've never known it to fail." I asked him if anyone on the river had ever had a barometer, and he said there had been a fellow who had fished there a great many years who had had one, but after the first year he had not paid much attention to it. He'd generally look up at the gap in the hills, and if it was foggy there and he did not raise anything the first drop, he would wait until it cleared up. Jim allowed that, having spent his whole life on the river, he could tell better whether it would be a good fishing day by the way the air smelled in the morning, and by taking into consideration general weather conditions, than he could by the barometer, almanac or any other of the "scientific" things, as he called them.

I was now using a medium-weight leader, about .015 in diameter. Jim had suggested that I try a new pattern of fly and I had tied on a No. 6 Dusty Miller, of which I had heard the guides speak so much at the lodge in the evenings. It is a great favorite on that river. On the third drop a salmon rose and made the water seem to boil under the fly; it was the first time I had seen it happen. Every fish that had come to my fly before had made a big swirl. Jim thought he hadn't missed the fly, but that when he had got close to it he hadn't liked the looks of it, and turning quickly, made the water boil. He decided that we had better rest him and change flies over him. So, after filling my pipe and getting it going, I tied on a Black Dose in the same size and cast it over him. He boiled at it again, but there was less disturbance, and Jim said he hadn't liked that fly as well as he had the first one. So, tying on a No. 8 Dusty Miller and resting him two or three minutes, I cast again. There was no turning back this time, for he took it savagely. "We may have to do most of our fishing from now on with a No. 8," Jim remarked when we had gone ashore and killed my fish, which was a fourteen-pounder. "He came out of pretty deep water for that fly." The balance of the forenoon's fishing proved this to be the case, for we killed another fish and raised two others on it.

During the morning we had seen plenty of fish jumping, but nothing showed in the afternoon until about five o'clock. Then we saw two or three fish cruising around with their back fin out, behaving as I have seen large trout do when they are looking for insects on the water. Jim found in his wallet an old No. 8 fly that was pretty well worn; there were only a few wing feathers left hanging and very little body to speak of, and the gut loop did not look as though it could hold a fish. But I tied it on, and in five or six casts was into one of those fish. The gut loop held, and I brought my fish to gaff all right. When we were back in the canoe I asked Jim to let me see what other flies he had in his wallet. He handed it to me with the remark that though there was nothing there that looked like very much, he wouldn't take a great deal for them. I told him I thought they were the sorriest-looking flies of any kind I had ever seen. "Well," he replied, "there are days when an old worn-out fly is the best one you can use; at least it works out that way. The trouble with most of the new flies

CAMEL'S RUN ON THE RESTIGOUCHE

BARN POOL ON THE KEDGWICK

JUNCTION POOL: LITTLE MAIN, KEDGWICK AND RESTIGOUCH

At the time of the lowest water within the author's experience on these rive you buy is that they are too bulky—too many feathers in the wings, too much hackle and too much body. It hasn't been until the last few years that we have been able to buy the kind of flies we fellows up here like. We can get flies now with small wings and slim bodies. Those are the kind of flies salmon like."

That evening we drifted along down river, fishing and talking salmon, until we came to water belonging to one of Jim's neighbors. There was no one fishing it, so Jim thought the owner wouldn't mind if we went over it once. A gravel bar in midstream divided the river at that point into two currents. Jim ran the canoe up on the bar and told me to tie a No. 6 single-hook Jock Scott on the leader of my ten-foot single-hand rod, which I had brought along to break the monotony of casting with a two-hand rod. The water was quite shoal down through the run, and Jim thought they would come quicker for a fly near the surface than for one fished deeper. I had fished down the bar forty or fifty feet, when the biggest fish I had yet seen made a rush for the fly; but it was travelling too fast and he missed it. Jim told me to cast more downstream and to hold the tip of my rod in toward the beach to make the fly travel across slower; which I did, and the fish took it at once. This was my first experience playing a fish on a single-hand rod, and in a few minutes my wrist began to get pretty tired holding him. Then I remembered the false butt which I had in my pocket; I slipped it on the rod, which I then held as I would a two-hand rod, and it made a great difference. I took longer killing this fish than any I had killed before. The tackle was lighter, and I was probably a great deal easier on the fish than I would have been otherwise. From the first, Jim had instilled into me the fact that the way to kill a salmon is to go right after him. I suppose we had this fish on for half an hour before we brought him in, but I noticed that the hook was as firmly embedded as it had been in any of the others. He was the best fish we had taken, weighing twenty-five and a half pounds, which Jim said was a big fish for the river. I noticed that Jim was peculiar about this hook business. He admitted that he thought in low water single hooks would raise the most fish, but he seemed to be afraid of their pulling out. He said he liked to fish them, but he was always afraid of them.

When it began to get dusk, Jim suggested putting on a larger fly and fishing until dark. He asked me if I had ever heard of a salmon fly called the "Fat Mary." I told him I hadn't and asked him about it. He said that it was a famous fly on Colonel Rogers' water on the Restigouche. When I told him I'd never heard of it, out of another old wallet he produced a No. 2/0 fly which had a fat, spindle-shaped body, wings similar to those on a Silver Doctor and a blue hackle. Tying it on the leader of the twelve-foot rod, I began casting. On the third drop, when it had begun to get so dark that I was losing sight of the fly on the water, I felt a strong tug and was into my fish. From then on we had rather an exciting time, for he did a great deal of running and jumping. It was so dark that we could not see him, but we could hear him splashing, and from the sound we guessed that he was big. When we finally got him close to the beach, the only way Jim could locate him was by my lowering the tip of the rod until he found the line and then followed it down with his hand to the leader. But each time he got his hand on the leader, off went the fish again. "We'll never get that fish," he said finally, "if I don't build a fire on the beach, because I can't see to gaff him." In a few minutes he had a fire going, and when I brought the fish in next time, Jim could see to gaff him. But he had to find the leader first, to be sure he did not cut it off with the gaff. This was the best sport we had had with a fish.

When I had been on the river two weeks, I had killed twenty-eight fish, which, Jim said, was ordinary fishing for this water.

I had been asking him about his experiences with greased line fishing and the dry fly, and he said he had never done a great deal of either until the past few years, when a man had been coming up every year for that kind of fishing. He came about the middle of July, when the water was low enough to wade. The only difficulty, as Jim explained, with that kind of fishing, is to find a pool where you can wade out within casting distance of the fish. "Pools like that are scarce on this river," he said, "but I know of three where we can take fish that way, and we have the two rocks just below the bridge."

He explained how he would run the canoe along the edge of a pool, looking for fish and sometimes, usually at the lower end, finding one that could be cast over by wading. "At any rate," he added, "it's so warm now and the water is so low that I think we'll do better that way than with the wet fly. But first I want to go up to the big pool for a while, because one of the fellows just came by and said he saw a couple of fish rising there, and I think we can take one right away."

When we set in at the head of the pool, Jim asked me if I knew of any way of getting money out of the bottom of a river. "No," I said. "Why?"

"Well," he replied, "there was a fellow who fished here for a number of years, and every time he would set in in this pool, right where we are now, he would toss a bright new ten-cent piece over his left shoulder into the river. It was an old custom, supposed to bring good luck. Every year he brought five or ten dollars worth of new dimes up here with him, and there must be enough right below us now to make it worth our while, if we knew how to get them." I allowed I thought salmon fishing was expensive enough without doing that.

The third drop we hooked a fish that made a short run and then jumped. "When this fish is ready," Jim said as we beached the canoe to land him, "bring him in to that little smooth beach just below, and I'll show you a new way of landing a salmon." I walked down to the beach, and after about ten minutes got my fish within fifty feet of it. "Now lower your rod," Jim called, "so there will be some spring in it and there won't be a jerk on the reel if he makes a run, and reel him in about twenty-five feet more." Which I did. "Now," he said, "back up and drag him right out on the sand. You'll be surprised how easy he'll slide up." It was surprisingly easy—my salmon slid out of the water right up on the beach. Jim told me that they often land salmon this way when they have forgotten to bring the gaff, and that you simply must be sure to choose a smooth beach and to keep the fish coming after once starting back with him.

This particular fish did something while I was playing him that none of my other fish had done. Three or four times, after making a run, he gave a succession of sharp jerks. Jim told me that he was what is called a "jigging" salmon, and that the jerks were caused by his standing on his head at the bottom and driving his nose into the gravel in an effort to rid himself of the hook. This is said to be the most dangerous sort of fish to play; some fishermen say you should ease up the strain on them, others tell you to hold them hard. Whatever you do, you often wish you had done otherwise, for they very frequently get off.

We fished down through the pool without seeing any more fish, and decided to go back to the house and rig up for our greased line and dry fly fishing in the afternoon.

When I put together the ten-foot single-hand dry fly rod and handed it to Jim, he said that it felt good but that you couldn't tell very much about a rod until you got the reel and line on it and did some casting. The line for this rod was a trifle lighter than the line I had been using for wet fly work with my other ten-foot rod, as this rod had more action in the tip. On the twelve-foot rod I left the same line I had been using for wet fly fishing, but I had an extra line which was lighter, in case we decided the other was too heavy. The lines for both rods we gave a good greasing with a preparation called Cerolene, which we applied with pieces of felt and rubbed well into about fifty feet of each line, being careful to wipe off the surplus. I put some of my finest nine-foot level leaders, about .012 in diameter, and a few twelve-foot leaders tapered to .010, in the leader box to soak, and we were ready. I carried the boxes which contained the dry flies and the very lightly dressed wet flies.

About three o'clock in the afternoon we went out on the bridge to see if there were any fish behind the two rocks; there was one of about twelve pounds which Jim thought I could reach with a fly by standing on the bar. I chose the ten-foot rod, since it required a cast of only about fifty feet to reach this fish. The line, being greased, did not run out through the guides very well at first, but as soon as I had thirty of forty feet out, there was enough weight to pull it through. Jim meanwhile had gone back on the bridge to tell me where my fly was in relation to the salmon. When one of my casts finally went over him, he turned downstream after it. Jim shouted, "He's coming for it!" but I had forgotten that the current was taking the line down to the point where it should be looped upstream again, with the result that the line dragged the fly around and the fish turned back to his rock. On the next cast I made sure that the line was well looped upstream when I knew the fly was going over him, and he took it just as though it had been a dry fly, with a head and tail rise. Jim had told me simply to raise the point of the rod, if a fish did rise, and to reel in the slack until I felt him, and to make no effort to hook him. He said the chances were he'd hook himself; which was the case. When I finally made contact with him, he was on, and on his way down river.

He was more fun than any of the fish I had caught before, as I distinctly saw him come for the fly and take it. He took a No. 4 Blue Charm, which Jim said was the best low-water fly he knew of. He declared that when they wouldn't take a Blue Charm fished this way, they wouldn't take anything. This fish took us about a quarter of a mile down river, where we finally got him in behind a little island in some quiet water. When Jim went to the canoe to get the gaff, he called, "I'll have to 'tail' that fish for you—I've forgotten the gaff. I don't think you'd better try to beach him with that light leader and rod. He's too big." So, when the fish began to show that he was about finished, Jim waded out a little over his knees and told me to lead the fish up to him, which I did. Just as the fish was passing him, Jim reached down in the water and grasped him by the "wrist" of the tail. That salmon certainly came to life quickly, but Jim, being very strong in the hands, held him and brought him ashore. "I wouldn't like to have had to hold him much longer," he announced when he got to shore. "A fish like that kicking so hard could break a man's wrist. We should have played him a little longer." Though I had read about it in books, this was the first time I had ever seen a fish tailed.

That seemed to be the only fish there, so we went on down river to a pool where Jim thought I would have a better opportunity for this sort of fishing and more water to cover, though we wouldn't be able to see our fish and hence would have to do a lot of fruitless casting before the fly finally went over one. There was a good beach on the right-hand side, and the fish, Jim told me, lay out in the edge of the current, which was a cast of about sixty feet. He thought we had better fish down through the run first, and then take the canoe along the edge of the lower end and look for a fish. So I began at the top of the pool, casting almost straight across. There was more current here between my rod and the fly, which bothered me a bit at first; I wasn't looping the line enough upstream and as a consequence had to loop it back too often, with the result that I sometimes lost control of the fly. I began to get the knack of it finally, so that the fly would ride for quite a distance along the edge of the current. Before long a small fish rose, took the fly and started up river. With such a lot of slack lying on the water and the current pulling it, I knew there would be no question about his being hooked. Fighting on up river as he did, he soon tired, and we brought him to gaff in fifteen minutes by Jim's watch—a minute to a pound.

We fished on down to the end of the rapid water, and then drifted along the edge of it at the lower end, with Jim standing up in the canoe looking for a fish. He finally spotted one at the very tail of the pool, in about two feet of water. I got out of the canoe below the fish and across from him, and waded upstream toward him; Jim poled upstream on the other side to where he could see the fish. It was some time before I could see the fish, and when I finally could see him, he wasn't more than twenty-five feet from me. After about ten minutes of fruitless casting over him with a Blue Charm, Jim suggested that I wade back carefully and get the twelve-foot two-hand rod, which was rigged for dry fly, and try him that way; which I did. I tied on a gray hackle called the Colonel Monell, and, wading back to within forty feet and a little below him, I put it over him. On the fourth or fifth cast he came up and, I thought, tried to take the fly. But Jim, who could see it all quite plainly, said that when he got close to it, he seemed simply to slap his tail at it. I thought I'd rest him for a while, but Jim told me to go right on casting, for it was likely he'd come right back at it. He did, after a few casts, and did the same thing again. Then we decided that he didn't fancy that particular fly, or that it was too early in the season, or that the water was too cold. But Jim believed that he would take a fly of some kind, and suggested I go back to the other rod with the wet fly and greased line, and not to get quite so near the fish this time. Casting from about sixty feet, I raised him again. After casting over him a few more times and not bringing him up, I fished the fly faster as it went past him, which brought him up at once, and he took it in a most business-like way. Not having seen Jim handle a fish, I asked him to take the rod and see how quick he could kill this one, which he did in about six minutes. The fish weighed fourteen pounds and, as far as I could see, was as good a fighter as any we had killed. But I could see that Jim was not as gentle with him as I had been with my fish. When I asked him whether he hadn't handled this one pretty rough, he said that that was the way to treat them if you wanted to get them in the boat, and that he thought ten or twelve minutes was enough time for killing almost any fish in that river, provided, of course, it wasn't an old sulky one.

Two or three times that night I waked up and heard it raining hard, and when I came down in the morning Jim told me that it had rained all night and the river was up two inches. I asked him how that would affect the fishing, and he thought that the rise of water would freshen them up. When the water gets very low and warm, a little rise in the river, even if only a few inches, starts the fish moving, and then they take well until the fresh water runs off. We killed four fish in the big pool that morning. But when we went out in the afternoon at four o'clock, the water had run off, and although we raised two or three fish, none of them rose at all decisively. But we had had a good forenoon's fishing and were satisfied.

Before we started out the following morning I asked Jim if he didn't think we might have caught that salmon the day before if we had used a longer and finer leader. He said we might have raised him and hooked him, but that he would have been surprised if we had ever landed him. He thought that the

SLOW RISE

GOING FROM THE BOAT

DONE!

FINALE

FROM PHOTOGRAPHS BY DR. A. B. FLETT, EDINBURGH

leaders we were using, tapered to .010, were as fine as could be fished successfully; he believed in using tackle which was in proportion to the fish for which you were angling. He told me he had seen a number of good dry fly men use sixteen- and eighteen-foot leaders tapered as fine as .007 or .008, and he believed they raised more fish than they would have with heavier ones. But it was only once in a great while that someone, who had an extremely whippy rod and was willing to play with the fish an hour or more, ever landed one. At that, he wouldn't land more than one out of every ten or twelve he hooked.

But I was interested in seeing whether finer leaders would raise more fish, so we drove down river several miles to a little store that carried fishing tackle, where I got three eighteen-foot leaders tapered to .007 and three tapered to .008. I also bought half a dozen hackle dry flies which were much larger than any I had—some of them, in fact, were almost as large as a walnut. Jim said he had seen salmon rise to them once in a while.

When we finally started down river in the canoe, Jim said he thought I had just the right tackle, for I had brought my thirteen-foot dry fly rod, and planned to use the twelve-foot rod for wet fly fishing with greased line. The big hackle-flies we were fishing dry offered so much resistance to the air that it really took something like a thirteen-foot rod to drive them out.

When we got down to the pool where we had killed the fish the previous night, we drifted along the edge of the run at its lower end, looking for a fish, and found two in the same place as we had the night before. So, having Jim set me down as he had before, below the fish, I waded out to within casting distance of them with the dry fly rod. There was a slight breeze down river, which caught the light hackle-fly and put a great curve in my cast, relieving me of any necessity for casting a curve. After eight or ten casts I put the fly over one of the fish. He came up and splashed at it, but I didn't hook him. This same thing happened four times more, which I thought was strange, for he rose as though he wanted the fly. Then Jim called, "I know what's the matter. The fly is riding too high. Wade down and over here to the boat, and we'll change to one that has softer hackles and will set lower in the water."

"But," I said, "I thought these flies should be tied with stiff hackles to be successful."

"They do to raise fish," he replied, as he examined my box of dry flies. "But very often fish coming for them on the surface or very near it, push the water ahead of them, and when they get to the fly there is enough motion of the water to push the fly over so that they miss it. That's what I think this fish is doing. If it is, a fly with soft hackle, that sets down on the water, will be just the medicine for him." He told me that this had been proven by Mr. George Bonbright, one of the best salmon fishermen on the Cascapedia River, who had his dry flies dressed with soft hackles.

We finally found the fly we wanted, and the first time I put it over these fish, one of them came, and this time I hooked him. After killing him and putting on a fresh fly, I waded back to see if the other fish was still there, and found that he was. After the fly had floated down over him five or six times without result, Jim called, "Now is a good time to try one of those eighteen-foot tapered leaders." But before wading back to the canoe to make the change, I thought I would try this fish with a fly dressed with stiff hackles. I put it over him six or eight times, but failed to raise him. Having waded back to the canoe and tied on an eighteen-foot leader and a soft-hackled fly, I cast over him again and hooked him on the fifth cast. Stripping in the slack and keeping the tip of my rod well up—in fact, higher than usual—I tightened very carefully. He had been on, I suppose, five or ten minutes, when all at once the line went slack and he was gone. "That's the way it goes with those leaders," said Jim. "Hook 'em and lose 'em. I think if your cast had been better with your first leader you'd have raised him on that."

While I was putting on a fresh leader, he told me of a fellow he knew down river who fished dry fly a great deal. One day he was casting over five fish he could see, but though he thought he was casting well enough, he couldn't raise them. Finally, in order to find out whether the fish weren't rising to anything, he cut the hooks off twenty-five flies with a pair of gut-clippers. Then he went upstream about two hundred feet above the fish, and waited for half an hour to let everything get good and quiet. At last he began dropping the flies on the water and letting them float down over the fish. They rose to fourteen of them. Then he said he knew his casting wasn't good.

We went on downstream two miles to another pool, where we thought we might find a fish, and where we did find one lying at the edge of quite a strong current. After I had tried him with a dry fly for a few minutes without being able to get him up, Jim suggested taking the other rod and seeing what I could do with the wet fly. Standing about opposite, I cast across just above him, and there I discovered something new. The current between the rod and the fly was a great deal slower than where the fly was landing, and the fly, of course, was going downstream much faster than the line. Jim told me to loop the slack over downstream, rather than upstream as I had always previously had to do with the greased line. This was a little awkward at first, for I was fishing from the left bank, and in order to loop the line over downstream, I had to do it backhand. But after a few casts it went better, and I finally got the fly to go over the fish the way I wanted it to. He took it the first time, and just the way the other had taken the dry fly. On our way back up river, I told Jim I liked wet fly fishing with the greased line better than fishing dry, because you could do so many different things to your fly while you were fishing it. He said it was undoubtedly the most deadly way he knew of to fish a wet fly, and only wished there were more water suitable for it.

When we arrived at the landing Jim suggested going out on the bridge to see whether there were any fish around the rocks. There was one small one there, which I thought would weigh about eight or nine pounds. When we went back to the canoe, I invited Jim to take the thirteen-foot rod and cast a dry fly over him. He stood much farther back and cast a much longer line than I had; it was a pretty sight to see him roll it out. In five or six casts he got just the right length of line out, and the fly went nicely down over the fish. I was up on the bridge where I could see everything happen. When the fly got down to him, he rose about half-way to the surface and let it pass over him, but turning like a flash, went after it. He got it about fifteen feet below his original position. When I told Jim later what the fish had done, he said they often did that—let the fly float over them and then turn and go after it. He always let the fly float on quite a distance if he could, after it had passed over a fish.

Because the two pools down river and the one at the bridge were the only ones nearby which we could wade, we gave them close attention for the next week, averaging slightly better than a fish a day with wet fly and greased line and with dry fly. I asked Jim if there was much dry fly fishing farther down river, but he said there wasn't, because there was so little suitable water. He told me that many fishermen cast dry flies from canoes, and that in doing so cast a loose line across and downstream.

At last there were only a few more days before the end of my month on the river, and I was in hopes I might have one or two days' good fishing before

I had to leave. Jim thought that what we needed was about two days of rain to bring the water up a couple of feet or more, which would bring plenty of fish along from down river. "It looks like rain now," he added, "and I wouldn't be surprised if we had some tonight." The following morning it was raining hard, and it continued for three days; all we could do was stay in the house and talk salmon. The third day it stopped, and Jim said, "Tomorrow the river should begin to drop and clear up, and I guess you'll have that big day's fishing you wanted before you go back."

The next morning, taking the twelve-foot rod, because Jim had said he thought a No. 1 or No. 1/0 fly would be large enough, we went up to the big pool. That forenoon it seemed as though every cast brought a fish; the pool was full of them and they were all taking well. After we had killed two on a No. 1/0 Jock Scott, Jim suggested changing flies. "Put on any pattern you want," he said. "I don't care what—as long as it's the same size. I think you'll find they'll take it just as well, and this will show you that it's size and not pattern you must be particular about in salmon fishing." I tied on a No. 1/0 Dusty Miller and killed a fish. I killed another on a No. 1/0 Night Hawk. Then Jim said, "Now tie on a No. 2 Jock Scott and see what happens." I fished it out as far as I could cast, without a rise. "Now," said Jim, "go back to a No. 1/0 again." Which I did, and in three or four casts hooked another. This satisfied me that he was right and that size was the all-important factor. That day we killed six fish, though none of them was more than twelve pounds.

The next day we killed two in the big pool and one at the rocks, and Jim suggested that we go down to the lower pools later to see if we couldn't find some larger fish. That evening we killed one which weighed eighteen pounds. I raised one that was very much larger, but I couldn't get him up again. Jim thought he had been frightened, because he had risen for the fly very close to the boat.

The next day we fished down through the big pool without a rise, nor could we get anything at the rocks or in the two pools down river. The water had cleared up, but as we poled back upstream we didn't see a fish in the tail of any of the pools. "The fishing will probably be poor," said Jim that night, "for the next week, or at least until a new run of fish comes along. This last run has apparently gone on up river. The grilse should be along next week, and I wish you could stay, because they're good fun on light tackle. Your ten-foot rods would be just right." But he had another fisherman coming the day I was to leave, and my staying was out of the question, as his water really accommodated only one rod.

But early the following morning Jim had a telegram from the other fisherman, saying that he would be delayed a week in coming, and we decided that I should stay and try for some grilse. That night Jim called up some of his friends down river and asked them whether there was a run of grilse as yet. One man ten miles below reported having killed two that day and that there seemed to be a lot of them in the river. "They should be here tomorrow," Jim said. "They'll come right along in this water."

When we went out on the bridge next morning, there were five grilse lined up below the rocks, but they looked small indeed compared to the salmon we had encountered—about two pounds, I thought. Jim said they would weigh four or five. Choosing the ten-foot wet fly rod, I tied on a nine-foot level leader and a No. 6 Silver Grey, and we set in above them. The first time the fly went over them they must have all started for it at once, there was so much commotion on the water. But one of them beat the others to it, and off he went down river, jumping a couple of times on the way. No salmon we had caught had taken out line as fast or as viciously as this grilse did. Before Jim had the killick up, the casting line and about a hundred yards of the backing were gone, and he was still burning up the reel. When Jim finally got the canoe under way, we soon overtook him, but he was still full of fight. He hung out in the heavy water and kept jigging as the big salmon had done—only he was more persistent and vicious about it. Jim allowed that if big salmon fought as hard as some grilse did, it would be a pretty tough job to land them. Even after I got this little fish up where Jim could dip him with the net, there was still plenty of fight left in him. These fish are of course too small to be gaffed, and the majority of fishermen beach them. But Jim carried a large trout net on a long pole, which was safer.

The following morning there seemed to be grilse everywhere. There were five of them lined up below a big salmon that had his nose up against one of the rocks at the bridge, and there must have been at least forty between the piers. I was quite excited, but I didn't think Jim seemed too enthusiastic. "All they'll do is just spoil our salmon fishing," he replied when I asked him why. "With that salmon there, there must be more like him up in the big pool. But these grilse can beat a salmon to the fly every time, and when you get one on he splashes around in the pool so much he puts the salmon down."

It worked out just as he said, for that day we saw any number of salmon swimming about with their back fins showing, and killed only one. But we killed ten grilse. There was one I thought we could never stop. He kept fighting on down river till Jim urged me to hold the line and let him break the leader rather than drag us half a mile downstream.

He told me that the only time he liked to catch grilse was late in the season when they're better eating than salmon, for then the salmon have been in the river a good while and are getting heavy with spawn, and are fit to eat only in a chowder with lots of onions. Grilse are split down the back, like mackerel, the backbone is taken out, and then they are broiled with bacon strips over them. I thought grilse cooked this way was much finer than salmon.

Jim told me that day that I was fortunate to have taken so many fish on a a dry fly so early in the season. The reason for my success, he said, was that the weather had been so warm, although the water was still very cold, there being a lot of snow and ice left in the woods up river. He had once had a dry fly fisherman there who had claimed that salmon would not take dry flies until after the middle of July, when the water gets quite warm, but Jim did not think it made much difference provided the air was warm. In other words, I understood him to think that if the air was warmer than the water they would take all right.

Several days later the big pool seemed to be full of large fish, but we could not raise any. Jim advised me to keep changing flies, for, he said, there were times when salmon showed a decided preference for a certain pattern, and if I kept changing I might find the one they would take. "Try that Bastard Dose," he said finally, after I had tried seven or eight different patterns. "It's not fished much on this river, and will be new to them. They've been looking at flies every day for a hundred and fifty miles before reaching us, and I think they must be tired of seeing the same ones day after day." That pattern proved to be the one they wanted, for we killed two fish on it almost immediately, and that evening killed another and raised three others.

I had noticed from time to time that the tails of some of our fish were bloody, and upon examining them found that they were split in a number of places. When I asked Jim about it, he said it was caused by their kicking the leader, and that fishermen used to claim they could tell how many times a fish had jumped by the number of splits in the tail. But fish that have not jumped at all are often cut by their kicking the leader in the water. Some fishermen tell you to lower the tip of your rod when a fish jumps, so he will not kick or fall back on the leader, but Jim thought that when a fish was on a long line the leader was never tight enough to be dangerous. On a shorter line, he thought, it was better to hold the tip high.

It had occurred to me that I had a great many flies but had been using only a very few of them. I asked Jim why it was necessary for me to have so many. "Well," he replied, "suppose that it was a No. 6 Bastard Dose they wanted, and nothing else, as it was today. You have only half a dozen, but you have been fishing well and have been lucky with your leaders. If you had struck your fish instead of tightening on them you'd have lost a lot of flies. Jigging fish often break hooks on rocks, and that hasn't happened to you. But the best reason for having a collection like yours is the satisfaction of knowing that if they'll take a fly at all, you have the right pattern in the right size and on the right type of hook."

I had now been on the river five weeks, and had killed forty-three salmon and twenty-one grilse. Jim's other fisherman was coming on the morrow. When I settled with Jim I felt that it had been the best and least expensive fishing trip I had ever had. I had certainly learned a great deal about salmon and salmon fishing. Before leaving I arranged with Jim for a month's fishing the following year, though it was to be two weeks later in the season, when conditions would be more suited for the dry fly and greased line fishing.

Courtesy of Joseph P. Knapp

NATASHQUAN SALMON

CHAPTER XI.

LIFE HISTORY

THE more we know about the fish, the better chance we have of taking him; so let's look into the salmon's life from the time he leaves the ocean until his return to his native river. That he does return to the river in which he was spawned has been proven beyond any doubt. The few instances where salmon have been found in rivers other than their own mean nothing; but we shall consider that later.

Salmon leave the ocean, where they have been feeding, for one reason, and one reason only; to propagate their species; and when the spawning instinct strikes them, they start. They may have to start from many miles at sea, depending on how far out the tides have carried the bait, which consists of herring, sand eels, caplin and crustaceans, on which they feed. There is also a thick broth in the ocean, made up of minute marine life, called plankton, which contains nourishment, and it is reasonable to suppose that salmon follow this and the bait wherever the tides carry it.

We know very little about the salmon's life in the ocean. Some fish have been taken by trawlers a considerable distance out. A Pacific coast fish has been taken in a river in Siberia, and a few years ago one was said to have been found in Florida waters. When salmon find food in sufficient quantities near the mouth of their river, it is reasonable to suppose they do not go any great distance; and the fish in early runs on certain rivers, such as the St. Marys and Medway in Nova Scotia, probably come from nearby. Fish from any number of different rivers may all leave the ocean for the coast together; but on reaching it, each one will enter his own river when he comes to it. His troubles begin from the time he starts following the coastline, because there he encounters nets as far as the mouth of his river; and in one river I know of, a salmon must pass about a hundred nets in the first one hundred and ten miles up from the head of tide. He is also fished over with flies at every pool or favorable place along the river, and it's a lucky fish that reaches the spawning ground alive. Salmon spears and nets have been pretty well eliminated from most of the rivers, and poachers today are few and far between.

The fish in Canadian rivers spawn during the last of October and the first part of November, and it is an interesting sight. One would never think that they were the same fish he had been catching during the summer. They are now slim and black, and show very little life. Once, on a deer hunt at the headwaters of a salmon river, I had a good chance to observe all that was happening. The female does not consort with any male fish that comes along, but chooses one to her liking, and will fight off any others. A warden near my lodge on Restigouche once told me that for days he had watched a female prepare the bed she had selected for spawning. Then a sea trout of about seven pounds came along and wanted to be friendly; but every time he came near, she would go for him with mouth wide open and drive him away. After a few days he got discouraged and left. Several days after, a salmon of about thirty pounds came along. The warden said he was a beauty. But she would have nothing to do with him and fought him off as she had the trout. Shortly afterwards, a very ordinary-looking fish of about fifteen pounds showed up, and everything was all right. She had found the one she wanted, and was quiet and contented.

The fish I saw spawning were at the head of a pool that dropped off into fairly deep water. You could see that the gravel had been fanned around and made ready for the eggs. The female would go to the bed, and after twisting and curving her body over it for a while would drop back into the deep water; the male would then swim over the place where the eggs had been dropped and deposit the milt. We could paddle the canoe around through the spawning fish, reach down in the water and touch them with our hands, and they paid very little attention to us. About ten days later, coming down river on our way home, we passed a lot of them on their way back to the ocean. They were doing very little or no swimming, except in the dead water places; where there was any current, they let it carry them along, and in all the rapids they were going down tail first. This was so the water could not enter their gills slits. They appeared to be in terrible condition, especially the males. They had lost a third of their weight, and were a sorry-looking lot. When we thought of all that they had gone through, and recalled the fact that, although the females had each deposited eight hundred eggs for every pound of her weight, the maximum return that could be expected was two fish for each spawning fish, it seemed to us that nature was not giving them a square deal. From fifteen to twenty-five per cent of these kelt would return again.

The incubation period of salmon eggs is about ninety days; but I don't believe they hatch out in Canadian rivers as soon as they do in the rivers of England and Scotland, because of the fact that our rivers do not open up, nor does the temperature of the water get warm, as early. When the fish are first hatched they are called alevins, and are less than an inch in length. That first summer they will grow two or three inches. The next summer they are called parr, and grow to five or six inches; and the following summer, in June and the first part of July, they are ready to go to the ocean as smolt. The great majority of these fish go to the ocean when they are two years old, but any number stay in the river till they are three or four. I have found a great many Tobique fish whose scales showed three years of river life, and some four. I have examined the scales of probably three hundred fish from this river, and fifteen per cent of them, I would say, showed three years of river life, and over twenty per cent showed that it was their second return to the river.

One perennial discussion is about the speed at which salmon travel up river. This speed depends entirely on the height of water, the distance to their spawning ground, and the time of season. If it is early in the spring, the river is high, and they have a long way to go, salmon don't waste any time. Tom's Brook on Restigouche is thirty miles up river from Matapedia, and, to get things ready for the season's fishing, I always planned to be there a week before the first fish arrived. The mail-boat men kept me posted, and when they told me that the first fish had been taken the day before at Matapedia, I would look for fish that night; and they almost always showed up. That's thirty miles in twenty-four hours. Those particular fish belonged in the Kedgwick River and had a hundred miles or more to go before reaching their spawning ground. This would be about the first of June, and the river high.

Another fish that has a long way to go and starts early is the Serpentine fish of the Tobique. He has to make a trip of two hundred and fifty miles up the St. John and Tobique before reaching his river, and has been seen on his way up as early as the tenth of April. These early fish do not stop for any perceptible time in the pools; and the best way to catch them is to anchor in some stretch of water in which you know they always travel upstream, and keep casting—as the Indians do. As a rule they take the fly readily.

As the water drops off and becomes warmer, they are more inclined to loaf along and to take things easy, and you can then look for them in the pools. If you raise one and don't hook him, you know he has gone back to the same spot he rose from, and you can be pretty certain of bringing him up again. It is safe now, and much better, to give him a few minutes rest before casting back at him; earlier in the season, during the high water, the chances are he would have gone along up river if you had waited.

At Plaster Rock, New Brunswick, there is a roll dam across the river with a fishway in it, and when there is a run of fish on, the salmon can be seen jumping. If there is water enough running over the dam, they don't bother with the fishway, but jump the dam. This dam is twenty-five miles up from the mouth of the river, where the Melicete Indian Reservation is situated. When a run of fish enters the river, they always do a great deal of leaping, and are seen by the Indians at the mouth of Tobique. When it is reported that the first fish have entered the river, we expect to see them at Plaster Rock dam the next day, provided there is a good run of water. So I think one is safe in saying that at times salmon travel twenty-five to thirty miles a day. However, the fish that run in July, or August, take a week or ten days to travel this same distance. There are times late in the season when they stay in a pool indefinitely, and the only thing that will move them up river is a rise of water. They seem lifeless and are hard to raise; but if the river comes up even two or three inches, it freshens them and puts new life into them. Then they go on upstream and will take the fly. I have been at the Mowat lodge at the mouth of the Kedgwick River for a month without seeing one fish in my water, while in the Rogers water, one and two miles below, there would be three or four thousand, none of which I could expect to come upstream till we had rain to raise the river.

The parr stage of a salmon's river life is the most interesting to the fisherman, because at that stage the fisherman comes into real contact with him. He is

FIFTY-FOUR-POUND SALMON

CAUGHT BY HENRY NADEAU ON THE GRAND CASCAPEDIA, P.Q.

Length: 48 inches. Depth: 13 inches. Thickness: 6 inches

at your fly constantly. The size of the fly makes no difference to him; he will take a 6/0 double hook, almost as long as himself, as readily as he will a small one. There are times during the season when it is impossible for a salmon to get your fly. A parr will have it first. It is very much the same when they become grilse, after one year at sea. A salmon has very little chance at the fly in a pool that holds a lot of grilse, which will beat the big fish to it every time.

A boy told me one day that there was a very large fish lying under the bridge at Perth, so I went down to see if I could take him with a dry fly. But first I had a look at him from the bridge to see just where he was. About fifteen feet beyond him were two grilse, both of which I caught. The boy watching on the bridge saw the salmon start twice for the fly; but each time the grilse got to it first. At times they will ruin a pool for salmon fishing. When you get one he does so much splashing around that he puts the big fish down. But after the first of August they are much more fun to catch than the big fish and are better eating, and fishing for them with a trout rod is good sport. The big fish are then beginning to get dark in color and have lost a lot of their fight; about the only way they are good to eat from then on is in a chowder.

Some rivers have very few grilse. There are hardly any in the Grand Cascapedia; but the Tobique and Little Main on Restigouche have large runs. They begin to come usually during the first part of July, and by the fifteenth or twentieth there is a good supply in the river. They run in weight from two and a half to five pounds, and are full of fight. A No. 8 Jock Scott or Silver Grey is a good fly to use.

I tagged fifty large parr in the Restigouche one year and gave the numbers of the tags, which bore my initial, to Mr. Percy Baker, the club secretary; but to my knowledge none of the fish were ever taken afterwards. I also tagged about the same number in the Tobique, with the same result. A good place to see smolt, which are bright and silvery, is at Flatlands, the head of tide on Restigouche. You can easily wipe off this silver surface and see the red markings of a parr.

Alex Mowat of the Fishery Department, told me of taking in the nets a grilse that contained both eggs and milt; the eggs were fertilized with the milt from the same fish, and they hatched out all right. He said it was the only case on record. Mr. Max Mowat, a brother, is and has been head guardian of the Riparian Association on the Restigouche for years, and his son Fred is superintendent of the Grand Cascapedia. They are a great salmon family and know a very great deal about the fish. They have given me very much valuable information.

In some of the Canadian rivers the fish that have spawned stay there all winter, going down in the spring. This, in a number of instances, is because they are a late run, and the river is either frozen over by the time they have spawned or the water is so low they cannot get down. In the last few years some fishermen have been going especially to catch them, but I have yet to hear of any real salmon fisherman doing it. These kelt, or well-mended fish, as they choose to call them, look plump and are bright like tin—not like silver, as a fresh fish is—and some of them fight well. But five minutes after they have been killed and laid out on the bank they all cave in, since that plumpness was nothing but absorption of moisture. Their flesh is a pale color, dry and tasteless, and numerous cases of poisoning have resulted from eating it. To a salmon fisherman they are "slink," which seems to me an appropriate name. In other times a man who did this sort of fishing was considered as unclean as the fish he caught, and his neighbors would have nothing to do with him. I consider a fish unclean until he has returned to the ocean, and so do most other salmon fishermen.

The greatest disappointment I have ever had in salmon fishing was with one of these fish. Mr. Knapp and I were fishing the Grand Cascapedia. It was early in the season and lots of kelt were in the river. I hooked a very large fish that looked like a fresh one when he jumped; and when I brought it to the gaff both men in the Gaspé with me thought it was a fresh-run fish, but refused to gaff it until they had given it a good looking over. The more they looked, the more suspicious they became. But I insisted I knew best, and told them to gaff it. When I saw it laid out I judged it would weigh not less than fifty pounds, and the guides agreed, provided it were a fresh one. I ran up river to where Mr. Knapp was fishing and brought him down to see what I had caught. I was gone perhaps fifteen minutes, and when I came back my fish looked as though he had been put through a wringer. He had all fallen in, and had nothing to recommend him but length. It was a blow to me, but the guides felt worse, because it's considered a crime to gaff a kelt on that river. One of the natives happened to come along and I asked him if he would like it. He looked at the fish, then at me, and went on without even speaking. I met that man in the village a number of times afterwards, but he never would look at me. I had insulted him.

It is well known that salmon which belong in a certain river do roam off to some other, and at times at a great distance away. For instance, several fish that had crossed the North Sea were caught in rivers in Scotland, and one salmon tagged in Scotland was caught in Norway. There are various cases like this, and some seasons it is not uncommon in some of our Canadian salmon rivers to take fish which do not resemble the typical fish in those rivers at all; undoubtedly they belong somewhere else. I distinctly remember one such case eight or nine years ago. Altogether we must have taken a dozen fish which looked entirely different from the rest of the run. The superintendent of the club, who had been on the river over thirty years and was a close student of salmon, was positive that they were not our river's fish. They were a much deeper fish and had a more pronounced wrist to the tail. Their fins were proportionately not as large and the tail was proportionately much smaller.

If one gets the opportunity to see a number of different rivers' fish all piled together, several hundreds of them, as I did once in a fish house at Bathurst, New Brunswick, he will quickly discern what is meant when we say that fish are geared for their own river. And knowing which particular river they belong in, you can readily understand why they are each geared in a particular way. For instance, if a fish belongs in a river that has a lot of heavy water to travel, such as big rapids, falls, etc., he is built for just that sort of work; whereas if his river is an easy one to travel, he is built very differently.

Fish coming into a river late in the season—the middle of August, for example—when the spawn is commencing to develop, are loath to travel heavy water even if they are built for it. A friend of mine has a pool with about a hundred and fifty yards of very heavy rapids at the head, which flow off into twenty feet of water. Of the fish that come there about the middle of August, the large ones will not go up through the rapids, but stay in the deep part, remaining in that vicinity until spawning time. The fish I speak of are very large, a great many of them forty pounds and over, and the only way they can be caught there is with angleworms. A large 4/0 hook loaded with all the worms that can be strung on it, which is carried to the bottom by a very heavy sinker about six or eight inches above it on the line, and sixty or seventy feet of line, is the only rig that will catch them. Speaking of angleworms, I might mention that most of the grilse caught on the upper waters of the Miramichi River are caught with worms.

A salmon's life seems to be a very short and a very hard one. He lives, on the average, about eight years; and from the time he is spawned in the river there seems to be something or someone continually at him. When he is in the fry stage other fish like trout feed on him, as do shelldrake ducks, kingfishers and other birds. In the parr stage not only are the shelldrakes and kingfishers after him, but the native trout in the river are taking his insect food away from him. When he goes to the ocean, seals, porpoise and other fish feed on him. It does not seem as if he were getting fair treatment. All you can expect back is four fish from every pair that has spawned, although each female gives from eight hundred to nine hundred eggs for each pound of her weight. For example, a twenty-pound female can potentially produce sixteen thousand fish.

The figures which Mr. Griswold gives in his book on salmon, under the heading "He who does not sow cannot expect to reap," states very clearly the tremendous loss in salmon life:

3,000 males	
6,000 females at 8,000 ova per fish . .	48,000,000
Loss in fertilization, 55%	26,400,000
	21,600,000
Loss in fry stage, 90%	19,440,000
	2,160,000
Loss in smolt stage, 79%	1,706,400
	453,600
Loss at sea, 96%	435,456
(The author estimates 98%)	
	18,144

Artificial hatching of salmon was first done in England by Frank Buckland in 1861; at that time he said he hoped it were true that salmon returned to their birthplace, since many thousands had been hatched in his kitchen!

The principal question in connection with the hatchery business is: how much can we improve upon nature? That improvement is not to be measured by the results of artificial hatching only, since successful artificial methods do not prove the success of fish culture. It has been proven that no matter how many hatchery fish are put in a river each year, that river will not thrive without natural spawning.

What information we have shows nature's waste in salmon to be tremendous; but Mr. W. C. Calderwood, the eminent Scotch authority, does not believe it is as bad as we imagine, and the fact that the salmon were once in such numbers in our rivers, before artificial hatching was ever thought of, would seem to bear out his statement.

Whether artificially-hatched salmon, kept in rearing ponds until they reach the parr or smolt stage and then put in the river, are a success or not, I don't know; but I very much doubt it. It is a well-known fact that they do not take readily to confinement, and need a lot of space and water. Furthermore, a salmon returns to the place where he was born and spent his childhood. If he spent it in a rearing pond, I'd expect him, when the spawning instinct struck him and he reached the coast (salmon are known as coast travellers), after his feeding in the ocean, to look for an overland route back to that rearing pond rather than a river to which he had made only a short visit. Let us suppose that one hundred thousand salmon were kept in rearing ponds until they reached the smolt stage and were then put in the river; all that could be expected back after they had gone to sea would be two thousand, as the loss at sea in the smolt stage has been proven to be ninety-eight per cent.

The value of kelt does not seem to be recognized on some rivers, because they are making a real job of catching them in the spring. The argument in favor of this fishing is that kelt hardly ever return and that most of those caught are put back. A kelt has reproduced his species in the river and will try to do so again if let alone; it seems too bad for him to have to fight a rod in the spring before he can get clean and recuperate in the ocean after the weakening process of spawning. One of our best authorities on salmon states plainly: "There's nothing to be made of a kelt after he's caught," meaning that he is worthless. Menzies, one of the leading Scotch authorities, says: "With the recovery of color in the well-mended stage there is also an apparent recovery in condition; this is an optical illusion due partly to the recovery of tone in the walls of the abdomen and partly to the fact of light and shade." The plumpness in the fish at that time is nothing more or less than the absorption of moisture, and even though these fish look better they are still losing weight. Menzies also states: "It's difficult to get exact records of the weight of marked kelts on recapture as the angler can only estimate this as he is in such a hurry to get the dirty brute away again so he may proceed with his legitimate business of catching fish."

It seems to be the general opinion that only four to six per cent of these kelt ever return; but while that is true of kelt in English and Scottish rivers, it is not true of the fish in Canadian ones, which show a return of from fifteen to as high as twenty-five per cent. The scales I examined from three hundred Tobique fish showed that very nearly twenty-five per cent had previously spawned. About two hundred from the Restigouche, and the same number from the Grand Cascapedia, showed that a trifle less than twenty per cent had spawned before.

An interesting letter from Mr. J. Arthur Hutton, the eminent English authority on life history of salmon, reads as follows:

From J. A. Hutton,
Woodlands,
Alderly Edge, England.

Dear Mr. Phair:

In this country it is illegal to kill kelts, and the law is very strict about it, and with very good reason. In the first place they are hardly fit for food and in any case are very poor "eaters." During the war we were allowed to catch them when we were really short of food. I tried them on two or three occasions and one or two mouthfuls were sufficient, even if it was a "well-mended" kelt. Then again a certain number will survive to return to spawn a second time, and if they do they are generally big fish—twenty pounds or over—and are fine sporting fish for they are generally harder fighters than maiden fish. Also they are quite good eating though not quite so good as maiden fish.

To show how they can recover and that they are worth preserving I may mention that I "marked" a kelt caught on Feb. 27, 1914, thirty-three inches long and weighing eight pounds. It was recaptured in a net on May 10, 1915 and then weighed twenty-eight pounds and was forty inches long. Thus in fourteen and a half months at no cost to us Nature had turned eight pounds of poor food into twenty-eight pounds of valuable food.

In Canada certainly they ought to be preserved and even more so than in this country, because for some reason which I can't explain, there is a much higher "survival-ratio" than on this side of the Atlantic. Here one does not expect the proportion of "spawned-fish" to be more than four or five per cent of the total catch, at the outside say ten per cent. It is a rather remarkable fact that of all the collections of scales from Canada which I have examined, the proportion is very much higher, from fifteen to twenty-five per cent. Therefore if kelts are worth preserving here, they have much more potential value in Canada.

Nor can I understand anyone who calls himself a sportsman wanting to catch kelts. They may splash about a bit for a minute or two, but it is soon over. If I hook a kelt when I am salmon fishing I put my rod down and draw the line in with my hand so as to get it back into the water as soon as possible.

The term "well-mended" is a misnomer. All they have done is to get bright in colour and to absorb a good deal of water, which makes them look plump. After a short time the water evaporates and their sides drop in and then one finds that they are quite thin. Until they get back to the sea they get no food worth mentioning, if any at all. I have known of a case where people have been poisoned by eating a kelt.

Yours sincerely,

J. Arthur Hutton.

Salmon are known during the different stages of their life as:

(A) Alevin: From time of hatching until the yolk sack is absorbed, generally about six weeks.

(B) Fry: From the end of the alevin stage until the end of the first summer.

(C) Parr: From the end of the fry stage until they are ready to go to the sea.

(D) Smolt: Parr just before entering the ocean, and silver in color. This silver color is put on as they reach the lower end of the river and at the head of tide.

I have seen these fish on their way to the sea, as far down the Restigouche as Matapedia, four to seven inches long, and perfect parr; but just a few miles farther down at Flatlands, which is the head of tide, they are all silver.

When these fish return to the river they are known as:

(A) Grilse: A fish that has spent a summer, winter, and a part or the whole of a second summer in the sea.

(B) Small Spring Salmon, Small Summer Salmon.

(C) Large Spring Salmon, Large Summer Salmon.

(D) Extra Large Spring Salmon, Extra Large Summer Salmon.

We are most interested in the spring fish since he is the one that furnishes the sport. These early fish, which come into most of the rivers of Canada the first of June, are the best fish to catch, being fresh from the ocean and full of fight, in good condition and at their best for eating. These fish start early because they have farther to go, like the Serpentine fish in Tobique and the Kedgwick fish, which is the first to come into the Restigouche. When a river is overfished or netted, these early fish are the first to disappear, a good instance of which is the Miramichi. As the season advances the fish that come in the river loaf along and stay longer in the pools; they grow dark in color, don't fight as well, and after the first of August are poor eating, a chowder being the best way to cook them. Most salmon fishermen are through with their fishing August first. After that about all the fish are good for is to make boots, the skin having grown tough like leather. A number of rivers, whose early run has been wiped out, are dependent, however, on their late fish; but they give poor sport to the fisherman who has caught them early in the season. It has been claimed by good authorities that salmon lose one third of their weight from the time they come in the river till they get back to the ocean, but today the loss in weight is placed at twenty-three per cent.

In spite of all the money spent in salmon hatcheries, and our experience, over a long period of years in Canada and the U. S. A., in hatching fish, we don't know today whether artificial hatching is any improvement on the natural process. One hundred spawning fish will produce two hundred mature fish by natural hatching; and the question is: if we caught those hundred fish, stripped them and hatched the ova artificially, would we get enough more mature fish to make the expense and labor worth while? Remember, we get only two out of every hundred smolt back; the other ninety-eight are lost at sea.

Scale Reading

An interesting feature of this spawning business is that ova from spring-run

Scale showing two years of river life prior to first descent to sea

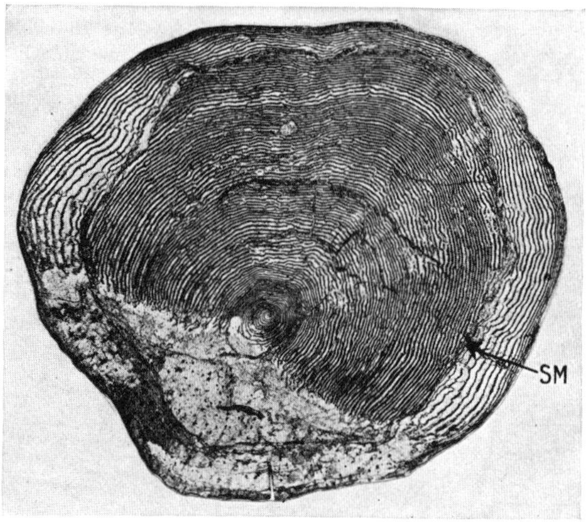

Scale with one well-defined spawning mark

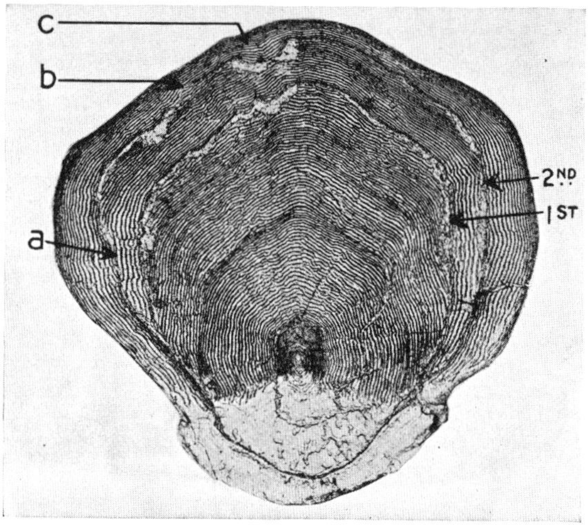

Scale with two spawning marks and evidences of ocean feeding

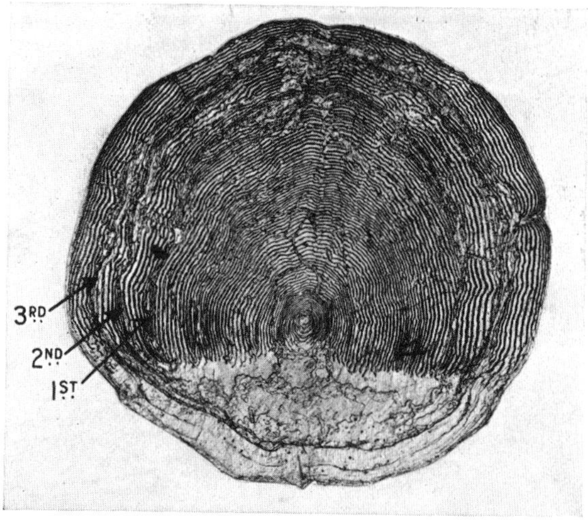

Scale showing three spawning marks

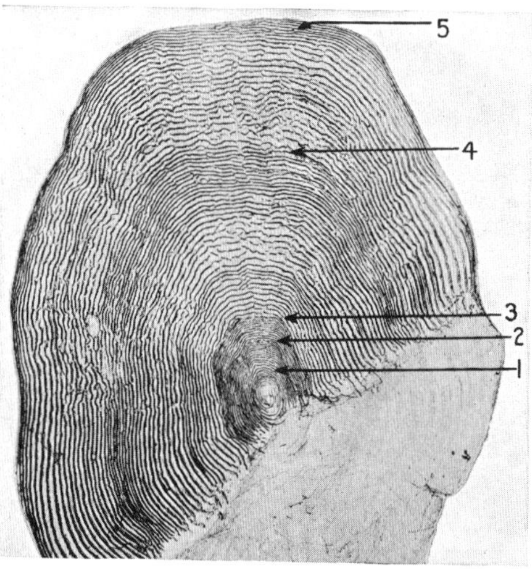

Scale showing *three* years of river life prior to first descent to sea

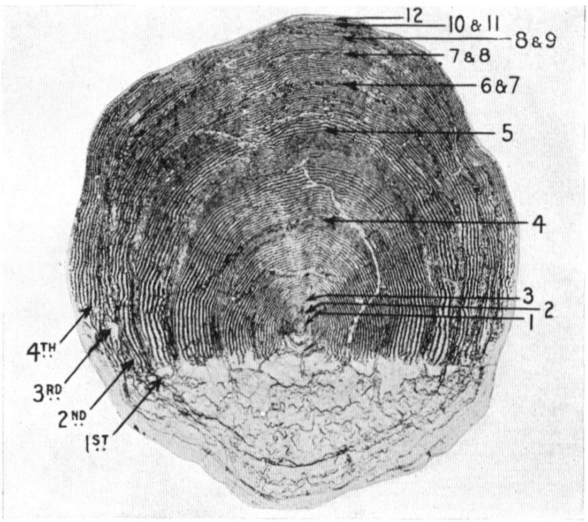

Scale from Moisie River fish showing four spawning marks

Photographs courtesy of J. Arthur Hutton

SALMON SCALES

fish will produce spring fish, and ova from late-run fish will produce a late-run fish. Early in the nineteenth century it was known to a certainty that the life history of a salmon is written on its scales; and the fact that salmon stop growing when they enter fresh water is only another proof that they do not feed there. The stop in growth of the scale then, and the beginning again of its growth when the fish gets to the sea, leaves a scar or spawning mark, as it is called. Eight years is about the life of a salmon; and it is usually the males which live to that age, since they remain fertile longer than the females. From the scales may be learned the fish's age, the number of times it has spawned, the number of years it spent in the river before going to the ocean, whether the fish belongs to an early or late run, and also, by certain measurements of the scale and the length of the fish, together with a mathematical formula, the fish's length at any time during its life.

For examining salmon scales I have a small magnifying glass, underneath which there fits a glass slide on which to put the scale. It folds up and can be carried in the pocket. It is of low power and I use it only to see if the scale is perfect and not scarred as many of them are. The scales should be taken from the shoulder of the fish, where they are more likely to be in good condition for reading. I also have an ordinary microscope, which can be bought for four or five dollars, of higher power than the pocket glass. This, with boxes of glass slides, with isinglass covers, on which to mount scales permanently, completes the outfit. The glass slides can be purchased of any dealer in surgical instruments.

A scale is taken and the silver film on it wiped off with a damp cloth. It is then placed on the pocket glass under the magnifying one. If the circular lines all show plainly, it is then transferred to one of the glass slides, an isinglass cover put over it and each end wrapped around with narrow strips of gummed paper. The isinglass cover is put on to keep the scale from curling up.

Upon examination the scale shows a number of rings like the rings of a tree, some of them heavy and well defined and quite widely separated, others much finer and closer together. The heavy, widely spaced lines show the heavy feeding in the summer when the water was warm and food was abundant; the fine ones, close together, indicate winter growth when the water was cold and food scarce. It is by separating these winter and summer growths that the age of the fish is determined. The center of the scale shows the river life before the fish went to sea, and the first year's feeding, when the fish was in the fry stage, is very indistinct. The second year, during the parr stage when the fish was large enough really to go after food, is plainly shown by the feeding ring. If this fish then went to sea and came back the next year as a grilse, the rings which designate this period of his life are much more pronounced, being heavier and more widely separated. He had done some feeding this third year when he reached the ocean where food was plentiful, and had grown from three or four ounces to three, four or five pounds. If he went to the ocean again (and if he ever returned), the scale then shows very heavy feeding. Salmon have been known to put on fourteen pounds in one year.

This separating of the summer and winter rings is not easy on some scales and a number of scales from the fish have to be examined to determine them. The contractions will be most pronounced, as a rule, on the sides. The old theory that sixteen rings on the scale constitute one year of the salmon's life won't hold water, as different scales from the same fish vary. The old saying is: some salmon come back once, hardly ever twice, and almost never the third time, although scales have been taken from fish on their fourth return, and one on its sixth.

When I first began trying to read salmon scales I would take them to a doctor who lived next door to me, and who was rather famous for his work with a microscope; but I couldn't interest him in them, nor would he read the literature or letters I had from England on the subject. He claimed such a thing was impossible. That winter he was ill in the hospital for three months, and while convalescing asked me one day to bring up those papers and letters I had on salmon scales; which I did. About a month after he had come home, he called me over and excitedly showed me a lot of different scales under his microscope. He said it was wonderful and that he wouldn't have believed it. I asked him where he found salmon scales at that time of year, and he told me that he had gotten them from frozen salmon in the ice box at the fish market. I had no trouble getting him to help me read scales after that; and I thought that if a high-class doctor would go digging into an old fish box for evidence, there must be something to it.

Collection of A. M. Barnes, Esq.

LEAPING SALMON

FROM A WATER COLOUR PAINTING BY OGDEN M. PLEISSNER

CHAPTER XII.

IMPROVING, PROTECTING AND STOCKING SALMON RIVERS; TOGETHER WITH ETIQUETTE AND CUSTOMS

IT might be interesting before we take up the subject of the improvement, protection and stocking of salmon rivers to observe what has taken place in the last one hundred and thirty-five years on the Restigouche, which is undoubtedly the best river in Canada, and also how the country around it has been affected financially.

The Bay de Chaleur is bounded by the counties of Gaspé and Bonaventure on the Quebec side, and by the counties of Gloucester and Restigouche on the New Brunswick side. It is about two hundred miles long, from the entrance to the head of tidal water. Gaspé has three salmon rivers of considerable size and two small ones. Bonaventure has the Grand Cascapedia and two smaller streams. Gloucester has the Nipisiguit and Restigouche, the latter having two branches, and also the small Jacquet River. These rivers are nurseries for the salmon which are caught on the coast and which afford fishing for the angler.

About a hundred years ago the salmon taken in these rivers and at the mouths were salted, barrelled, and sold to the lumbermen or sent to Halifax. Half of the fish killed were taken with the spear, the Indians having license to go where they chose. Few if any restrictions were imposed on netters, nets near tide head in some instances extending from shore to shore, and the channels, where at all practicable, being barricaded. Netting was confined to the estuary of the Restigouche. The inhabitants living on the rivers used the drift net. Few took more than necessary for winter use, for the low price of about $6 per barrel was not sufficient temptation to take more. Such was the state of things in 1837; and at that time the statement was made that the salmon were gone. It was told that thirty years before one thousand salmon had been brought in at one haul. At this time the catch fluctuated very much, poor in some years, good in others; and "Two bad years and one good" was a general saying among the fishermen. Some netters got from twenty to thirty barrels during a season, others as little as five barrels; and the best years from 1837 to 1857 did not yield over five hundred barrels.

Such was the general state of the fisheries during that period. Fish gradually decreased in numbers and some of the netters abandoned their stations. About that time a canning station was opened near tide head, which took all the fish caught by the Indians, as well as those handled by the netters, within a radius of twenty miles or more. The quantity canned would be about 200,000 pounds at the most, but it was often as low as 50,000 and in 1864 the whole product of this cannery was only 37,000 pounds. The sale of fresh salmon now became an extra inducement to the Indians, and for ten years they paid every attention to it and speared and netted the rivers up to their headwaters. About 1864 it became known that when there were any salmon in the river they would rise to a fly. In 1869 the Department of Fisheries took charge and the Fisheries Act came into force; and a few anglers then fished the rivers with some success. With the coming of rod fishermen, the headwaters had better protection against the St. John spearers; the Indians were restricted as to limits, and shortly afterward totally prohibited. Then, about 1869, salmon gave signs of increasing. In 1871 the rivers were leased; the protection given by the lessees was of great benefit. Pisciculture was started in 1873, but no fry of any consequence were deposited in the rivers until 1875. The opening of the I. C. R. railroad in 1876 gave another impetus to the fresh-fish trade, and, although it was not a very good year, one firm in six days shipped 80,000 pounds to New York. Freezers now began to be constructed, only two having previously been in existence. From 1876 to 1882 the yearly catches varied a great deal. The netters often had a poor season though the river held a fair supply of fish. This happened when the water remained high late in the spring, preventing nets from being set; sometimes, when they had been set, a June freshet swept them away just as the fish were running up. The records from that time show that the heavy run of fish did not last more than three weeks, as a rule; and some years the whole run was known to pass in ten days. Since 1883 there has been a steady increase in both river and net catch, due to protection and stocking. It was known that a great many of the naturally spawned ova were destroyed each year by heavy ice jams and freshets, which washed away the beds in which the eggs were lying just at the most critical stage of their existence, some seasons being much worse than others. To remedy this and to assist nature, artificially-raised fry were planted; and, which shows how artificial hatching was first regarded by some, a great deal of influence was brought to bear upon the Minister of Fisheries to abolish the hatchery; otherwise, it was claimed, there would be total extinction. Records show that in 1885 and 1886 over 2,000 salmon were taken with the rod, some ladies running a score of from thirty to fifty fish, and the men from fifty to a hundred and twenty, with an average weight of twenty-three pounds, which is about five pounds more than it is today. In 1886, Mr. Charles Hallock, an authority on fish and fishing in the United States, wrote in *Forest and Stream* that the Restigouche fish had degenerated in size and had lost their fierceness and courage, due to their artificial propagation. This statement led Mr. John Mowat, who was at that time in charge of the hatchery at Dee Side, to doubt that Mr. Hallock had ever been on the river; and he made the statement that if he had been there he would have found that the fish broke just as many leaders and lines as ever.

That the salmon fisheries were improving is indicated by the fact that the market value of salmon shipped to the United States in 1886 was $1,066,000; of which $1,001,000 was accounted for by fish taken in nets, $45,000 by fish taken by anglers, who killed 2,000 salmon on the Restigouche alone, and $20,000 by fish caught by anglers in Bonaventure and Gaspé counties in Quebec.

Mr. Mowat was told to get a price on the holdings of twenty-three of the netters in the estuary of the Restigouche, not with the idea of re-selling for profit, but to do away with the nets and to give free pass to the salmon to enter the river. He found that the project would cost the modest sum of $130,000, which would surely indicate that salmon were on the increase.

Now let us have a look at the rivers. The New Brunswick Government offered at this time to lease the rod fishing on the Restigouche River for five years at an upset price of $3,900 per year. This same river had been let in 1871 for nine years to Messrs. Fleming and Brydges at a yearly rental of $40. Private properties with from half a mile to two-and-a-half miles of frontage on only one side of the river were valued at from $15,000 to $25,000, and pieces which a few years ago had not cost more than $400 or $500 were priced from $5,000 to $8,000. Yearly rentals of $50 to $150 were paid in 1887 for a season's fishing on a single front of fifty rods. There were then three clubs on the river, with a combined membership of sixty, whose expenditures amounted to about $27,000, with twenty guardians employed for the season at an average of $40 per month. At that time the Indians in the little town of Campbellton went around, after a month's fishing trip, with new clothes and $150 or more in cash in their pockets. Not a chicken, lamb, pound of butter or quart of cream could be produced by a settler that was not sold at New York prices. Mr. Alex Robertson, Superintendent of Rivers, made the statement in 1887 that no living man of that generation had ever seen anything approaching the number of salmon seen on the main Restigouche River during the last two years.

Let us see what has taken place since. At the auction of salmon rivers in 1917 the upset price of the anglers' rights for a single year on the whole Restigouche River was $17,700. Little Main was sold then for $500, and in 1927 brought $5,100. At the auction of 1922 the upset price for twenty-five different stretches of the Restigouche was $29,790. The Patapedia, the upset price of which was $200, did not receive a bid. At the 1927 auction seventeen stretches alone on Restigouche brought $81,500, and one stretch on the Kedgwick of about twenty miles, the upset price of which was $1,000, was sold for $12,800; the balance of the Kedgwick, the upset price of which was $1,000, brought $3,150, making a total for this river alone of $15,950. The whole river, only a few years before, had been leased to a friend of mine for around $300. At the 1932 auction, due to the depression, these rivers failed by about $15,000 to bring as much. Bear in mind that it was 1864 when it was first discovered that Restigouche fish would take the fly, and that the above figures are yearly rental prices.

Since the incorporation of the Restigouche Salmon Club in 1880, well over $1,000,000 has been spent there for protection alone. From 1912 to 1932 it cost approximately $650,000 to guard the Restigouche, Kedgwick, Little Main, Patapedia and Lower Restigouche.

CASCAPEDIA CLUB LODGES

SAGE LODGE—OLDEST ON THE RESTIGOUCHE

LODGE AT TOM'S BROOK ON THE RESTIGOUCHE

JAMES C. COLGATE'S LODGE ON THE MIRAMICHI

On the Restigouche and its branches there are about seventy wardens employed for five months each year, going on duty around the end of May. Each man patrols about one mile of river where there are settlements and about five miles of river above the settlements.

The Restigouche Riparian Association was formed in 1911. This Association is comprised of the various clubs and lessees along the river system, who pay proportionately their share of the expenses. This Association was formed for the river's protection; it holds a Dominion charter, though it is entirely non-political. Approximately $30,000 is expended each year. The president of the Association was formerly Henry De Forest and is now Robert W. Goelet. Mr. Max M. Mowat has been head warden for the past forty years. He is an old friend for whom I have a very high regard. He comes from an old family of salmon fishermen. His father, Mr. John Mowat, was the first to have charge of the hatchery at Dee Side, Quebec, which was burned about sixty-five years ago. Alex Mowat, his brother, took over from his father in 1882, and continued until 1923, when W. A. Mowat took charge until superannuated in 1935. Mr. Max Mowat took charge of the Restigouche River in 1897, and to him I owe a great deal for whatever knowledge I have of salmon. He was always most kind and instructive during the years I fished the river. He tells me that he would judge that there are about 125 per cent more fish taken nowadays than there were in 1897, but grants, of course, that there are many more rods on the river today. Even at that he estimates that there are fully 50 per cent more fish in the river today than in earlier times. This he attributes to stocking and the protection of the river.

As can be readily imagined, a club such as the Restigouche has a heavy investment on the river. This includes such items as twenty-three club houses in New Brunswick, valued at $161,000; fifty-six guardians' shanties valued at $16,800; and boats and accessories valued at $15,000. The upkeep of the lodges, half in New Brunswick and half in Quebec, is about $15,000 a year. Guardians' pay and other expenses are approximately $40,000. On the Quebec side the holdings amount to about $200,500.

Improving

Very little has been done in regard to improving salmon water on Canadian rivers as compared to what has been done in England, and with one exception, the only instances I have seen have not been very successful. I have never known of an attempt being made to divert the current (as they do in England), by building an obstruction with rocks, in a stretch of water where the current is slow, to make a faster run on the other side. But I have seen the large point of a ledge, which projected thirty or forty feet into very fast water, blown about half away, to flatten out the current. In this case, the point of ledge, running out as it did, narrowed up the river, making the current so heavy that fish would not lie in it or near it. By blowing off enough of it, so that the water flattened out, a very successful pool was formed. The ledge I speak of was right in front of the lodge, and in the spring when it was struck by the high water, it made such a continuous roar that it was impossible to sleep in the lodge. Though it was only about a hundred yards from the mouth of a good cold spring brook, we did not get the advantage of that cool water running for any distance down along the shore, for when it hit the ledge it was distributed all over the river. After the change, however, we had good fishing along that shore.

I have seen a number of places in salmon rivers where the owner of the land, not having any pools on his water, had put in a number of rocks here and there, in hopes that fish on their way up river would stop to rest behind some of them. But I only know of one instance where this turned out well. A friend of mine who had no pool, but had a stretch of river about a quarter of a mile in length, with a good pool on his neighbor's water above and another on his neighbor's below, put in three rocks which he thought would be in the line salmon travelled on their way up river. He, being a guide, and having a good idea of what salmon want for a resting place, got all three of those rocks in the right places. And after that we could go out at almost any time during the season and find a fish behind one of them.

Another friend of mine, who had some leased water, chose, to experiment upon, the pool which he considered his poorest. This particular pool, while not yielding very many fish each year, was always good for a few. During the winter he had a farmer haul rocks on a sled out on the ice to certain places he had designated the summer before, and by cutting holes through the ice put these rocks down. As I remember it, they put a dozen or fifteen rocks in different places in the pool. And the result in this case was that there have been but few fish taken there since. The new rocks evidently changed the bottom in a way that fish don't like, for they refuse to stop there now.

I would not think it advisable to disturb a pool that provided any worthwhile fishing at all, but would very much prefer to do as my friend did in the first instance: to take a stretch of water that was not producing any fish and to make places there for them to lie. One very often sees single rocks here and there in a not particularly good-looking piece of water where the current is slow, but there are often salmon behind them. And I don't know why a lot of water which now is never fished could not be made to produce something. It would be very inexpensive to do on most of our Canadian rivers, since most of the farmers have rock piles; you could select the size rocks you wanted, and in the winter they could be loaded on a low sled or sledge and hauled down to the river; holes could then be cut and the rocks put into the river. It would be well worth trying.

In England concrete or cement blocks are built in the desired sizes; a lot of good fishing has been made in just this way. I think that if one selects some place which resembles another he has seen, with a rock here and there in it, and imitates it as nearly as he can, he will not go very far wrong. I have always wanted to try it, anyway.

Protection

A great many things enter into the protection of a salmon river; I would consider first the removal of anything that interferes with not only the grown salmon but the fish in its fry, parr and smolt stages as well, if there is to be good fishing.

Salmon like good clean water: it was pollution that ruined the rivers of the United States. A grown salmon can stand a certain amount of pollution in a river, but when in the fry, parr and smolt stages, they cannot. For one reason, pollution destroys what food there is in the water, leaving the fish nothing on which to live. Water is said to clean itself in six miles, but that depends on whether it is six miles of fast broken water or water with slow sluggish current. Brook trout and other fish feed on the fry and parr; sea trout practically live on parr, and a decided effort was made in one river I know of to clean out the sea trout, so destructive were they. The river should be kept clear of shelldrake ducks and kingfishers. In the spring when the shelldrakes hatch out, the mother will be seen with a closely-bunched flock of fifteen or twenty; a warden then, with one shot, can clean up most of the brood. Kingfishers can be destroyed by driving a pole at the edge of the water and setting a small steel trap at its top. They will always alight on the top of such poles. If there are any heron on the river they also should be cleared out.

I like the idea of counting or making an estimate of the number of fish on the spawning beds each fall, as in that way you can estimate how many to expect back.

Dams in salmon rivers should have fish-ways placed where they can be easily found by the fish, and so arranged that they can be easily ascended. They should extend to the bottom of the river, where the fish are likely to be, not up so high as to be completely out in low water, like one I have seen. It has been repeatedly proven that salmon will not jump or go through white water early in the spring when it is cold. Nor will they jump over anything they can swim over. Of course, when the water is a good pitch over some of the low roll dams, which we have on some rivers, fish will be seen going right on up and over them, and not bothering with the fish-way; and a salmon has been known to jump eleven feet four inches. This latter feat was witnessed by Mr. W. C. Calderwood of Scotland, who measured the leap. But, when it is cold, salmon do not like rough, broken water, and it should be avoided in placing the mouth of the fish-way, which should be put, rather, in quiet water where the fish would naturally lie. Care should be taken that it does not get clogged up with snags and rubbish which come down river.

The wardening service on salmon rivers is very important, but not always an easy thing to handle. It is the custom on some rivers, when there is a poacher who cannot be made to stop his illegal fishing, to give him a job as warden; in some instances this has worked out all right, but I think that if a man is once a poacher and a good one he will always be one. I would consider the ideal warden for a stretch of water, a man who has lived there all his life and who is interested in salmon; if he likes to fish them with a fly, all the better. I think he should have the privilege of taking a fish on a fly for his table once in a while, when the water is not being used; and it is also a good idea for whoever is fishing that water, whenever he kills fish in it, to give the warden one. I have known instances of men who, having owned the water originally and sold it, or leasing their water, never have a salmon to eat all through the season. I don't think I'd blame those men for taking a fish once in a while.

Whoever has charge of a salmon river should give his entire time to it and

TOM'S BROOK POOL ON THE RESTIGOUCHE

Point of rock at left has been blown away to spread current

Photo by Acme

STEPS FOR SALMON AT AROOSTOOK FALLS, MAINE

Courtesy of Dr. A. B. Flett

ICELAND

Courtesy of Joseph P. Knapp

4TH FALLS, NATASHQUAN RIVER

LEAPING SALMON

do nothing else. To be a success, he should not only know something about the fish but should be deeply interested in them.

One of the best instances I can remember of good wardening on a salmon river was done by the late Thomas Allen, superintendent of the Tobique. I had four pools leased on that river for a number of years and used to fish the entire season each year. At the end of one season's fishing, Tom asked me how many fish I had killed, for, he said, he wanted to check up with me. I asked him if he meant to tell me that he had a record of my fish. "Yes, sir," he replied, "and where you caught every one of them." And he did have them all recorded, with the dates they were taken, the pools, the number I had shipped, and the number I had given to the natives or put on the table at Hayden's Inn. I called that good wardening because I considered anyone smart who could keep track of me on a salmon river in those days.

A salmon river can be protected and well wardened without having trouble and disagreeableness with the natives that live on it, but it does not always happen. The fact that you have leased a man's fishing and it is yours to fish as you like, is no reason why you should ignore him; and I do not know of any place where little things count as much as they do on a salmon river. It is a good plan, for example, to buy from the natives whatever things you can for the lodge, such as spring lamb, chickens, butter and eggs. Perhaps they do charge you a little more than you would pay somewhere else, but what of it? Everywhere else along the river others are making a little money out of the fishing: why shouldn't they? After all, they once owned the water and could go out and take fish whenever they wanted to.

I know of two rivers not five hours apart, on both of which there is plenty of money to spend for protection. On one there is always trouble and poaching; on the other, such things are never known. You cannot antagonize people and expect them to do things for you. I have known of one bad warden upsetting a whole river, and turning members of a once peaceable community into a gang of poachers. Just as I was bringing a fish in to the gaff one evening, on a certain river, the fly came untied, and the fish got away with it in his mouth. That night at the place where I was staying, I happened to remark that I hated to lose that fly, since I did not have any Jungle Cock feathers with which to tie another. A little while afterwards a man standing there said to me, "Would you give $5 to have that fly back?" "Yes, quick," I said. The next morning that fly was on the table beside my place when I came down to breakfast, and I know it was the same one because I tied it myself.

The Restigouche is the best managed river I have ever fished.

The banks of some pools should be watched carefully, and if they start to cave in and wash away during the spring freshets, cribwork should be put in at once, or the pool will probably fill up and be ruined.

Stocking

As the supply does not meet the demand, stocking is carried on on practically all of the rivers.

It has been proven that, by stocking and protecting, a depleted river can be brought back and made a success; but the stocking has to be done on an enormous scale. Instead of a few hundred thousand each year they must be put in by the millions, which, of course, is expensive. It has been estimated that a hatchery capable of handling nine million eggs would cost in the neighborhood of $7,500, with $3,000 necessary to maintain it. Good judgment is not always used in choosing the places along the river where fry are put in. I have seen a truckload of fry in cans from a hatchery hauled to one of the bogans and all dumped in together; naturally most of them stayed pretty much in a bunch together in this quiet water. For how long I don't know, but I thought at the time that if a shelldrake duck should come along they wouldn't last long.

I like the way fry were formerly distributed on the Restigouche, which was from pontoons which were towed up the rivers by horse-scow; the fish were liberated at such places as the superintendent desired. It used to be quite an event on the river when this fishery boat came along manned by a crew of men and a superintendent, with the British and Canadian flags flying. There are approximately 2,000,000 fry distributed in the river and its branches each year. They are three months old when liberated. *And this work and protection has been going on for sixty-five years.* That is why the Restigouche is one of the greatest rivers in the world today. The fry are taken by motor truck in large cans and are distributed in all parts of the main river and its branches along the shores. The parent fish are bought by the Federal Government from commercial netters in the Bay de Chaleur in the months of June and July at about $3 per fish, only prime fish being acceptable. They are towed in pontoons by motor boat to the rearing pond at New Mills where they are kept until spawning time near the end of October. The number of fish retained each year runs from 400 to 600, and about three-quarters of these are females. After they are stripped of from 1,500,000 to 2,000,000 eggs they are liberated in the bay; the eggs are then taken to the Dominion Government Hatchery at Flatlands by motor truck, where they are hatched out during the following months of April and May, and they are distributed from there.

Etiquette and Customs

If you have leased fishing on a river with which you are not familiar, it is well to get in touch with the superintendent of the club, if there is one, and to find out from him what it is customary to do, about not only your fishing but many other things as well. Clubs on the different rivers establish certain customs it is well to follow, since your guides and others in your employ will naturally expect you to do so. My first year on the Restigouche I fished from a Gaspé boat, which requires two men. The day I arrived I wanted to cross over to an island in front of the camp, only about seventy-five yards away, with just an ordinary quiet piece of water between. Going down to the river where one of my guides was at the boat, I asked him to set me over on the island, which he said he would do just as soon as he could find the other man. He wouldn't put me across on that island, though he could have easily enough, because it was not the custom for one man to handle a Gaspé boat.

On some rivers, even if your lodge is only a small one and there is no one fishing from it but yourself, the chances are that your cook will want someone to help him and to wait on the table. And he will expect you to supply the camp with the same sort of foodstuffs the club camp has, and any number of other things, too numerous to mention. But if one follows club ideas, everything will go on more smoothly; and as the club is in a position to do you a great many favors if it sees fit, it is well to follow along in its footsteps.

A mail-boat service such as is maintained on the Restigouche is very convenient; the men bring not only the mail for the Lodge but any small packages, and on the trip down take fish to be shipped. A tag bearing the name and address is tied through the fish's mouth, and when it reaches Matapedia it is boxed and iced before shipping. Manzer Howard, who was guiding me, once stuffed a lot of sheet lead down the throat of one of my fish, to beat the weight of a fish killed by a certain member of my party, and when we shipped the fish down river by the mail boat that particular one was addressed to the late Ezra Fitch. Two weeks later I had a letter from Mr. Fitch thanking me for the fish, and asking, "why the hell all the sheet lead in him."

There is one thing which must never be forgotten, provided you may ever want to go fishing again, and that is to tip the cook, guides, mail-boat man and what other help you have had. It does not necessarily have to be a large amount, since it is really a way of showing them that you appreciate the many things they have done for you during your stay. Above all, don't forget that a guide is a guide and a cook a cook. The guide takes care of your fishing tackle, looks after his boat, and handles it for you while you are fishing. The cook cooks for anyone who may be at the camp. Don't ask either of them to run errands and to do things that are out of their line. If you do, they won't like it.

An instance of how much guides and cooks will stand before blowing up is the case of one of my guides, who was once doing the guiding and cooking for a fisherman. The first morning Jack brought in fried eggs and bacon for the man's breakfast; the gentleman allowed he did not want his eggs fried, but boiled, so Jack took them back to the kitchen and boiled some. Next morning, naturally thinking he preferred boiled eggs, Jack cooked them that way, but that morning he wanted them fried. For dinner one night Jack served canned beans; the man wanted to know what brand they were. Jack said he didn't remember, having thrown the can away, whereupon he was told to go find the can, which he did; when Jack returned with the tin, the gentleman said he did not like that brand at all and told Jack to heat up a different one.

This went on for a week, until one morning for breakfast Jack brought in the fry pan full of beans; when the man saw them, he told Jack he did not want his beans in the fry pan. And Jack replied, "You are going to get them in the fry pan whether you want them or not," and brought the pan down over the man's head, beans and all.

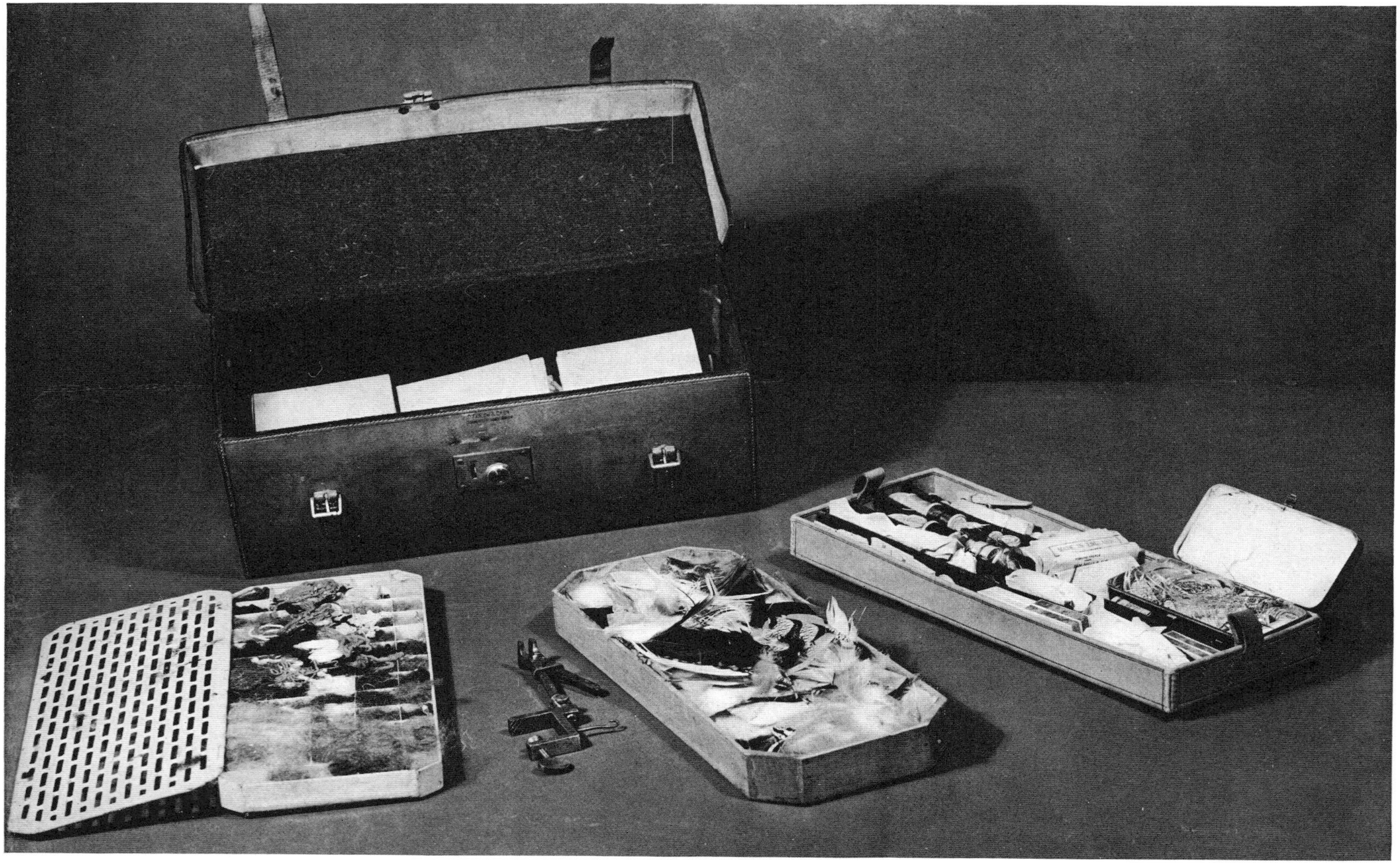

THE AUTHOR'S FLY TYING KIT

CHAPTER XIII.

SALMON FLY DRESSING

IT is best to have a case which will hold your vise, tools and all your materials for dressing salmon flies; otherwise they get misplaced and badly mixed up. The hackles should be sorted and sized for hooks of different sizes and, if you want to tie flies fast, everything should be where you can put your hand right on it. Otherwise, it takes longer to find the materials for a fly than to tie it.

I had a leather case made in London for my materials. The bottom part was designed to hold hackles and feathers in large square envelopes, each one marked and just fitting. There was a tray with a perforated top and compartments for wools, seal's fur, chenille and body material; with a dubbing needle you could pick out whatever material you wanted. The next tray held jungle cock, golden pheasants' necks, pieces of Indian crow, toucan, chatterer and other plumage needed in most of the standard patterns. The top tray held Pearsall's tying and floss silks, an airtight nickel box for all tinsels, hooks, pliers, vise and other tools.

At home a cabinet is all right, but when you start on a fishing trip you cannot take it with you; you pack a lot of things in miscellaneous boxes, and when you arrive your materials are not only all mixed up, but you find you have left home half of the things you want most. With a case such as I have described you always have everything and everything is in its place.

Tying flies on a fishing trip affords much more pleasure than tying them at home, because you can go right out and try your new flies over fish and change the dressings as the water changes. Best of all, there is a group of guides looking on and suggesting how to make the flies look the way they like them. On a salmon river you generally lunch at one o'clock, and from then until four there is nothing to do except sleep, a habit which almost all salmon fishermen acquire before they have been at it a great while; so there is always plenty of time each day to devote to fly tying. You will do better developing and experimenting with new patterns on the river than at home. On the river, salmon is all that you think or talk; and new ideas occur to you and many of your observations lead to new conclusions.

I have purchased fly tying materials everywhere across the water, and the ones I have had from C. Farlow and Co., 11 Panton Street, Haymarket, London, are easily the best. I think Farlow salmon flies are the finest tied and the best proportioned of any I know, and the materials that go into them are the best that can be had. A good thing to do, which simplifies matters a lot, is to select the patterns and sizes you wish to tie, and which you know you will use a great deal—flies like Jock Scott, Black Dose, and Silver Grey—and send Farlow a list telling them you want all materials for dressing so many flies of each size and pattern. When the materials arrive, you will find the throat and body hackles separately sized for different sized hooks, and everything not only of the very highest grade materials possible but arranged in an orderly manner. They specialize in filling such orders, and everything they send out is most satisfactory.

The way fly dressers work across the water is interesting. The best flies are dressed by men whose fathers, grandfathers, and great-grandfathers were fly dressers before them, and who are proud of the fact that their art has been handed down to them. These fly dressers are no longer assembled, as they used to be, in one large room, furnished with materials and told what patterns and sizes to tie; that method of production was not at all successful. I know of no other profession in which there is so much jealousy and it is so impossible for people to work together pleasantly. Now, each fly dresser or family is given an order for so many flies of each pattern and size. The dressers then make requisitions on the firm for the necessary materials, which are furnished them, and they do the tying at home. If you select some fly dresser, for instance, whose work you like, and hire him at so much an hour to give you lessons, it is more than likely that while he is teaching you he will tell you that his family is the only one in which the art has really been handed down from father to son. If you mention some other dresser whose flies you have admired, it is likely he will tell you that the man's father or grandfather was a butcher, or engaged in some other line of business, and that it was not possible for him to tie good flies. If a stranger happens in on a family who are tying leaders, they all stop work immediately until they find out that he does not want to learn how they do their work. They have secrets about the tying of knots.

When I went to England I looked forward to meeting a certain dresser of trout flies who had a great reputation in this country and whose flies were supposed to be the best. I found out when I arrived there that there was no such person; it was only a trade name.

I watched one man tie some Jock Scotts, and from the way he worked in the different colored feathers and materials, it seemed more as though he were painting a fly than tying one. That man was an artist, and, I was told, a fine salmon fisherman.

The tools required are: first, a vise; and this should be one of which the jaws and top part can be turned and moved forward and backward so that you can see the bottom and sides of the fly while the work is progressing, to ascertain whether the ribbing is being rightly spaced, etc. I like the one made by Wesley Richards, the gun manufacturer, of London. It is such a vise as I describe. Some dressers dispense with a vise and hold the hook in their fingers, which is not easy to do, especially with small flies. It is difficult to tie on wings and get them to stay right when holding the hook in your fingers, and it is almost impossible to dress such elaborate patterns as Popham, Nicholson or Jock Scott, which have jointed bodies, without a vise. Then again, in tying without a vise, the silk must be more heavily waxed to keep it from slipping; this wax gets on the feathers and hackles when you hold the hook in your fingers. It is well to have a half dozen pairs of pliers handy, since they get misplaced and knocked on the floor; when you want a pair you want it quick, so it is well to have several on the table. Some of these should have an extra solid grip to hold tinsels when winding them on, or other materials from which you particularly wish the pliers not to slip while winding. A good dubbing needle for picking out bodies of seal's fur and wools has numerous other uses as well. You should also be provided with several pairs of forceps for picking up hackles, feathers and other materials from the table. The table, by the way, should have a large piece of white cardboard on it, because against this background you can see better the fly on which you are working, and can more readily distinguish different feathers and hackles. Have several pairs of scissors; be sure not to cut tinsel and the ends of hackles with the pair you use for cutting strips of feather for wings. You will need a manicure pair with curved blades for trimming the ends of wings before finishing the heads of flies, and also a sharp knife for splitting the quills of certain feathers, such as jay feathers, that are to be used for hackles. Fly tying should all be done in the daylight, as it is ruinous to the eyes to tie by artificial light. Pearsall's gossamer tying silks are best and come in all sizes and strengths. Buy your wax ready to use. I tried to make mine at first from Kelson's recipe in his book THE SALMON FLY. I once had a quart bottleful corked up and standing in a pail of warm water, at one stage of the proceeding, which exploded, ruining a first-class kitchen that had just been done over in white enamel. I like cobbler's wax, and the tying silk drawn through a piece of it a few times will last out if the temperature of the room is warm. Keep a small bottle of alcohol or turpentine on the table and a towel which you can easily reach, hanging at the side, as you will have to keep the wax off your fingers or it will get on wings and hackles. And do not try dyeing your own feathers. I dyed not only my feathers but everything else in the house! It is cheaper and better to buy them.

I am taking it for granted that whoever is beginning to dress salmon flies has had experience tying trout flies. If not, he should learn to tie them first and get used to handling the feathers and other materials. Trout fly materials are inexpensive, and a great many of them can be had for nothing, while those for salmon flies are very expensive. It is a good plan at first to practice the different styles of winging with ordinary feathers on a bare hook. Practice tying on different styles of tags again and again, until you are proficient, and do the same with silver bodies, using old tinsels that may be lying around. Do not try using the real materials for a salmon fly until you know how. It is much too expensive.

One of the most difficult parts of dressing a fly is getting the tail, which is a topping, to set right, and not to cant to one side or the other. The topping which goes over the wings of most salmon flies will tend to do the same and the cheeks, which are of jungle cock or chatterer, will seem to want to go everywhere except flat against the wing. But there is a knack, and a number of little tricks to make them go right the first time, which cannot be explained on paper. The only way to learn is to watch some fly dresser at work and to have him explain these things as he goes along. After one once understands how to do them, all these things are a matter of tying continually until you become familiar with them. Keep plenty of barnyard hackles and feathers from turkeys, ducks and geese with which to practice. If you are a gunner you will pick up any number of feathers and hackles from woodcock, grouse, snipe, geese, widgeon and black duck; even the crow gives you feathers to wing a Night Hawk fly, and the blackbird furnishes wings for a Greenwell trout fly. In fact, everything you shoot yields something that can be used in flies; it costs you nothing, and not only can be made into successful flies, but gives you the practice of handling the feathers.

The collecting of feathers and other materials is very interesting. I had a friend in the Bird House at the Franklin Park Zoo in Massachusetts, who once a month used to send me a box of the feathers dropped in their cages by rare birds, and when one of the birds died he would send me the skin. Good white-tipped turkey tails can be easily procured at Thanksgiving time, as can some of the badger hackles used in place of the silver coch-y-bonddu for ribbing certain patterns.

I first learned to tie from the descriptions in Kelson's book, THE SALMON FLY, but my flies were pretty bad. The heads were too large and the wings too bulky—two faults which must be overcome. It is only natural to use too much of everything at first. In winging a fly which requires five or six strips of different feathers one gets too much of all of them, and it takes a lot of tying to learn just how much of each to use. It is a good plan to begin tying on a large-sized hook, say a 1/0, because you can see better what you are doing, and your first work will not look quite so bad. I knew Kelson's methods by heart, and all the feathers and materials he advocated, but I just could not tie them on the hook so that they looked well. About that time, I heard of a man who was a good tier of salmon flies and who tied for the market, so I took the first train and spent a week with him. I learned a few little tricks from him and that was all, but he told me of another man farther on who tied good flies, so I kept on going and hunted him up. He could really tie a fly, and I learned quite a lot from him; but my wings were still bad and continued bad until I found a salmon fisherman who tied his own flies. At last I began to make progress. I had been tying about two years then, and still my flies did not suit me. But some of them would take fish, which was encouraging. At this time I got a copy of Pryce-Tannatt's book on dressing salmon flies. After tying his way for about three months, I began to tie what might be called a good-looking fly. After watching a man in England dress Jock Scotts, I knew that if I could have had some lessons from him in the first place, I would have accomplished in a few months what had taken me three years.

Things like marrying strips of feathers become easy with practice, but unless one keeps at it his fingers get clumsy and the strands will not go together well at all. You will tie better flies if, in starting to tie a dozen, you tie the bodies of all of them first, instead of completing each fly in turn; then wing them all and last tie on the topping and cheeks. You will tie better flies this way because you are doing the same thing over and over, and you will tie much faster. In my case I simply had to tie good flies because two of the severest critics in the salmon fishing game were watching me most of the time, the late Thomas Allen and Mr. Claude Knapp. They knew flies and what they must be to raise fish, and it was a long time before I could produce a fly that satisfied them. When I did, I was happy and well repaid for all the time I had spent.

Pryce-Tannatt's book on fly dressing is the best thing on the subject I have seen. Everything in it is clearly explained and quite intelligible. Since obtaining a copy, I have tied my flies pretty much his way. In England I learned the Crossfield method of tying in wings. This way of doing it accomplishes what he intended it to, that is, shows all the different feathers in the wing, instead of leaving some of them covered up as they are in most salmon flies. I saw a lot of Crossfield's flies in England; they were beautifully tied, but what appealed to me most about them was that they looked like *fishing* flies. There is a great difference between flies tied to sell to the general public and those tied by a fisherman to catch fish.

Tying the Fly

It is best to start with eyed hooks, for gut loops make the body too bulky and the head too large, unless one has had considerable practice. To prevent the hook from being scarred in the vise, place a small piece of leather between the jaws; with the hook in place, start by tying on the silk, which has been well-waxed, where the bend of the hook begins (see Figs. 1 and 2). Now you are ready to tie in the tag. Take two turns to the left and with two more turns of the silk, tie in the tinsel on the side of the hook nearest you (Fig. 3). Then, attaching a pair of pliers to the silk and letting it hang, attach another pair of pliers to the end of the tinsel and wind four even tight turns to the left, then back over and tie down with two turns of the silk. The end of the silver tinsel should be opposite the barb of the hook. Now either cut off the waste end of tinsel close or break it off by bending back and forth (Fig. 4). The latter way is perhaps preferable. If your work now looks as mine did at first, you will find that you have used twice as much tinsel as was necessary and that where you turned it back over itself the coils are not quite together and tight. So unwind it all and do it over and keep doing it over until you get it to look like the specimen fly which you should have laid out before you on the table as a sample. I always keep a lot of cheap tinsels of different widths for practicing. Constant tying will enable you to tell at a glance what width tinsel to use for any size hook on which you are going to dress a fly. Practice tying this tag of flat tinsel until it looks like the one on the specimen fly.

If the tag is to be of silver or gold thread, first unwind about an eighth of an inch of the fine wire that is wound around the floss, break it off and tie the floss in close to where the gold or silver winding is to begin (Fig. 5). This prevents your having a bunch there when it is tied. In tying a tag of this silver or gold thread, wind the tying silk to the left until it is opposite the barb before you start to wind. Then carry the tying silk back in even coils. Next wind the silver thread in four neat tight coils to the right and tie off (Fig. 6). These tags are more difficult, and require a good deal of practice to make them neat; it is much finer work than when using tinsel. Be sure to keep the work cleaned up as you go along; that is, cut off at once all ends that should be cut off; or, if they are to be tucked in to form part of the body of the fly, do it as soon as possible. In other words, keep your work neat as you go along, and do not be in a hurry to tie a fly; you cannot tie one that will look well until you can do all the different parts of it, so practice each part faithfully. This is a real job you have tackled now; don't make any mistake about that. Unless you are willing to devote plenty of time and patience to it, you will never tie a good-looking fly.

I like the tags of my flies, if tied on ordinary hooks, to extend from a point opposite the barb to one opposite the point of the hook. If the hook is a long-shanked one, I tie it farther back, as a fly must be tied in proportion to the hook, or it will look badly. If a salmon fly is to be good-looking, proportion is everything. In some patterns this silver thread or flat tinsel completes the tag, and the topping for the tail is tied on next. But for patterns like Jock Scott, tie in a small piece of yellow floss silk, or whatever the color may be, close to where the tinsel is finished off. Cut off a piece of floss about one inch in length and, because the whole piece is too thick and would not tie flat with the silver, split it. Smooth all the strands flat by drawing them between the fingers, then tie in one end on the near side of the hook (Fig. 7) and wind two turns to the left up to the tinsel, then back over to where you began, keeping it flat all the way by smoothing out the entire length through your fingers on each turn. This should always be done in winding floss silk if you wish it to lie smooth with no lumps in it. In building foundations for silver bodies one must be very particular in this respect. Now tie down the floss silk and cut off the surplus; if this waste is to be used for part of the foundation of the body, make two turns to the right with the tying silk to form a foundation for the tail (Fig. 8).

A golden pheasant's topping, its length in correct proportion to the hook, is next tied in for the tail. But this needs some preparation if it is to set upright and not cant to one side or the other. In selecting toppings for tails, or to go over the wings of flies, be sure to choose one that has not been bent out of shape. Lay aside any that are bent to be steamed and straightened at some later time. Instead of stripping off the extra fibers or fluff at the butt of the feather and leaving the quill bare, cut it off, leaving just a little on each side of the quill; this helps keep the feather in position while tying. Remember to do this also to other small delicate feathers like chatterer and jungle cock if you want them to lie right. Next bend this topping against the dubbing needle at the place you intend the silk to go over when tying on (Fig. 9). Now, holding the topping as you would a pair of wings, tie down in the same way, being careful not to get one turn of the silk over another (Fig. 10). At every stage of dressing a fly keep the turns of silk tight and next to each other, never one on top of the other. If the topping does not go on right, and it probably does no more than the tag did, untie and do it over. One's fingers have to become accustomed and trained to holding feathers of any kind before they can be tied on satisfactorily. If the tail requires a couple of Indian crow feathers or chatterer at the base, prepare them as you did the topping, cutting the waste at each side of the quill and leaving a little, instead of pulling it all off. Lay these two feathers one on top of the other and tie down on top of the piece of the topping. This completes the tail.

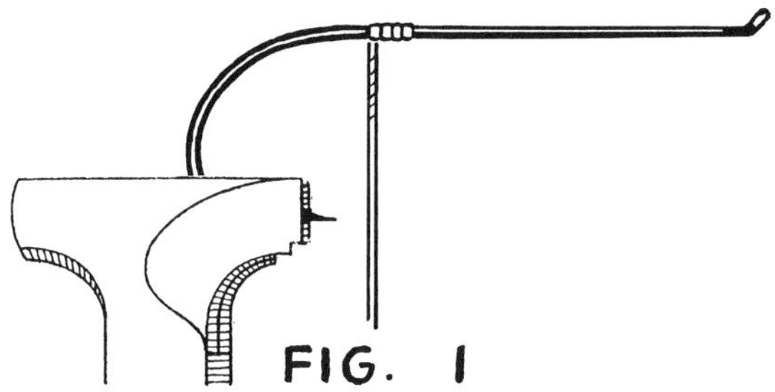

FIG. 1

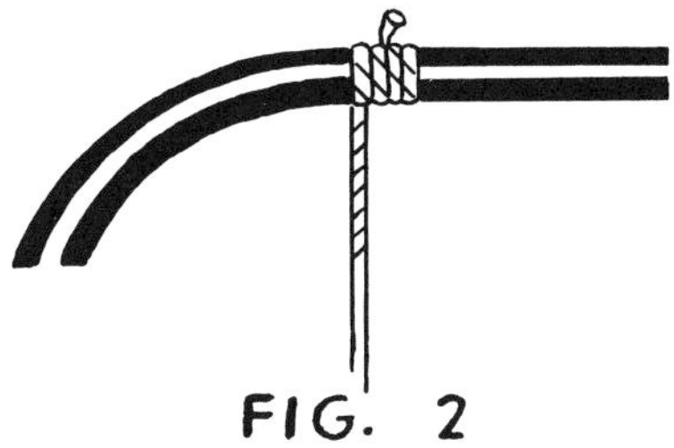

FIG. 2

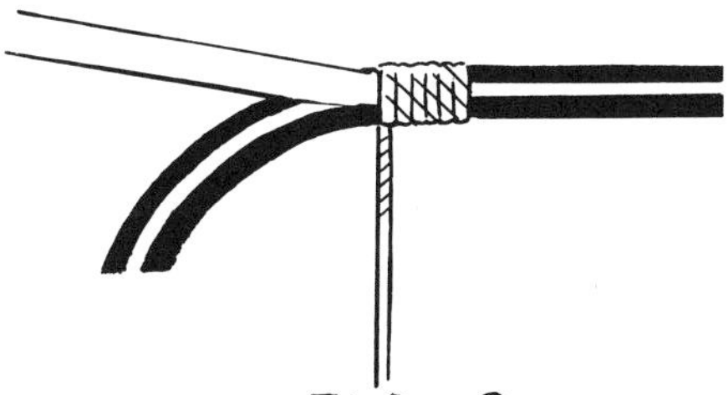

FIG. 3

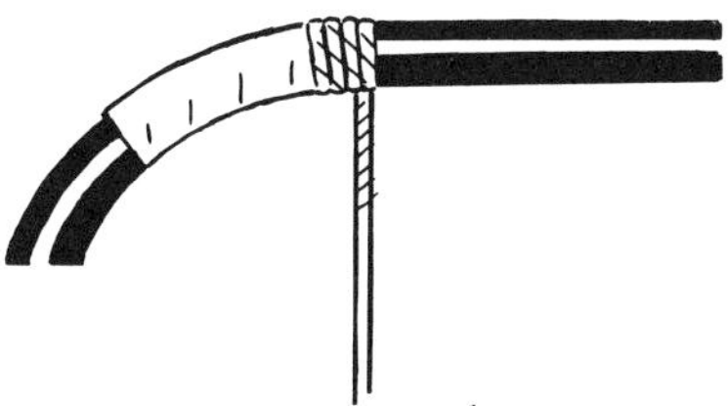

FIG. 4

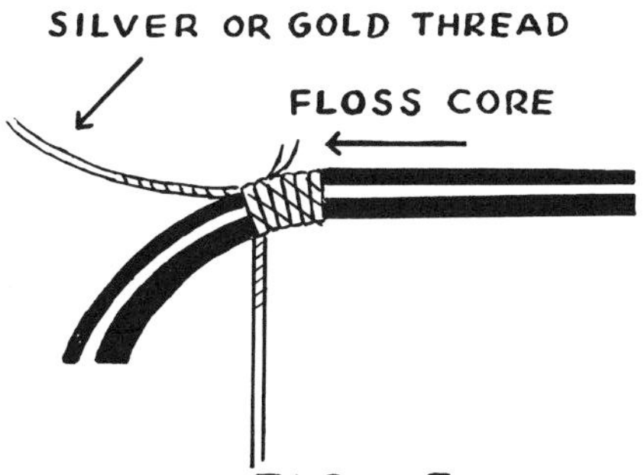

FIG. 5

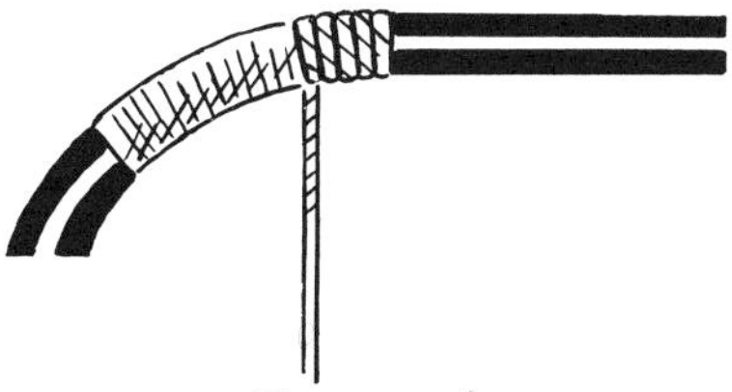

FIG. 6

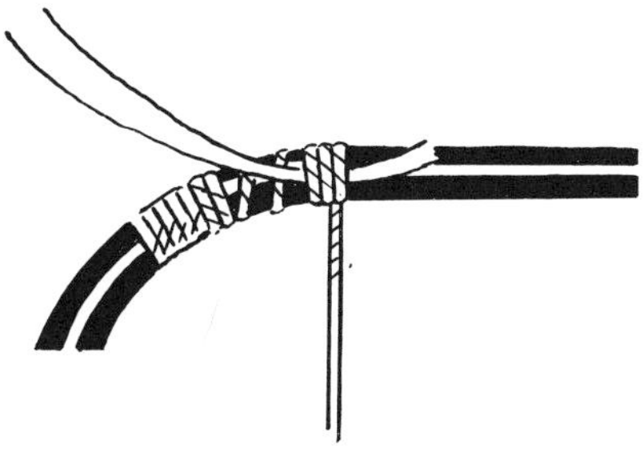

FIG. 7

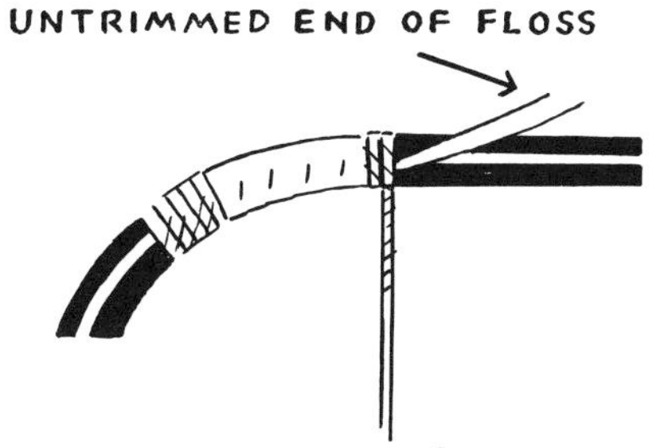

FIG. 8

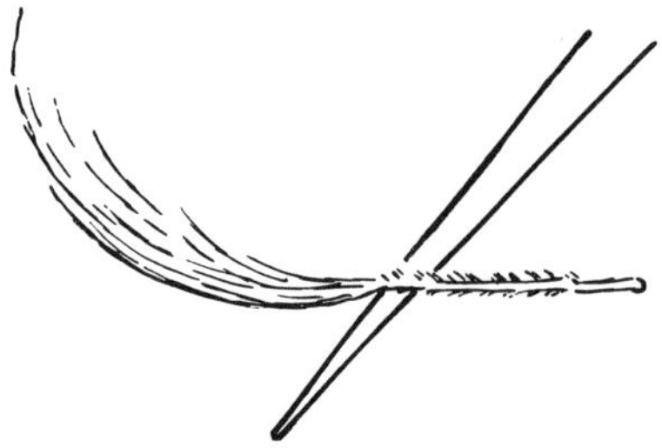

FIG. 9

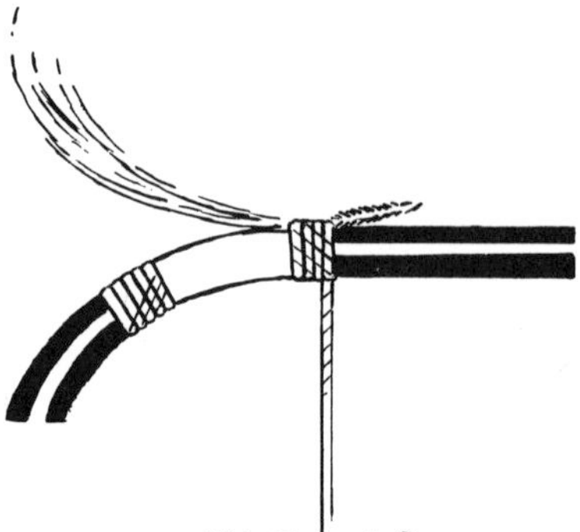

FIG. 10

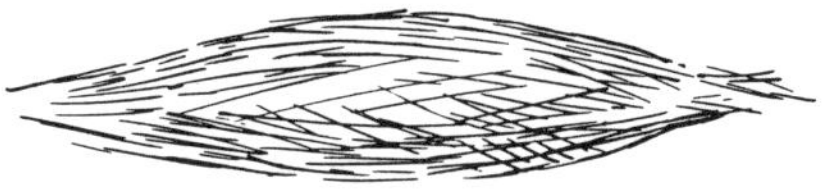

FIG. 11

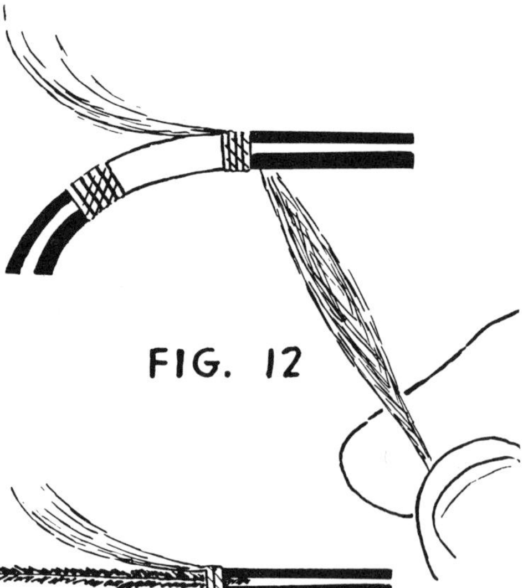

FIG. 12

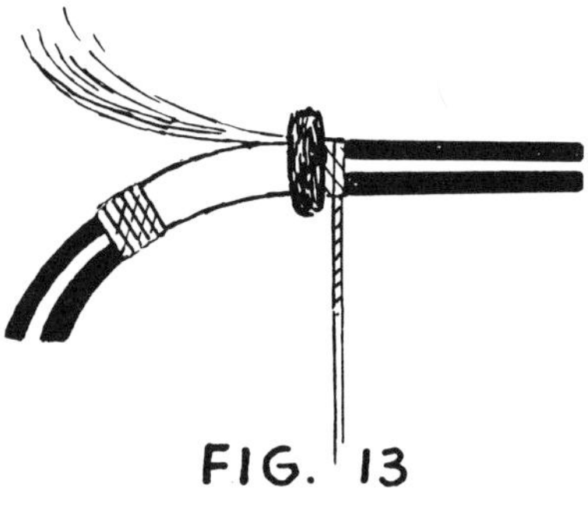

FIG. 13

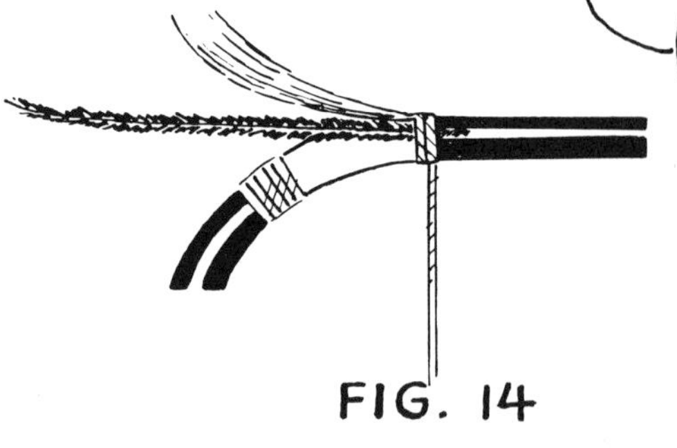

FIG. 14

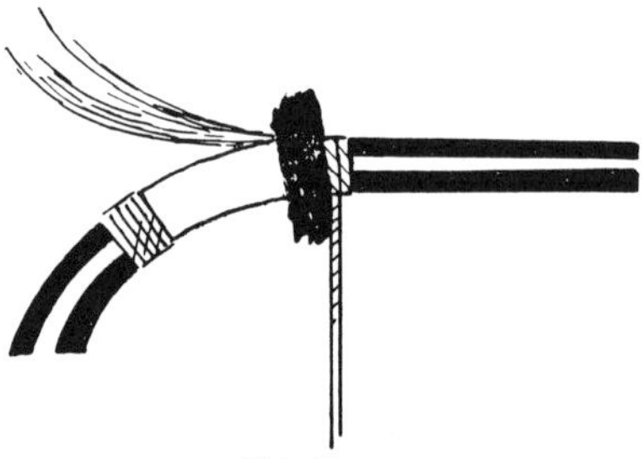

FIG. 15

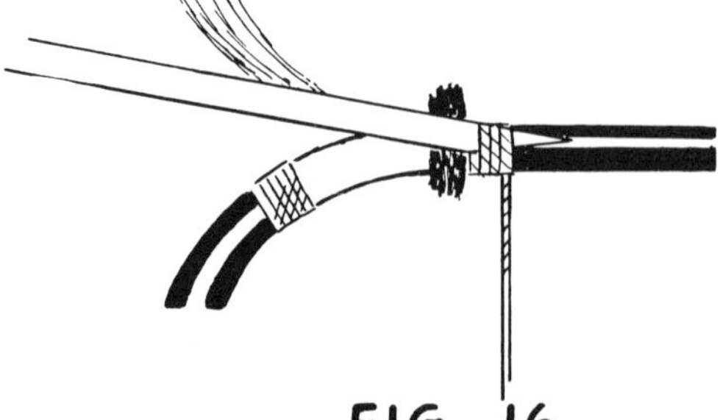

FIG. 16

If the topping used for the tail looks too long after it is tied on, take it off and select one that is right. *Do not trim any feathers that have been tied on;* so doing ruins the fly. It not only spoils the looks of the fly, but it discloses that you are a poor fly dresser in not being able to select topping or feathers the right length for the hook. I have always thought that the tail of a fly played a very important part; and it certainly does when composed of a topping. After I tie on a fly while fishing, I always try it on a short piece of leader in the water at the side of the boat to see how it rides. And I have always noticed how that topping flashed.

The butt, which is tied on next, may be composed of wool, chenille, seal's fur or ostrich herl. If of wool or seal's fur, place a *very* small piece in the palm of your hand and roll it out so that it tapers at each end (Fig. 11). A very small piece will do, so be careful not to get too much. Lay one end of it against the far side of the hook and against the tying silk; now, holding the other end of it against the silk in your other hand, spin it on the thread by twirling the silk away from you (Fig. 12). Wind two turns of the fur one over the other, as the butt is not supposed to lie flat like the tag but to set up. Tie it off with two turns of the silk (Fig. 13).

If the butt is to be of ostrich herl, tie down one end on the side of the hook (Fig. 14) and take three or four turns close up against each other, not one on top of the other, and tie off with two turns of the silk (Fig. 15). Because herl breaks easily, I hold it in my fingers rather than with the pliers while winding.

It is amusing to watch a salmon fly dresser tie trout flies. A trout fly no longer looks to him like a fly at all. He wants to dress up the plain patterns with elaborate tags, Jock Scott and chatterer cheeks, etc. It is good practice to do this, though, and it adds much to such patterns as Parmacheene Belle, and Professor. The pattern Tomah Joe, a famous fly in Maine, can be made to look like a million dollars, and bucktail flies can be made to look attractive in the same way instead of looking like just a mess of deer hair.

On the flies I tie for my own fishing, the tags are of flat gold and silver tinsel and not of thread. It is certainly brighter and more attractive, although it does not look as nice or show quite the same skill in work. But they can be tied much faster.

In the collection of materials, I suggested ordering of Farlow and Co. Their tinsels are as untarnishable as it is possible to get them. I have some that are eight years old, and they are as bright as ever. Of course, they have been kept in an airtight box. You can probably get such a box from some surgeon friend who generally has one in which his instruments were packed. Being airtight, it is the best thing I know of in which to keep tinsel. In your collection should be every variety, gold and silver in all widths, gold and silver thread in different sizes, solid wire and embossed silver and gold thread.

On short dressed salmon flies, as for instance a No. 6 dressing on a No. 4 hook, the tag should be farther back from the barb of the hook. Its position all depends on what type of hook is to be dressed. If it is built too far down on the bend, the tail will not set right. Nice judgment must be used in placing the tag. When dressing low water flies I often tie them without a tag to keep them as plain and lightly dressed as possible. Floss silk of the right sort for tags may now be obtained on spools, and there is no necessity for splitting it to get it fine enough.

In some patterns, strands of tippet feathers are used for tails and a dresser can add anything he thinks would make the topping more attractive; but chatterer and Indian crow are the best of the lot. Sometimes, however, a few strands of scarlet ibis help. For my own flies I use seal's fur spun on the silk for butts; ostrich herl breaks easily, and occasionally, when the hook is taken from a salmon's mouth, it is found hanging. In flies in which herl is used, if the butt must be very pronounced two strands of herl are tied in at the same time.

Bodies

The bodies of flies are composed of floss silk, seal's fur, wool, chenille, silver tinsel, dyed gut, rabbit's fur, mohair, dyed quill and other similar materials. As a plain seal's fur body is probably as easy to tie as any, I shall describe that first.

Take a piece of seal's fur the size you think would be right for the hook and roll it in the palms of your hands, as was done for the seal's fur butt, until it tapers off at both ends. Lay it on the table. Now take about two inches of flat silver tinsel and tie in on the near side of the hook close up to the butt (Fig. 16), and attach pliers to hold it down out of the way while you are spinning and winding on the body. Lay one end of the fur against the tying silk on the far side of the hook, holding it there with the forefinger of the left hand. Lay the other end of the fur against the silk and hold with the thumb and forefinger of the right hand, then twirl the seal's fur and silk away from you with the right thumb and forefinger (Fig. 17). Do not twirl or twist it too tight. The fur should be firmly twisted on the silk but in such a way that it can be picked out afterwards if necessary to make the body look fluffy. Tie the seal's fur off with two turns to the right, then back two turns (Fig. 18). If, when the body is finished, there is some of the fur left on the tying silk, simply pull it off.

Next the silver tinsel is wound in an even spiral around the seal's fur and tied off with three tight turns of the silk to the right; then three turns back. And to be sure it holds, for tinsel is slippery stuff, take a half hitch and attach the pliers. After this silver ribbing is wound on, the seal's fur should stand out well and look fuzzy (Fig. 19); if not, take the dubbing needle and pick it out to look that way, for then it catches the light better.

Perhaps this fly is to be hackled down the body. In this case the hackle should have been folded and ready, and the tip tied in before the tinsel (Fig. 20). To fold a hackle requires quite a little practice, but can be done quickly once the knack is acquired. To fold a hackle, wet the thumb and forefinger of the right hand, and, holding the hackle by the tip with the thumb and forefinger of the left hand, stroke the fibers down and out at right angles to the quill. Now attach the pliers to the root end of the quill and let them lie in the palm of the right hand with the hackle bent over the forefinger, *under side up*, and held quite tight by the tip. With the moistened thumb and forefinger of the right hand stroke the upper fibers down to the horizontal, and the under fibers up and horizontal. In other words, stroke the upper and lower fibers together and coax them to stand at right angles to the quill (Fig. 21). Every hackle used on salmon flies should be folded before being tied in, except in the case of some salmon dry flies. After the flat tinsel ribbing is on the hackle is next wound around up close to it and tied off with two turns of the silk to the right, then two turns back, and the pliers are attached (Fig. 22). In winding on the silver ribbing, use a strong pair of pliers and wind tight; this is better than holding the ribbing in your fingers as it slips easily.

If the body is to be of floss silk, cut a piece about three inches long and smooth it out flat by stroking its full length a number of times with the thumb and forefinger. Then tie it in close to the butt, first tying in whatever tinsel is to be used for ribbing. Perhaps in this case there is to be an embossed silver cord to be wound on close to the tinsel. If so, tie it in right after the flat tinsel

(Fig. 23). The metal winding of the cord should be pulled off for an eighth of an inch first; then it is tied in over the core, which is floss. The order of winding would be, first, the floss silk, then the flat ribbing tinsel, and finally the embossed cord up close to each spiral (Fig. 24). Most bodies, though, are ribbed with oval tinsel, which is also used for ribbing silver bodies. An eighth of an inch of the wire should be pulled off any tinsel which has a core of floss silk, leaving the floss core exposed to tie in. By tying in the floss core you eliminate a bunch which would result if the oval tinsel were tied in intact.

Silver Bodies

In tying silver or gold bodies a foundation must first be built. This is done by the use of white floss silk—white, because if there happens to be a coil of the flat tinsel that is not quite tight against the next coil the white foundation is not very noticeable. Cut off a piece of floss about three inches long, split it in two, and smooth it out until its whole length is smooth and even with no twists or thick parts in it. Tie in the oval ribbing tinsel first, not forgetting to strip an eighth of an inch off the end; then the flat tinsel, and last the floss silk. Now wind the floss up to the head, then back to the butt and back to the head again, smoothing it the whole length each time you wind it over, keeping it tight and even (Fig. 25). If the floss is not tight, it will be squeezed up and show between the turns of the tinsel. This is a rather delicate job, and lots of care must be taken if the silver body is to be smooth and look like one whole piece as it should. Use the strong pliers to hold the tinsel and wind it on tight and even, tie off with three turns of the silk and a half hitch, attach pliers to silk and let hang down. Wind on the oval ribbing tinsel tight and even close to each edge of the flat tinsel (Fig. 26). When trimming off the waste ends of flat tinsel it is better to break them off by bending back and forth, as then they are not so likely to pull through as they would be if cut off. The shape of the body depends on how you wind on the floss foundation; by pulling it tighter each turn as you near the ends, beautiful spindle-shaped bodies may be formed, such as used on the Fat Mary fly; by experimenting and practicing one soon learns just how tightly to wind at different stages of the work. If this fly were to be hackled down the body, as in a Silver Grey, the hackle, after being folded, should have been tied in at the tip, the last thing after the ribbing tinsel, and then wound up the body close to each coil of the ribbing. Care must be taken that the hackle,

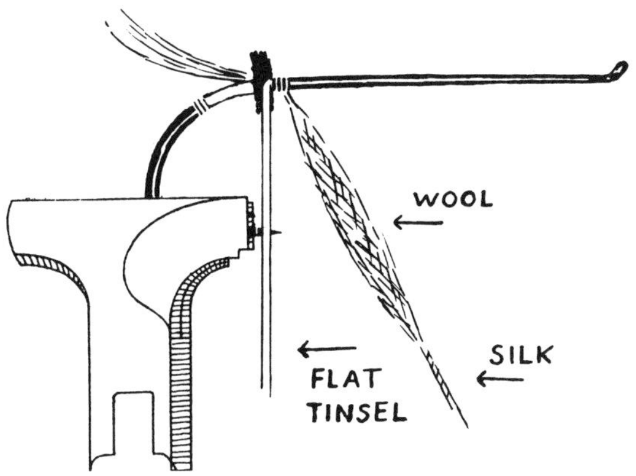

FIG. 17

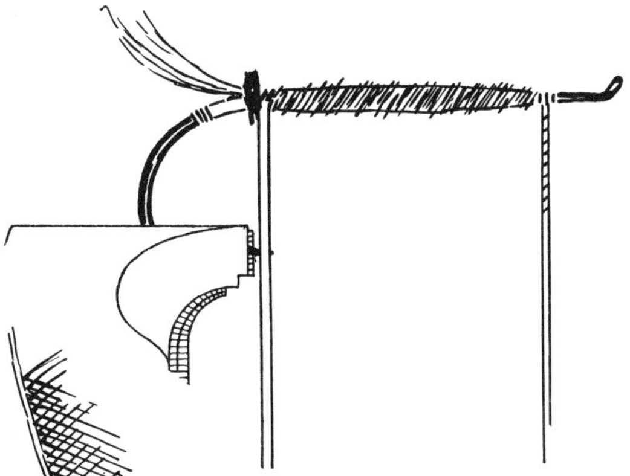

FIG. 18

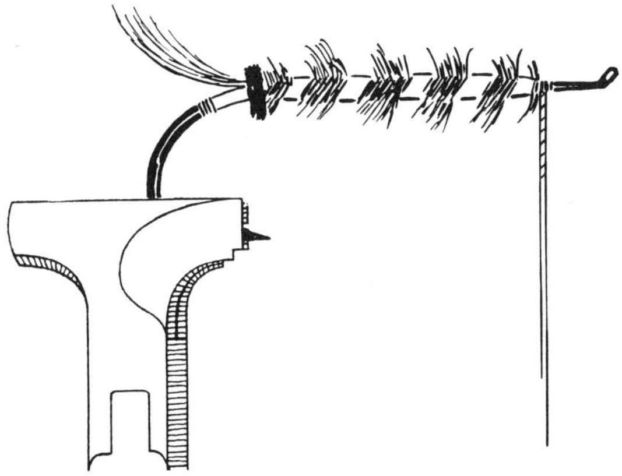

FIG. 19

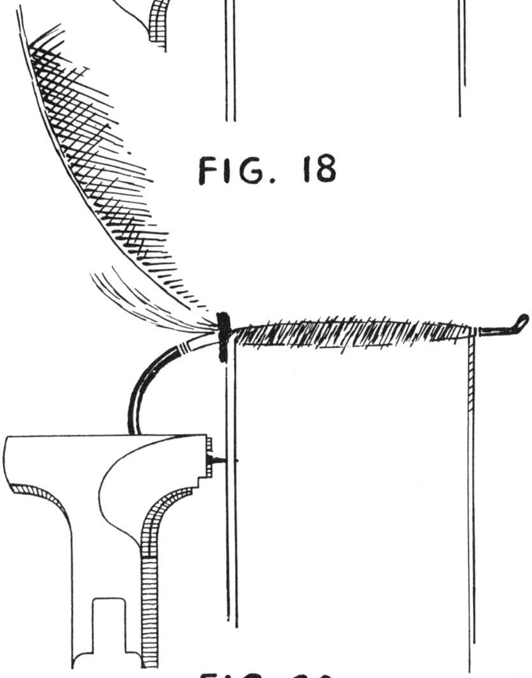

FIG. 20

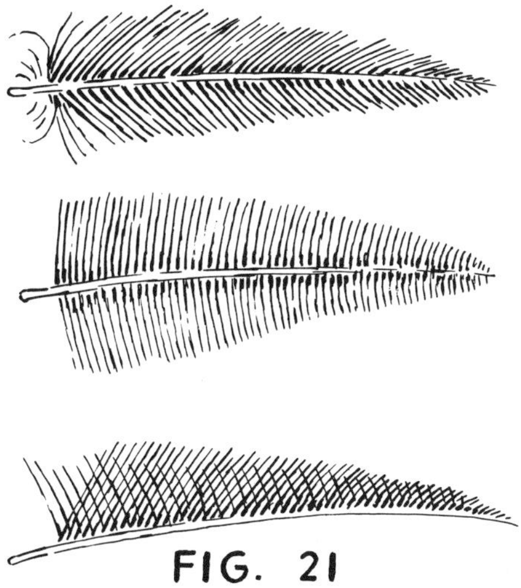

FIG. 21

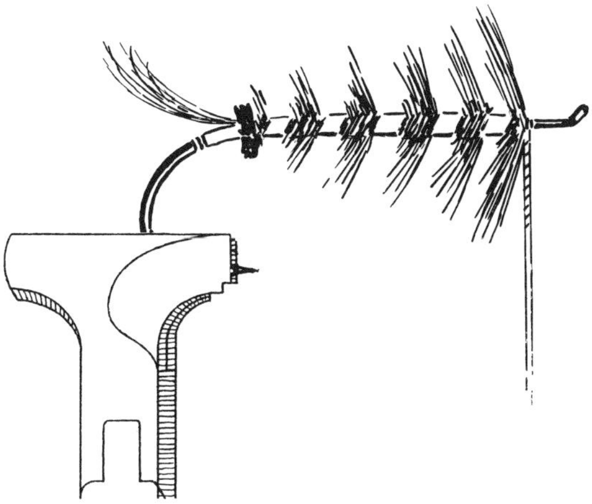

FIG. 22

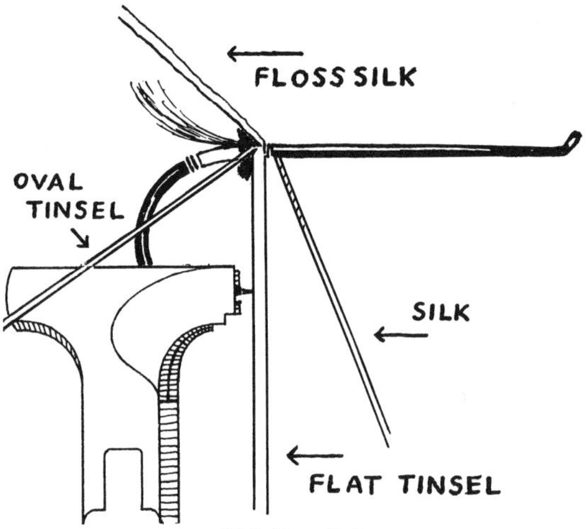

FIG. 23

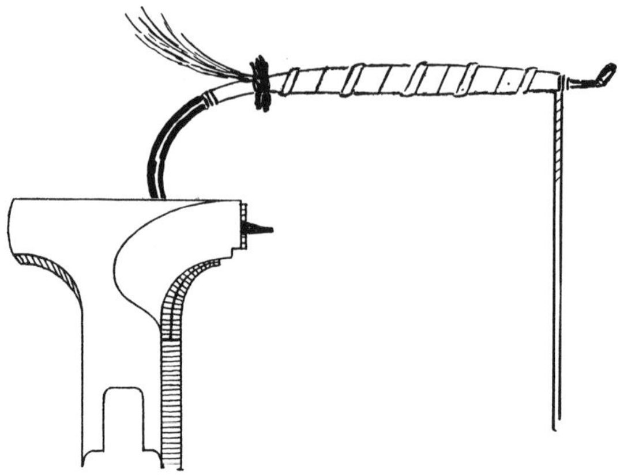

FIG. 24

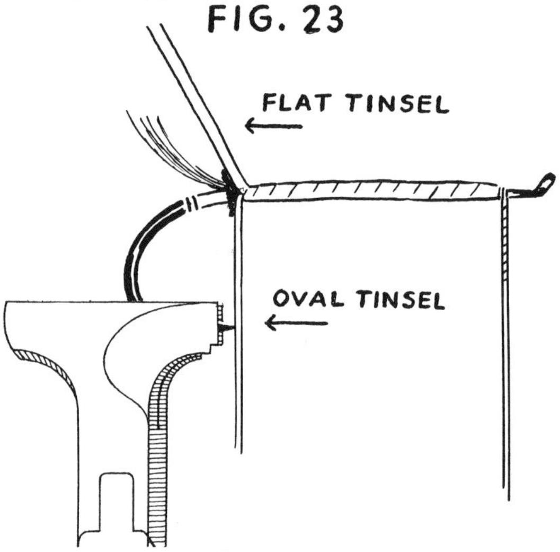

FIG. 25

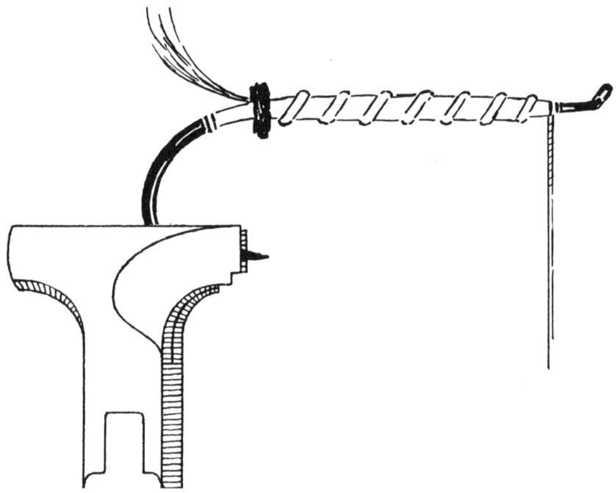

FIG. 26

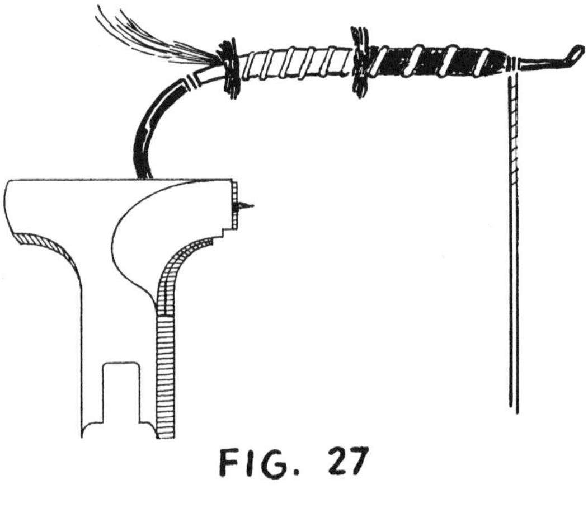

FIG. 27

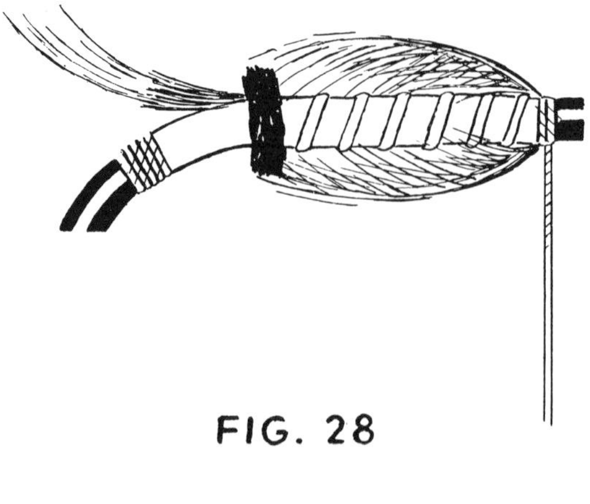

FIG. 28

when tied in, is not cut off by the flat tinsel. If the body is to be hackled only half way down, tie in the hackle with the flat tinsel when winding it, and again be careful that the tinsel does not cut it off.

Jointed Bodies

To tie a body of two joints such as a Jock Scott, tie in the ribbing tinsel, then a piece of yellow floss, about two inches long, smoothed out as before. Wind the floss not quite half way down the shank and tie off; rib this and tie off. Tie in one strand of black ostrich herl and wind a butt as you did in forming the one of ostrich herl for the tag, and tie off. Tie in oval ribbing tinsel first, then a piece of black floss about two inches long close up to this butt and wind on as before; then wind the ribbing tinsel and tie off (Fig. 27). In bodies with three joints, such as a Popham, tie materials on the same way, in this case simply adding one more joint.

The first thing you will notice about all the work so far is that too much of all the different materials has been used. The fly is too bulky and there is no taper whatever to the body; the body dressing has all been carried down too far toward the head, and there is not enough room for the throat hackle and wings. If there is not sufficient room left at the eye of the hook, a large bad-looking head results when it is finished off and varnished. It is better to have too much room for the hackle and wings than not enough.

Some fly dressers tie in the floss silk for foundations of bodies at the middle of the shank and wind both ways. This also works well. It can be done whichever way the fly dresser prefers.

If the joints of a body should be veiled, which is generally done with toucan feathers, as in a Jock Scott, they should be selected the right length to cover the joint. Take three small toucan feathers, cut the bottom edges, leaving a little of the waste on each side of the quill, wet them and lay them one on top of another, bending the quills over the dubbing needle at the point where they are to be tied on, and tie in on top of the joint. Prepare three more the same way, and, turning the vise over so that the bottom part of the fly can be seen, tie them on the bottom opposite the top ones (Fig. 28). Indian crow is sometimes used for this. In what tying has been done so far, the greatest difficulty has been in keeping the tying silk from breaking, but constant work with it soon teaches you just how much tension it will stand.

In dressing bodies of dyed gut, as in the Little Inky Boy pattern, the gut is tied in the same way as other materials were, close to the butt, and wound tightly around the shank in close even coils. When tying in flat tinsel for bodies, cut off the end to be tied in on a taper for an eighth of an inch. This will do away with any hump at the start in winding it on. In building foundations for slim bodies, such as the Silver Blue, the floss must be used very sparingly and great care must be taken in smoothing and winding on.

Body and Throat Hackles

There are two kinds of hackles used on salmon flies: those used for the bodies are what we generally know as hackles, but some of those used at the head of the fly, throat hackles as they are called, are body feathers from such birds as the guinea fowl, heron, teal, widgeon and cock-of-the-rock. Undyed hackles are very little used except for the dry flies, though a few are used for wet flies, such as silver coch-a-bonddu, with which the body of a Silver Grey is hackled. Hackles dyed lemon, red, dark red, burnt orange, magenta, fiery brown, blue, green and claret are used most. Long-fibered hackles such as used in Spey and Dee patterns are little used on Canadian rivers. Blue jay wing coverts are used in the Popham and some other flies, but is a very difficult feather to prepare for a hackle, as the quill must first be split and then scraped.

All hackles should be sorted into sizes for the different sized hooks—it saves a lot of time when tying flies—and all hackles which are to be used should be folded before the actual tying is begun. Lay out on the fly-tying table all the materials to be used in dressing the flies, placing on the right side of the table feathers for winging which have long fibers on the right side of the quill, and on the left of the table those with long fibers on the left side of the quill. Be particular about this, because, if you have these different strips to marry and get the rights and lefts mixed up, they will not go together. Rights will only marry with rights, and lefts with lefts. Remember, though, when placing the wing, that your lefts form the far side of the wing, i.e., *the right side as you look at the fly from the eye*, and your rights the left in conventionally dressed salmon wet flies. It might be well, while we are on the subject of wings, to say that all the time the body of a fly is being tied the fact should be kept in mind that there must be room for a pair of wings. If there is not room enough the result is a large unsightly head, which is the first symptom of a poor fly tier.

There should be not only enough room for tying on the wings but enough so that when the head is varnished all is left clear around the eye for tying on the leader. Otherwise the knot may slip off. When the throat hackle is tied on, carry the silk the full length of what is to be the foundation for the wings and back again, so that when the hackle is on, the whole foundation will be level (Fig. 29). If it slopes off to the eye the wings will set up and not lay curved along the shank. The throat hackle should be tied in by the tip, and the number of turns used depends on what type of fly is being tied. Four turns are usually enough for a heavily dressed fly, and one or two at the most, of a little hackle, for the lightly dressed ones. One must use his judgment about this.

Wings

There are many different types of wings for salmon flies, but the methods of dressing most of them are simply means of accomplishing the same thing in different ways. There is no difference between built wings and mixed wings; they are only two different ways of doing the same thing. I will describe them both, and the reader, after trying them, can select the one he likes best and with which he gets the best results. I learned to tie flies from four different men, and from reading the descriptions in Kelson's book, Hale's, Pryce-Tannatt's and others, and from all these sources I selected the ways which suited me best for tying the different parts. There are whole feather wings, built wings, mixed wings, and what are called strip wings. Whole feather wings and strip wings are the same as are used on trout flies and are easy to tie.

Whole Feather Wings

Whole feather wings in patterns like the Durham Ranger are tied on as follows. Select a pair of tippet feathers which you find, by trying, to be the right length for the hook. Lay them back to back. Cut the fibers on each side of the quills at the point where they are to be tied on, leaving just enough so that the quill ends will not roll over each other when being tied. Holding them firmly in the left thumb and forefinger at the point where the tying silk is to go over, bring the silk up between the thumb and the wing, over, and down between the forefinger and the wing (Fig. 30). This is achieved by means of just a suspicion of an opening between the thumb and the forefinger which are holding the wings in place. Now squeeze the wings together tightly with the thumb and forefinger of the left hand, being sure that the very top part of the fibers is held firm, and draw the silk straight down, take one more tight turn of the silk over and alongside the first one, *not on top*, then release the fingers holding the fly and see how the wings look. The chances are that they are on straight but that the top strands are pulled over toward the far side. In that case do not cut these strands off with scissors, which would be a natural thing to do, but unwind the silk and tie them on again, this time being sure to pinch the top part tightly together when the silk is pulled out. This time they should be on right. In tying on all wing feathers be sure that the turns of silk are carried along the foundation to the end and back when each of the separate feathers or combinations of them are tied in, and that the turns of silk are tight and close to each other. Never tie a turn of silk over another one; two tight turns of the silk side by side are better than ten piled on top of each other, and one must make every turn of silk count if the fly is to have a neat small head. Practice tying on this pair of tippets until they go on right every time. And by the time they do, they will be probably worn out, so discard them and start the real winging of a Durham Ranger (Fig. 31). First, select a pair of jungle cock feathers, one from each side of the neck, so they will both curve the same way down over the shank of the hook, and measure for length. Cut the fibers away from each side of the quill where the silk is to go over, and, pinching them tightly with thumb and forefinger of left hand, tie down in the same way you tied down the tippet feathers. Carry the silk to end of foundation and back. Next select a pair of tippet feathers which, when held over the hook, extend up to the last white spot on the jungle cock. Prepare the ends by cutting the fibers as before and lay one on each side of the jungle cock, being sure they are both even in length, pinch tight and tie down, again carrying the silk to the end of foundation and back. In this way the foundation is kept flat and even, and the feathers that go on next each time will lie flat over the hook. Now take a second pair of tippets, smaller in size, which will extend to the last dark band on the first pair, cut the fibers on the ends to be tied down, lay one on each side of the first pair of tippets, pinch tightly and tie down, and carry the silk to end of foundation and back. Select another pair of jungle cock feathers of a smaller size, measure so they will come to the last dark band of the second pair of tippets, cut waste off where they are to be tied down, lay one on each side of tippets and tie down, again carrying the silk along the foundation and back.

Some dressers tie in the throat hackle after the wings have been tied on. I like to tie in the hackle first, divide it on top with the fingers and press it down on each side, thus leaving a place for the wings to set in. I do not press the hackle all down under the hook as is done in most flies, for I like to have the hackle playing around the sides of the wings in the water.

Take a pair of small chatterer feathers, cut the fluff along the quill where they are to be tied in, place one over the lower end of the jungle cock feather on the far side, hold in place with the forefinger of the left hand and tie in. Take the other one, lay it against the jungle cock on the near side, hold in place with the thumb and tie in as before. These chatterer and jungle cock feathers on the sides of the wings are the "cheeks"; they will go on every way but flat against the wing if the fluff is all pulled off the quill at the point where they are to be tied on, but by leaving a little on, when it is trimmed off with the scissors, they can be made to lie flat where they belong. Whether these cheeks on a fly effect anything more than adding beauty to it, I do not know. I have caught a fish with a Jock Scott that was dressed with cheeks, then changed to a Jock Scott dressed without them and taken another fish. In any event, they help to sell flies.

Be sure to look carefully at the foundation before tying on any wing feathers. If it is not up level with the base of the throat hackle, build it up with successive turns back and forth of the silk. If it is a trifle higher than the base of the hackle it will do no harm; in fact, the wing will be more inclined to lie close over the body.

Strip Wings

Wings of feathers cut in strips from the right and left sides of quills can be tied on in four different ways (Fig. 32).

First: cut a right and a left strip from a cinnamon turkey tail, or from whatever feather is to comprise the wings. Lay the right strip, which will be the left wing, on the left strip, which will be the right wing, back to back, being sure they are even in length, then tie down on top of the hook. This is one way of tying upright wings.

Second: reverse the order this time, using a right strip for the right wing and a left strip for the left wing. In the first instance the wings curved closely over the shank of the hook, but tied this way the tips of the wings are more cocked up.

Third: cut strips as before, and first tie the right wing, cut from the left side of a quill, on the far side of the hook, holding it, rather than on top of the hook, about a quarter way down the side, tying it on with two turns of silk. Lay the strip cut from the right side of the quill on the near side in the same way partly over the shank and tie down.

Fourth: this time tie down in the same way, partly over the shank, but use a right strip for the right wing and a left strip for the left one.

By tying on wings the third and fourth ways described, the part of the wings near the head of the fly are made to hug the body of the fly more, while the tips, tied the third way, curve naturally over the shank and tied the fourth way, point up. By tying on the strips in the third and fourth ways, that is, by tying down on the side of the hook, one can wing a fly Sedge style, as those patterns of trout flies are tied.

After tying on the wing on the far side of the hook some tiers reverse the silk to tie the other on the near side. To do this, take a loop of silk around the dubbing needle, and, holding the loop tight with the needle, wind in the opposite direction back over the preceding coils to the wing (Fig. 33). The pliers are then attached to the silk and the loop cut away; then, holding in place on the near side the wing which is to be tied on, bring the silk up over it toward you and tie on. The head is finished off in this instance by winding the silk in the opposite direction. The object of reversing the silk is to keep from disarranging the fibers on top of the wing on the near side. There are some wing feathers, such as bronze mallards on a Brown Fairy fly, which require very delicate handling; unless the near wing is tied on by reversing the silk, some of the fibers will break away from the others and point in all directions.

In dressing some strip wings, you will find that the fibers are perhaps more inclined to stay in place while being tied on if each wing has some of the quill left on it; to prepare a wing this way split the quill with a sharp knife, and cut your wing feather, leaving the quill part on until the wing is tied on.

Built Wings

Built wings are those tied on in instalments, as one writer puts it, which means that the wing is built in sections, each of which is tied on separately and which slightly over-lap each other. The idea, though, is not to cover up any of the feathers in the different sections; and I think I would like to say something about that. A fly dresser may tie built wings in any way he can devise to show off all the different feathers, but the only place they will *all* show is in the show-case of some tackle shop. Certainly not more than half of them do when wet and being fished. It is the same with Jock Scotts, Silver Doctors, or any other fly that is dressed with built or mixed wings. When they are fished against the current, all the fibers are washed together and half of them are covered up. I have tied wings on Jock Scotts and Silver Doctors, Silver Greys and Dusty Millers, leaving out half the wing feathers the formulas call for, and I have killed just as many fish on them as I ever have on those patterns fully dressed. I never leave out jungle cock cheeks, however. Some of the feathers in a wing are necessary—there is no question about that. But others are there just to make a better looking fly.

Crossfield, years ago, had a way of tying in all the different fibers or sections by tying down each one in a place of its own on the shank, and working up along the shank in this way. But it made what I thought was a bad-looking fly, and, at that, half of the feathers would wash together in the current. It may be that when all the different feathers in a wing are washed together, they produce harmonious effects that are attractive to salmon, but I do not see how they possibly can do so when half of them cover up the others. A fly dresser ties on two or three sections of married fibers from different feathers to form the wing of a fly, then he tops it with a bronze mallard for protection, which covers up a good part of the work done. There is only one answer to all this, as far as I am concerned, and that is that the fly is tied to sell.

For years, in the flies I have tied for my own fishing, I have not used more than half of what is supposed to go into the wings of flies like Jock Scotts, leaving out the married strip of bright colored feathers to quiet the fly down. The flies tied by Crossfield, which I saw in London, particularly appealed to me for the reason that the wings only had the necessary feathers in them. They also were what I would call short-dressed in both wings and body, and I thought at the time that any fish coming short would certainly be hooked. They were the best fishing flies, tied by anyone, I have ever seen.

Cut two strips from a white-tipped turkey tail feather, one from each side of the quill, lay back to back and tie down to lie as low as possible over the shank of the hook. In order to do this last, hold the entire wing down low over the shank while tying in. The white tips of this feather should extend to the point where the tail was tied on (Fig. 34). Cut narrow strips, of about two strands, of yellow, blue and scarlet from the right-hand side of dyed swan's quills, and lay them on the right side of the table. Cut the same from the left side of the quills and lay them on the left side of the table. Lay the three strips from the right side of the table between the left thumb and forefinger right side up, with the edges touching or as near as possible together. Next, taking the roots between the right thumb and forefinger, smooth them together lightly with the thumb and forefinger of the left hand. This should make the little hooks on each strand catch each other and fasten the strands together (Fig. 35). Be sure to remember that right fibers will marry only with right and lefts with lefts. If one experiences difficulty in marrying the three strips all at once, lay one strip between the forefinger and thumb of the left hand and marry the others to that one at a time. Each strand should be a little longer than the preceding one in order to taper off the end. It is an object to tie in the first wing feathers as low over the body as possible, because in a wing of this kind there is so much to go on that if this is not done the wing will be too high when finished. Now take the married strips on the left side of the table and tie on the far side of the hook, flat against the lower part of the turkey tail which you have already tied on, with the tips of the married sections extending not quite to the tip of the white turkey tail and no farther. Take the other married strips on the right side of the table and tie those on the near side in the same way (Fig. 36). Next marry two fibers each from quills of bustard, florican and golden pheasant's tails, and tie in just above the other married section and against the turkey tail. The ends of this section also are tapered, each strand a little longer than the preceding one. Next two narrow strips of teal and barred wood duck are married together and tied on just above the last section. Two strands of peacock's sword feather may now be tied on top if you wish, but, as it will be broken off at about the first cast, there is not much object in doing it. Two bronze mallard strips must now be tied on top of the wing to cap it for protection. Cut right and left strips from right and left bronze mallard feathers wide enough to cap about a quarter of the sides of the wing and long enough to cover about a third of its length. These mallards should be tied on with the right strips on the far side of the hook and the lefts on the near side; they protect the wing better this way.

The wing is now finished except for the cheeks, topping and horns. Select two jungle cock feathers, one from each side of the neck, and measure them

FIG. 29

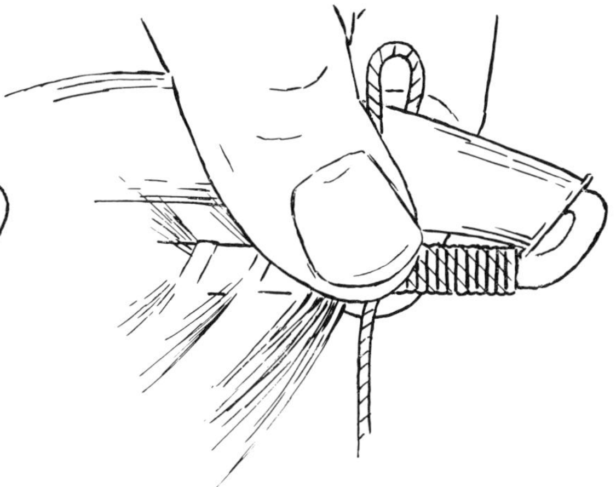

FIG. 30

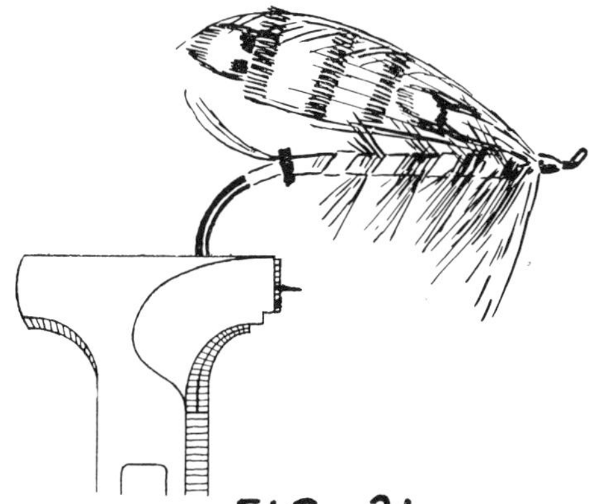

FIG. 31

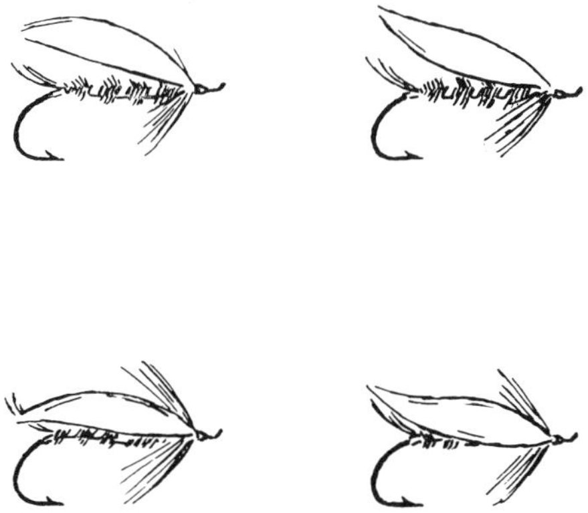

FIG. 32

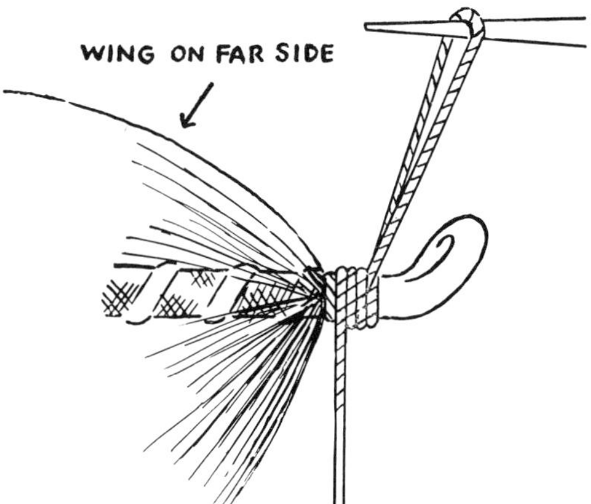

FIG. 33

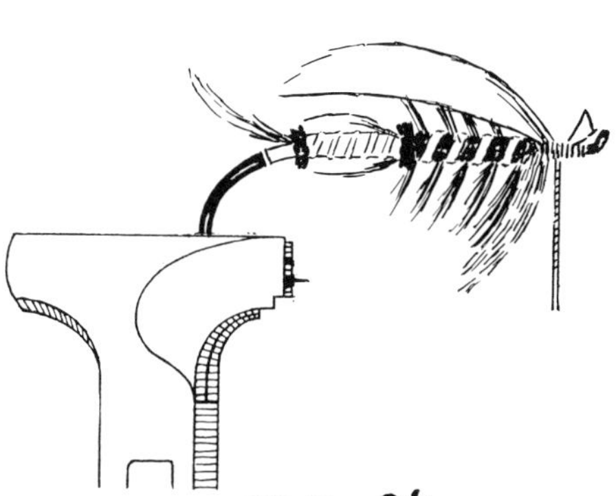

FIG. 34

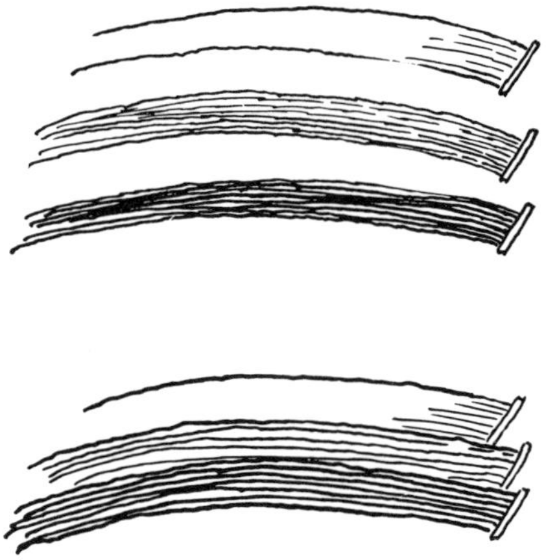

FIG. 35

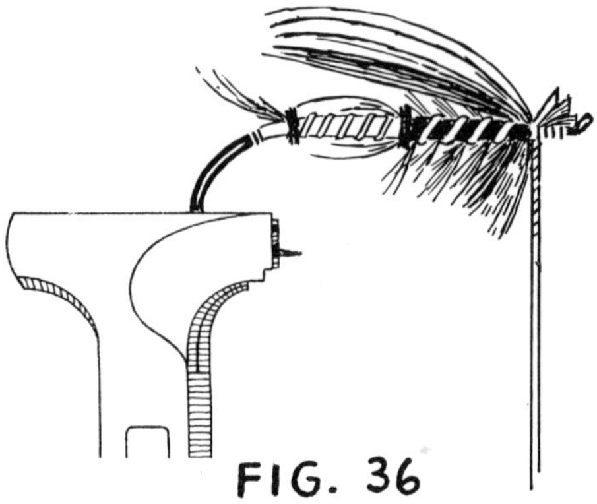

FIG. 36

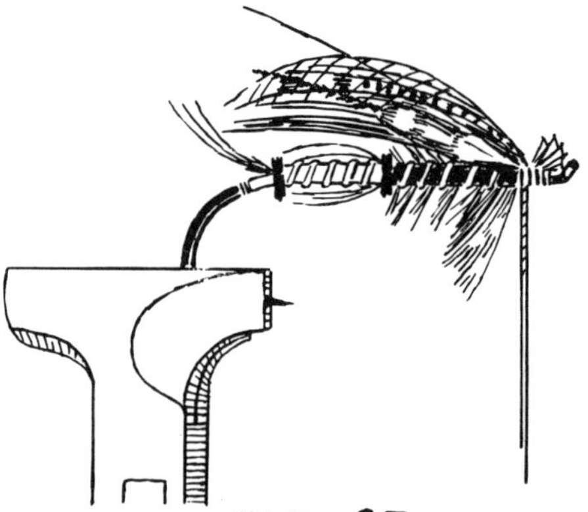

FIG. 37

FIG. 38

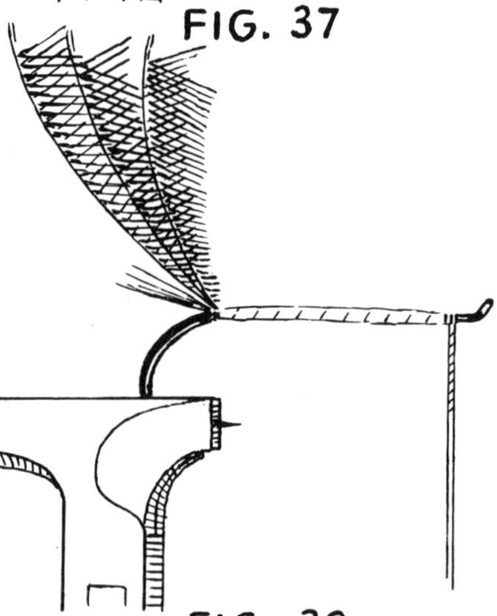

FIG. 39

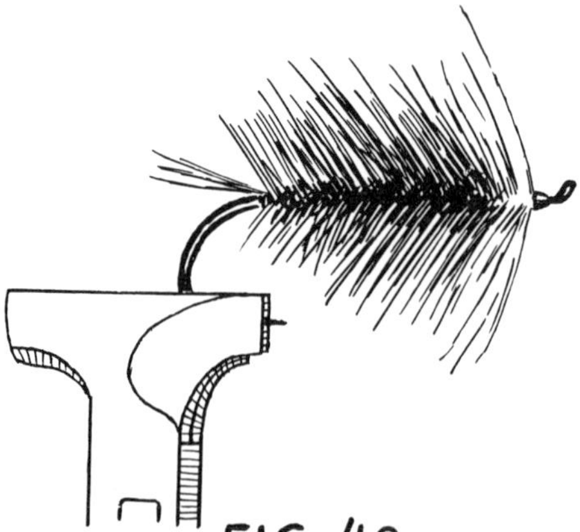

FIG. 40

WMW JR

for length against the wing. Prepare the butts by cutting away part of the fiber, as explained before, and tie on, the one on the far side first. By tying the one on the far side first it is easier to get them even and of the same length. Next, select two chatterer feathers, prepare the butts and tie against the base of the jungle cock cheeks. These complete the cheeks.

A topping should be selected that has a true curve throughout. If it is in good condition it will be champagne in color. Measure it over the wing so that when it is tied on it will curve over the wing and just meet the tip of the small topping that was used for a tail. Before tying on, trim the butt on each side of the quill as in the jungle cock and chatterer and bend a notch in it over the dubbing needle at the point where the tying silk is to go over. Finally, to add the finishing touch and make it more showy, take a fine soft-bristled brush and brush the long fibers on the quill down on each side. Take the topping in the left thumb and forefinger, hold it firmly in place over the wing and tie down tight with two turns of the silk (Fig. 37). Then look to see if it is on straight. If so, finish tying on. Two strands of yellow and blue macaw tail, tied one on each side and a trifle below the topping and to stand out away from each side of the wing, complete the wing. The head of this fly, or of any other whose wings are composed of so many feathers, is naturally large, but if care has been taken in bending the feathers over the dubbing needle before tying them on, and in carrying the silk back and forth over the foundation after tying on each feather or combination of feathers, the head will not be unsightly.

Mixed Wings

There is practically no difference between built wings and mixed wings, and the object of each is about the same. The whole feather wing, such as a pair of tippets, is tied on first, but, feeling as I do that the white tip of the turkey tail in a Jock Scott has something to do with the success of that fly, I generally tie on a pair of white hackles back to back. They are also just as good to build the rest of the wing against.

Take a pair of white hackles, place them back to back and measure over the shank of the hook for length, cut the fibers away from each side of the quill at the point where the tying silk is to go on, to keep them from rolling when being tied, and tie on, carrying the silk to the end of the foundation and back. Next marry three strips or four, if they go together well, of whatever the formula of the fly calls for, and tie on each section separately, the one on the far side of the hook first, then the one on the near side. These first strips should be tied on at the bottom edge of the hackles. Next marry three or four more strands, or the balance of those to be married, and tie on just above the previous ones. If there is peacock sword feather in the wing, tie this on next and then tie on for a cap whatever the formula specifies, probably bronze mallard. The cheeks and horns, if there are to be any, are tied on next, as was done in the built wing fly, and the topping last.

One may marry all the strips at once that are to go into the wing, and, provided you have good luck with them and can tie them all on at once, this will help keep the head of the fly smaller, as less silk will be used. If you wish to dress a thin wing, through which the light will pass more freely, leave out the two hackles that were tied on first. Low water flies are built this way, by leaving out certain feathers and using less of others.

When cutting off the ends of all waste winging materials, cut at an angle to the eye of the hook with a pair of curved manicure scissors. Do not cut at too great an angle, as the silk will keep slipping when you are finishing off to the eye (Fig. 38). Be sure each coil is tight and close against the preceding one.

Some fly dressers apply a drop of shellac to the foundation just before laying on the wings; if, in doing this, you get any on your fingers, be sure to clean them at once with alcohol or turpentine before the shellac gets on the wings or hackles. When a fly dresser ties flies for himself on the river, he never bothers with things like this, and is inclined to throw his flies together hurriedly, leaving out a lot of the materials; but they seem to kill fish just the same and hold together.

Transferring Wings

I often have flies with worn-out gut loops, but whose wings have been chewed to pieces by fish just as I like them for certain times. In that case I tie, on a new hook, a body as near like the worn-out one as possible and transfer the old wings to it. This latter is done by splitting the varnish on the head with a sharp knife and, holding the whole wing in the left thumb and forefinger, removing carefully all the old varnish; the wing is then tied on altogether in one bunch. Wings of this kind are valuable because fish will sometimes rise to them as long as there are just a few strands of the wing left hanging.

The following is the dressing of a very small low water wet fly that is worth knowing, as it is very deadly:

Hook: a light wire eyed double, No. 8 or 10
Tag: flat silver tinsel
Tail: four long black wisps from a black cock's hackle, not tied in a bunch, but separate
Body: black seal's fur, spun on lightly and well picked out
Ribbing: narrow silver tinsel
Throat hackle: black cock's hackle
Wings: narrow strips from wings of a crow, or any other thin black feather
Cheeks: small jungle cock with very white spots

I fish small flies like the above a great deal in hot weather and very low water, on a nine-foot trout leader tapered to .010, with a nine-foot five and three-quarters ounce trout rod, light in the tip, a Hardy three and one-eighth inch Model Perfect reel, about a D trout line with a long front taper, spliced to a hundred yards about three and a half pound test very fine silk backing, which just fills the reel. This same fly and leader fished with one of the ten-foot seven and a half ounce rods with the line that goes with it, will not raise nearly as many fish as it will with the trout rod and line. I suppose it is because the light rod casts more delicately.

Feathers for Winging Salmon Flies

The feathers that should be kept on hand for winging flies are:

White-tipped turkey tails
Cinnamon turkey tails
Golden pheasant's heads and necks, with all toppings and tippets
Golden pheasant's tail feathers
Hen pheasant's center tail feathers
Lady Amherst tail and sword feathers
Peafowl wings and sword feathers
Teal
Bronze mallard
Widgeon
Pintail
Bustard
Speckled florican

Jungle cock necks, being sure the spots are white and not a faded brown color
Cock-of-the-rock
Kingfisher, used in place of chatterer
Indian crow
Macaw tails, blue and yellow and red and yellow
Swan quills, dyed blue, yellow, burnt orange, scarlet, red, green and black
Crow wings, for Night Hawk flies in small sizes
Wood duck feathers, including the barred ones

If the fly tier is a gunner he should take a good supply of manila envelopes in all sizes on his shooting trips, for almost every bird he kills will yield feathers or hackles for trout flies and some salmon flies. Two of the most interesting things I know of in connection with salmon fishing are the collecting of fly tying materials, and the assembling of your own fishing library. As to the library, one can go as far as he likes in making the collection, but he should have at least a working library to refer to. Some of the old books are very interesting; among other things one of them states that salmon were first discovered in England by the Romans two thousand years ago. Salmon flies were first mentioned in 1746, although they had been in use for a considerable time before that. A vise for fly tying was first mentioned in print in the year 1800, and there seems to be nothing new about the long-shank hooks that have been popular with some fishermen in recent years, for in THE NORTH COUNTRY ANGLER, published in 1786, the dressing of a fly is given and it is specified that it be dressed on a long-shank hook. Michael Rogan, about 1880, appears to have been the first of the really great fly dressers, and established a method which has been used as a foundation by some of our best fly tiers in later years. Kelson came next, and was without doubt not only a wonderful caster, fisherman and fly dresser, but also possessed of a wonderful imagination; in spite of the fact that I was never successful with many of the things he suggested, I still get a great deal of pleasure from reading his books. Dr. Pryce-Tannatt's book on fly dressing, which came out in 1914, is to my way of thinking the best thing on the subject that has ever been published.

ALL-HACKLE DRY FLIES

If these flies are to be extra large, as they sometimes are tied, they should be dressed on long-shank hooks, which can now be had with a good-sized gap in the bend. The majority of these dry flies, however, are dressed on the regulation light wire dry fly hooks in sizes 4, 6 and 8.

First tie in the tail, which consists of seven or eight whisks of the same hackle of which the fly is to be dressed; then tie on a foundation of whatever material is desired, using only a very little of it.

Fold three or four hackles of a size in proportion to the hook and, starting at the tip, wind on evenly and tightly, being sure that no fibers are wound in, and finish off with two or three tight turns of the silk (Figs. 39 and 40).

The flies I like best for dry fly fishing are tied with a silver body over the bare hook. I first tie in the tail, of whatever hackle I happen to be using, then flat silver tinsel for a body over the bare hook, and tie in two folded hackles together at the same time. These I wind over the tinsel body, leaving as much of the tinsel showing as possible, but winding on enough hackle to make the fly ride high. If you tie only two hackles on a No. 4 or No. 6 hook, they must be very stiff. These flies will not last and ride up high as long as others dressed with more hackles, but I would rather change flies more often in order to have the silver body showing. I know that anything silver floating down on the surface is very attractive to salmon and that they will rise for it, for I can raise them every day during the season by throwing from a bridge I know of, pieces of silver foil from cigarette packages.

Correct Dressings of Favorite Flies

Blue Charm (summer series)
Tag: silver thread
Tail: topping
Ribs: silver oval
Body: black floss
Throat: blue hackle
Wings: mallard (caper); narrow strips of widgeon; topping

Silver Blue (summer series)
Tag: silver thread
Tail: topping
Butt: black ostrich (swan)
Ribs: silver oval
Body: silver flat over white floss
Throat: pale blue hackle
Wings: narrow strips of widgeon

Brown Fairy
Tag: gold thread and golden yellow floss
Tail: topping
Ribs: gold flat
Body: brown mohair; brown hackle on body and throat
Wings: turkey and mallard (broad strips)

Night Hawk
Tag: silver thread and lemon floss
Tail: topping and kingfisher
Butt: scarlet wool
Ribs: silver oval
Body: silver flat over white floss
Throat: black hackle
Wings: pair of black hackles; broad strips of black swan; jungle cock; chatterer (king-

fisher); topping; blue macaw (dyed turkey)
Head: scarlet wool

THUNDER AND LIGHTNING
Tag: gold thread and golden yellow floss
Tail: topping
Butt: black ostrich
Ribs: gold oval
Body: black floss; orange hackle
Throat: jay (dyed Guinea fowl)
Wings: pair of natural red hackles; broad strips of turkey, with mallard over them; jungle cock; topping; blue macaw (dyed turkey)

GRISWOLD GRAY
Tag: silver thread and yellow floss
Tail: topping
Butt: scarlet seal's fur, well picked out
Ribs: silver oval
Body: flat embossed silver tinsel over white floss
Throat: Guinea fowl
Wings: pair of grey hackles; bustard; hen pheasant; narrow strips of Lady Amherst; narrow strips of teal; jungle cock; chatterer; topping

BLUE CHARM
Tag: silver oval
Tail: topping
Ribs: silver oval
Body: black floss
Throat: blue hackle
Wings: pair of natural red hackles; turkey; mallard; pintail (narrow strips); topping

CANADIAN BLACK DOSE
Tag: silver thread and medium yellow floss
Tail: topping
Ribs: silver oval
Body: one-fifth black floss, remainder black seal's fur; black hackle on body and throat
Wings: pair of natural red hackles; tippet fibers; turkey; blue swan; Amherst; red swan; Spanish bustard; yellow; pintail; jungle cock; topping

MITCHELL
Tag: silver oval
Tail: topping and blue macaw (dyed white Guinea fowl)
Body: one-fifth orange seal's fur put on fine; one-fifth scarlet Berlin wool, picked out; remainder of body black floss ribbed with silver oval; medium yellow hackle over floss from first turn of ribs
Throat: black hackle
Wings: pair of black hackles; black swan; jungle cock; chatterer (kingfisher); topping

JOCK SCOTT
Tag: silver thread and lemon floss
Tail: topping and Indian crow (dyed tippet)
Butt: black ostrich
Body: in two equal sections. First joint: dyed golden quill over golden floss, ribbed with fine silver oval, butted above and below with two toucans (dyed hackles) and black ostrich. Second joint: black floss, ribbed with broad silver oval, black hackle
Throat: Guinea fowl
Wings: pair of grizzle hackles; mixture of blue swan, turkey, red swan, Spanish bustard, yellow swan; peacock fiber (sword feather); pintail; jungle cock; chatterer (kingfisher); topping

DUSTY MILLER
Tag: silver thread and medium yellow floss
Tail: topping
Butt: black ostrich
Ribs: silver oval
Body: silver embossed over white floss; light orange hackle
Throat: Guinea fowl
Wings: pair of grizzle hackles; mixture of Spanish bustard, blue swan, red swan, yellow swan; mallard; pintail; jungle cock; topping; blue macaw (dyed turkey)

SILVER GREY
Tag: silver thread and golden yellow floss
Tail: topping
Butt: black ostrich
Ribs: silver oval
Body: silver flat over white floss; silver coch-a-bonddu hackle
Throat: widgeon
Wings: pair of grizzle hackles; mixture of blue swan, turkey, red swan, Spanish bustard, yellow swan; pintail; jungle cock; topping

CHAPTER XIV.

THE ATLANTIC SALMON RIVERS OF AMERICA

THE SALMON RIVERS OF QUEBEC

The rivers of the Gaspé Peninsula are:

MATAPEDIA RIVER. Enters the Restigouche at the town of Matapedia. A beautiful salmon river, with very large fish. It was a favorite river of the Indians for spearing; some of the spears and irons seized by the wardens years ago, and now on exhibition at the main Restigouche clubhouse, are most interesting.

GRAND CASCAPEDIA RIVER. This river is noted for its large fish; probably more salmon of forty pounds and more have been taken here than from any other river in the world. The record is fifty-four and a quarter pounds, caught by Henry Nadeau. The average some years has been as high as twenty-eight pounds. The Grand Cascapedia, like the Restigouche, is an example of what good management will do; the river has been well protected and has never been over-fished. (The salmon rivers of Quebec are all under lease to prominent American and Canadian sportsmen.)

The following score, taken from the fishing records of Mr. W. B. Mershon, gives a good idea of the quality of the fishing on the Grand Cascapedia.

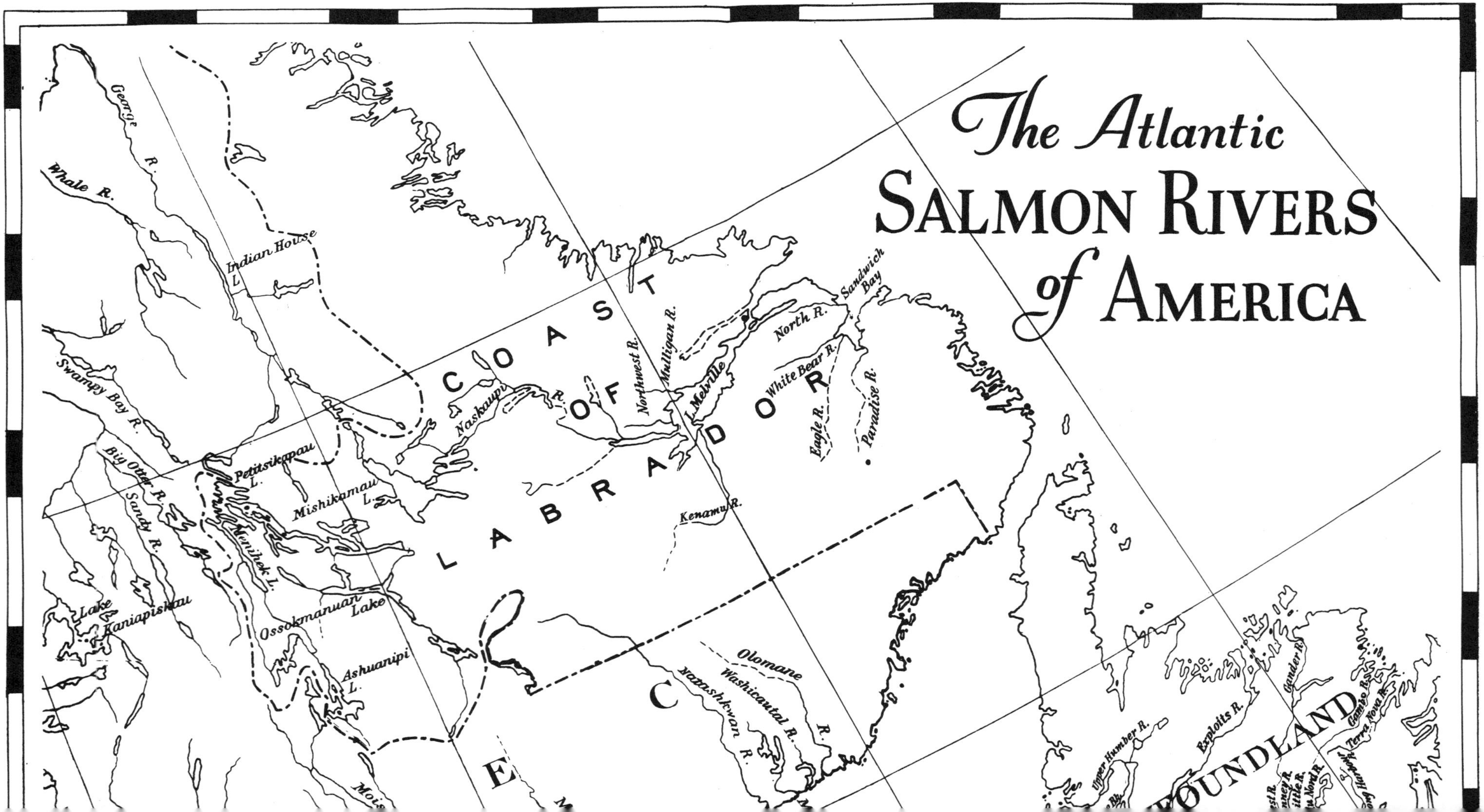
The Atlantic
SALMON RIVERS
of AMERICA
COAST OF LABRADOR
George R.
Whale R.
Indian House L.
Swampy Bay R.
Big Otter R.
Sandy R.
Lake Kaniapiskau
Petitsikapau L.
Mishikamau L.
Menihek L.
Ossokmanuan Lake
Ashuanipi L.
Naskaupi R.
Northwest R.
Mulligan R.
L. Melville
North R.
Sandwich Bay
White Bear R.
Eagle R.
Paradise R.
Kenamu R.
Olomane R.
Washicautal R.
Natashkwan R.
Upper Humber R.
Exploits R.
Gander R.
Gambo R.
Terra Nova R.
NEWFOUNDLAND

Mushalagan L.
Manikuagan R.
Trinity R.
Godbout R.
Betsiamites R.
Laval R.
St. Marguerite R.
Saguenay R.
River St. Lawrence
QUEBEC
MONTREAL
Anticosti Island
Gulf of St. Lawrence
Fishells R.
Robinsons R.
Middle Barachais R.
Crabbs R.
Highland R.
Codroy R.
Little R.
Dartmouth R.
York R.
St. John R.
Malbie R.
Grande R.
Madeleine R.
St. Anne de Monts R.
Grande Pabos R.
Bonaventure R.
L. Cascapedia R.
Gr. Cascapedia R.
Baie de Chaleur
Matapedia R.
Patapedia R.
Upsalquitch R.
Kedgwick R.
Restigouche R.
Tabusintic R
Nipisiquit R.
Renous R.
Miramichi R.
Tobique R.
St. John
Aroostook R.
NEW BRUNSWICK
St. John R.
FREDERICTON
Saint John
Penobscot R.
Bay of Fundy
Cape Breton Island
PRINCE EDWARD ISLAND
Margaree R.
NOVA SCOTIA
St. Mary R.
Ecum Secum R.
Moser R.
Salmon R.
Sheet Harbor R. E.&W.
Tangier R.
HALIFAX
Musquodoboit R.
Gold R.
Annapolis R.
Lahave R.
Wallace R.
Medway R.
Liverpool R.
Tusket R.
Salmon R.
Yarmouth

1925

June	W. B. Mershon	H. N. Torrey	J. B. Schlotman	Dr. C. R. Sumner
4.	Arrive at Cascapedia			
5.	River too high for fishing			
6.	Ditto			
7.	Sunday			
8.	34 lbs.	22, 22, 24 lbs.	31 lbs.	
9.	25, 32, 38	25	25, 27, 31, 41	
10.	29	22, 25	21, 20	
11.	24		25, 26, 24, 26, 26	
12.	22	22, 24, 26		
13.	24, 24, 26, 20, 22, 24, 21, 28	31, 34, 22, 27, 36, 22	15, 23, 25, 26, 27, 29	27, 20, 24, 23 lbs.
14.	Sunday			
15.	26, 22, 26, 26, 24, 29, 35, 24, 12			23, 13, 30
16.	25, 23, 25, 26, 23, 28, 22, 22			21, 27, 23, 20, 22, 27, 29
17.	12, 15, 23, 25, 13, 30, 26, 30			13, 16, 26, 13, 23, 13
18.	34, 27, 24, 26, 26, 21			22, 34, 28, 24
19.	30, 26, 14			27, 28, 21
20.	22, 29			14
21.	Sunday			
22.	32, 25, 25, 22, 26, 25			28, 22
23.	30, 24, 23, 12, 30			15
24.	25			
25.				28
Total	63	15	18	32

Mr. Mershon once took thirteen fish consecutively that averaged 30⅔ lbs.

LITTLE CASCAPEDIA RIVER. Very ordinary fishing; the salmon run small.
BONAVENTURE RIVER. Good-sized fish.
GRANDE PABOS RIVER. Fair fishing.
GRANDE RIVER. Good fishing.
MALBIE RIVER. Fair fishing.
ST. JOHN RIVER. Good fishing.
YORK RIVER. Large fish.
DARTMOUTH RIVER. The record fish of this stream weighed thirty-five pounds; the average is about fourteen. Good fishing.
MADELEINE RIVER. Large fish; forty-pounders are not infrequently taken.
STE. ANNE DES MONTS RIVER. Very fine fishing.

The rivers of the North Shore are:

STE. MARGUERITE RIVER. Enters the Saguenay; good fishing; the salmon run fairly large. There is another river of this name. See map.
LAVAL RIVER. Fair fishing.

BETSIAMITES RIVER. Fair fishing.

MANIKUAGAN RIVER. Good fishing.

GODBOUT RIVER. One of the most famous rivers on the North Shore, though the fishing is not as good now as it once was. During a great many years Americans could not get on this river, as a few Canadian and English sportsmen kept it to themselves; nor do I blame them.

TRINITY RIVER. Good fishing.

STE. MARGUERITE RIVER. Good fishing.

MOISIE RIVER. One of the great salmon rivers of the world; its fish run very large. I remember one season a few years ago when the average was about twenty-six pounds.

ST. JEAN RIVER. Fair.

MINGAN RIVER. A delightful river, but rather ordinary fishing.

NATASHQUAN RIVER. Mr. Joseph Knapp of New York, who has fished this river for a great many years, tells me that the average weight of its fish is about twelve pounds, but that in his catch each year there are sixty or seventy that average nineteen pounds. Thirty-one pounds is the river's record. (The alternate spelling, Natashkwan, is shown on the map.)

WASHICAUTAL RIVER. Fair fishing.

OLOMANE RIVER. Fair fishing.

THE SALMON RIVERS OF NEW BRUNSWICK

ST. JOHN RIVER. Free fishing and, as a rule, poor fishing, because of extensive netting.

TOBIQUE RIVER. A tributary of the Saint John. Fair fishing, but nets in the Saint John take many of this river's fish.

MIRAMICHI RIVER. There are several rivers which empty into Miramichi Bay. Though it is not good fishing, the best known of them is the Big Southwest. A great many salmon run up the river, but its water is so still and deep that they do not take well. Most of the fishing here is for kelts in the spring.

Little Southwest enters the head of the bay at Redbank. There has been a great deal of poaching here, but I understand that it has gradually been minimized. There are several camps on the river where a considerable number of salmon are taken at times.

The tidewater runs two or three miles above Redbank, and there the Northwest enters the bay. Mr. James C. Colgate of New York has a lodge at the junction of the Northwest and the Big Sovogle, and has good fishing. There is very good fishing at what is known as the Adams Camp a number of miles up the Northwest.

On the Sovogle, about eight miles above Mr. Colgate, there is good fishing at the Forks Camp, where the North and South Branches join at Square Fork and run through a very picturesque gorge.

There is very little poaching on the Northwest, as the various camps are interested in preventing it and the river is pretty well patrolled. There are a great number of set nets between the head of the bay and the town of New Castle, which hurt the fishing, but the chief harm is done by the drifters outside of the bay.

NIPISIGUIT RIVER. Once a famous river, but poor fishing now except at Grand Falls, twenty miles upstream. (The alternate spelling, Nipisiquit, is shown on the map.)

RESTIGOUCHE RIVER. One of the finest salmon rivers in the world, due to good protection and judicious fishing and stocking. This is a perfectly appointed river.

UPSALQUITCH RIVER. A tributary of the Restigouche. Good fishing at certain places, though the fish run small.

KEDGWICK RIVER. A tributary of the Restigouche. Good fishing. The fish run very large, any number of thirty-pounders and larger taken every year. The early June run averages about twenty-two pounds.

TABUSINTAC RIVER. This is a late river, the fishing beginning about the end of August. Does not amount to much.

RENOUS RIVER. Fair at times.

PATAPEDIA RIVER. A small tributary of the Restigouche. Not considered much of a salmon stream.

THE SALMON RIVERS OF NOVA SCOTIA

The season on Nova Scotia rivers opens February 1st and closes September 1st, except in Cape Breton, where it opens June 11th and closes October 1st, and a few rivers where it opens April 16th.

There are possibly two hundred salmon rivers in Nova Scotia, of which only the principal ones are listed hereinafter. The average weight of Nova Scotia fish is about fifteen pounds.

The principal rivers are:

ANNAPOLIS RIVER.
SALMON RIVER.
TUSKET RIVER.
LIVERPOOL RIVER. This river is good in May.
MEDWAY RIVER. Fish are taken here as early as February 1st, the opening day.
LAHAVE RIVER. Fish are caught here in the middle of February.
MUSQUODOBOIT RIVER.
TANGIER RIVER.
ST. MARY RIVER. Good early in May.
MARGAREE RIVER. A fish weighing fifty-two and a half pounds was taken here in 1927.

Some of the smaller rivers on the south coast are:

WALLACE RIVER. Good in May.
GOLD RIVER.
EAST SHEET HARBOUR RIVER.
WEST SHEET HARBOUR RIVER.
MOSER RIVER.
ECUM SECUM RIVER.

THE SALMON RIVERS OF NEWFOUNDLAND

There is no legal limit to the catch of salmon in Newfoundland, it being taken for granted that one is a good sportsman. The closed season is from September 15th to January 15th, and all the fishing on the island is free.

The following streams are within easy reach of the Newfoundland Railway system, and offer accommodations for fishermen:

UPPER HUMBER RIVER. Fishes well from the first of June to the first of September. Its fish run large.
CORNER BROOK. Large fish.
SPRUCE BROOK.
SERPENTINE RIVER. Fishes best in July and August, and yields large fish.
FOX ISLAND RIVER.

HARRY'S RIVER. Fishes best in July and August. Good-sized fish.

ST. GEORGE RIVER.

LITTLE BARACHOIS BROOK.

FLAT BAY BROOK. July and August are its two best months.

FISHEL'S RIVER. Small fish. (Appears on map as Fishells River.)

ROBINSON'S RIVER.

MIDDLE BARACHOIS BROOK. The fish run small here. (Appears on map as Middle Barachais River.)

CRABB'S RIVER.

HIGHLAND RIVER. This is a late river, fishing best in August and September.

CODROY RIVER. Some very large fish are taken here, occasionally a forty-pounder.

LITTLE CODROY RIVER. The fish run large here.

EXPLOITS RIVER. Fishes best in July and August.

GANDER RIVER. Fishes best from the middle of July to the middle of September.

GAMBO RIVER.

TERRA NOVA RIVER.

SOUTHEAST RIVER.

The following rivers on the south coast require camping outfits and are to be reached by coastwise boats:

BURNT ISLAND BROOK.

LA POILE RIVER.

GRANDY'S BROOK.

WHITE BEAR RIVER.

GREY OR LITTLE RIVER.

BAY D'EST RIVER. (Through error, appears on map as Brie D'est River.)

CONNEY RIVER.

LITTLE RIVER.

BAY DU NORD RIVER.

LONG HARBOUR RIVER.

THE SALMON RIVERS OF LABRADOR

The following rivers empty into Sandwich Bay:

NORTH RIVER.

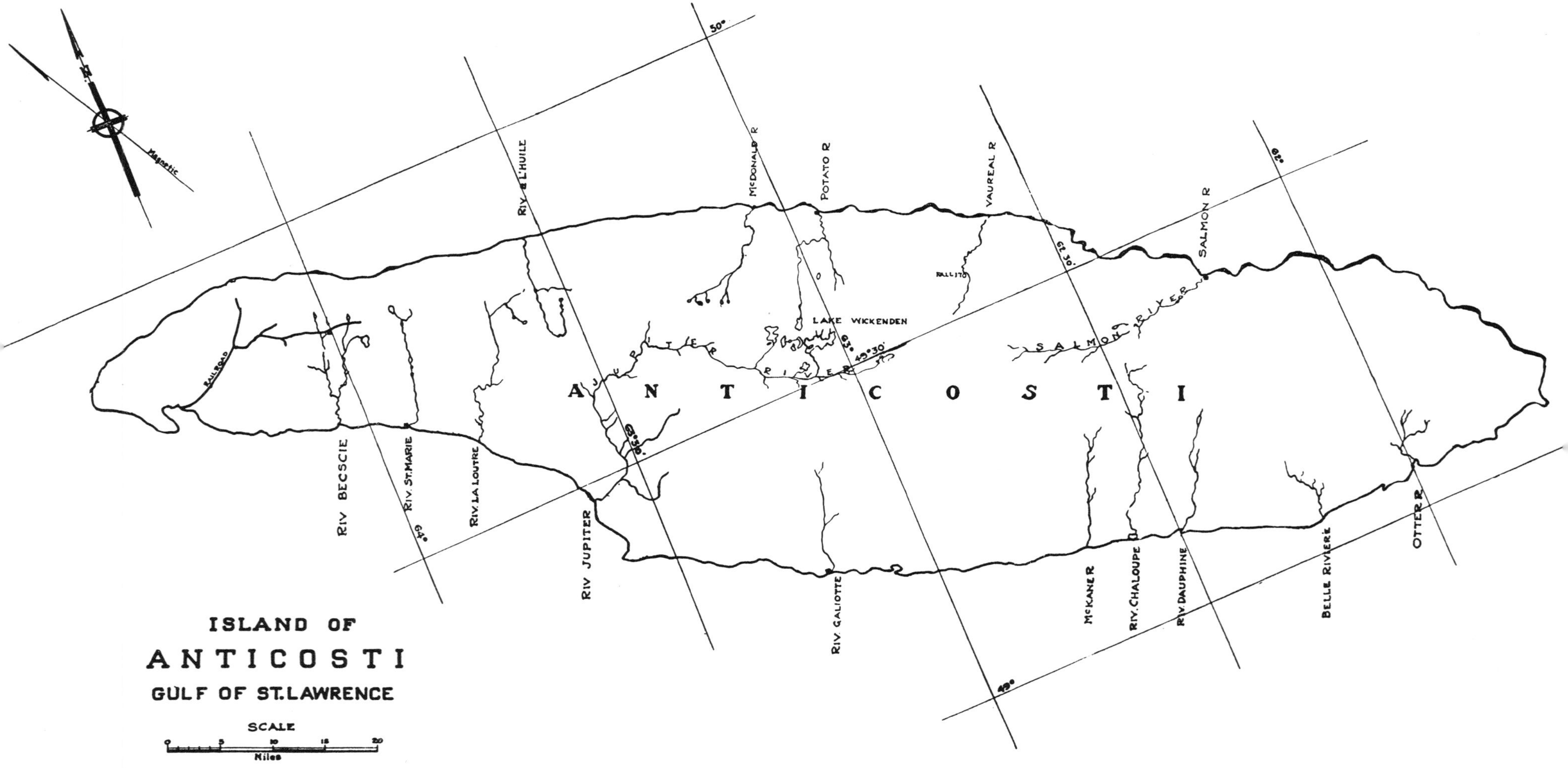
ISLAND OF
ANTICOSTI
GULF OF ST. LAWRENCE
SCALE
0 5 10 15 20
Miles
Magnetic
N
ANTICOSTI
RIV BECSCIE
RIV. ST. MARIE
RIV. LA LOUTRE
RIV. JUPITER
RIV. GALIOTTE
McKANE R
RIV. CHALOUPE
RIV. DAUPHINE
BELLE RIVIERE
OTTER R
RIV. à L'HUILE
McDONALD R
POTATO R
VAUREAL R
SALMON R
SALMON RIVER
JUPITER RIVER
LAKE WICKENDEN
RAILROAD
FALLS
50°
49°
64°
63°
62°
62 30'
63°30'
49°30'

WHITE BEAR RIVER.
EAGLE RIVER.
PARADISE RIVER.

The following flow into Lake Melville:

MULLIGAN RIVER.
NORTHWEST RIVER.
KENAMU RIVER.

Labrador salmon run small, a great many six- and seven-pound fish being taken. Small flies, dressed on Nos. 6 to 10 single hooks, fish best here.

Mr. George G. Williams of Farmington, Connecticut, who has fished more Labrador rivers than any other sportsman, tells me that he has had his best fishing on the following three rivers: the Eagle River; the St. Mary's River at St. Lewis Bay, ten miles from Battle Harbor; and a river at the head of Adlatok Bay, near Hopedale. (The latter two do not appear on the map.) The largest fish killed by Mr. Williams in Labrador weighed thirty pounds, from the Eagle River.

THE SALMON RIVERS OF THE STATE OF MAINE

PENOBSCOT RIVER. The Bangor Pool is the only salmon fishing on this river. Some years it yields a number of fish, but as a rule it is poor fishing. Most of the fish are taken by commercial fishermen. It has always been claimed by Maine people that a Penobscot River salmon has a finer flavor than fish from any of the rivers of Canada, but nothing could be farther from the fact. A Tobique or Restigouche fish, in my opinion, is of a much better and more delicate flavor. Salmon fishing in Maine has always been free, with poor protection, which is why there is none there today worth mentioning.

AROOSTOOK RIVER. A salmon river fifty years ago, but it has been ruined by dams built without fishways. Fishways are now being built, but it will require stocking on an enormous scale to produce any worthwhile results. A hatchery on the river, with a capacity of seven or eight million fry a year, and good protection would be the only means of restoring the river's fishing.

THE SALMON RIVERS OF ANTICOSTI ISLAND

Henri Meunier, who had amassed a fortune from his chocolate factories in France, gained control of the island in 1896 and established a private sporting preserve. The Meunier family retained possession of it for thirty-one years, until it was purchased by a group of newsprint companies who now own it.

The island may be reached by steamer from the city of Quebec in about thirty-six hours.

The best salmon rivers on the island are:

Rivière Becscie.
Rivière Ste. Marie.
Rivière La Loutre.
Jupiter River.
Rivière Galiotte.
Rivière Chaloupe.
Salmon River.
Potato River.
McDonald River.

There are comfortable camps and lodges to accommodate fishermen on the rivers listed above. The other rivers on the island, most of which are fished from tents, are:

McKane River.
Rivière Dauphine.
Belle Rivière.
Otter River.
Vaureal River. There is a comfortable lodge here.
Rivière l'Huile.

The fish at Anticosti weigh from six to twenty pounds, and the limit of twenty-eight fish a week is easily taken. The cost of fishing here is very reasonable for private water: $75 per rod per week.

INDEX

INDEX

A

Abbey fly, 45
Abe Moon Killer fly, 29-30, 37
  dressing of, 31
Accessibility of fishing, 6
Accommodations, 6
Ackroyd fly, 29, 37
Adams, Dan, 23
Adlatok Bay, 181
Alevin, 125, 133
Allen, Thomas, 35, 74, 145, 154
Almanacs, 108
Angleworms, fishing with, 129-130
Annapolis River, 179
Anticosti Island, 5
  salmon rivers of, 182
Aroostook River, 16, 181
Arthur Wood flies, 36, 39, 87, 89
Arthur Wood method, 35, 71, 87-91
  See also Greased line fishing
Atlantic Salmon. See Salmon
Atlantic Salmon Rivers of America, 175-182
  See also Salmon rivers
Atwood, Roy, 39
Ayer, F. W., 34, 37, 69-70, 80

B

Bag limit, New Brunswick, 59
Baker, Percy, 127
Bangor Pool, Aroostook River, 80, 181
Barometers, 94-95, 107-108
Bastard Black Dose fly. See Bastard Dose
Bastard Dose fly, 29, 36, 38, 98, 120, 121
Bay de Chaleur, 137, 146
Bay d'Est River, 180
Bay du Nord River, 180
Beaching salmon, 111
Bear, Newel, Indian guide, 16-17
Beauly Snow Fly, 29, 43
Becscie, Rivière, 182
Belle Rivière, 182
Betsiamites River, 177
Biddle, Moncure, 44
Big Falls, Nipisiguit River, 31
Big Sovogle River, 178
Black Dog fly, 29, 37
Black Dose fly, 25, 29, 36, 58, 98, 108, 150
  dressing of, 174
Black Gnat fly, 41
Black Goldfinch fly, 29, 37
Blue Charm fly, 36, 43, 89, 98, 112-113
  dressing of, 174
Blue Charm fly (summer series), dressing of, 173
Blue Doctor fly, 33, 37
Blue Dun fly, 44
Bogan Water, Nipisiguit River, 66
Bonaventure County, Quebec, 137, 139
Bonaventure River, 176
Bonbright dry fly, 34, 35, 44, 98
Bonbright, George D. B., 39, 44, 116
Broderick, Mike, guide, 15, 21, 32, 38
Brown Fairy fly, 29, 30, 36, 98, 166
  dressing of, 173
Brydges, 140
Buckland, Frank, 130
Bumble Bee fly, 38-39
Burnt Island Brook, 180
Burtis, George, 43
Burtis, Judge, 43

C

Calderwood, W. C., 131, 144
Camp cooks. See Cooks
Canadian Black Dose fly. See Black Dose
Canoes, 50, 55-56, 80
  Chestnut, 56
  equipment, 15, 99
  White, 56
Cape Breton Island, 178
Caribou Dam, Aroostook River, 16-17
Cascapedia River. See Grand Cascapedia River. See also Little Cascapedia River
Casting, 12, 47-53, 70-71
  developing accuracy, 48
  dry fly, 81
  fundamentals of, 48-50
  greased line, 88-91, 112, 116-117
  learning, 47-48
  practicing, 49-50

single-hand rod, 109
standing position, 107
wet fly, 56-57, 100, 102, 104
Casts, curve, 80-85
Galway, 51-52
loop, 50-51
"mending," 49, 100
overhead, 48, 50
Spey, 50-51
switch, 50-51
Wye, 51
"Cat's Whiskers" fly, 44
Causapscal fly, 29, 37, 38
Chaloupe, Rivière, 182
Chubb, Percy, 33
Clothes, fishing, advisability of inconspicuous, 14
cost of, 99
Club membership, 1-2
cost of, 1
dues and expenses, 2
Codroy River, 180
Cold weather, 106-107
Colgate, James C., 178
Commercial fishing, 137-139
Conney River, 180
Cooks, camp, 6, 14, 18, 147-148
Corner Brook, 179
Crabb's River, 180
Crossfield, 154, 167

D

Dams in salmon rivers, 16, 144
Dartmouth River, 39, 176
Dauphine, Rivière, 182
De Forest, Henry, 5, 43, 141
Dressing flies. See Fly dressing
"Dropping," 11, 100, 102
Dropping water, 95, 101, 105-106
Dry flies, 34, 35, 44, 79, 81, 98, 115-116
presentation of, 80-86
Dry fly fishing, 5, 25, 71-72, 79-86, 110, 113-114, 115-116
behavior of fish, 117
hooking, 116
leaders for, 112
rods for, 79-81, 111-112
seasonal considerations, 120-121
Dry fly water, 5, 80, 83-86, 110
Dunn, George, 2
Durham Ranger fly, 41, 61, 63
dressing of, 163-165
Dusty Miller fly, 25, 29, 30, 36, 98, 108, 118, 167
dressing of, 174

E

Eagle River, 181
Eagles, General, 32, 42
East Sheet Harbour River, 179
Ecum Secum River, 179
Eight Mile Pool, Little Main Restigouche River, 63, 77, 85
Elevation of rod while playing, 101, 103
Emmet, Col. Robert, 13
English Black Dose fly, 32
Etiquette and customs, 147-148
Exploits River, 180

F

Farlow & Co., 150, 157
"Fat Mary" fly, 32, 109, 160
Faulding, Percy, guide, 9, 71
Finnemore, Howard, guide, 38, 39, 64, 77
"Fish sense," 61-62
Fishel's River, 180
Fisheries Act of 1869, 138
Fishways, 144, 181
Fitch, Ezra, 148
Five Finger Pool, Little Main Restigouche River, 85-86
Flat Bay Brook, 180
Fleming, 140
Flies, all-hackle dry flies, 44
Arthur Wood, 36, 39, 87, 89
box for, 98-99
bright patterns, 63-64
cost of, 98
Dee patterns, 162
dressing. See Fly dressing
dressings of favorite, 173-174
dry. See Dry flies
earliest use of for salmon, 172
factors governing choice of, 42
favorite, 30, 173, 174
for evening fishing, 109-110
for various uses, 32-39, 40-45, 63-64
hair, 44-45
Kelson's, 32, 42-43
lightly dressed, 35, 42-43, 71, 109
low-water, 112-113
dressings of, 38, 171

number of patterns in use, 29
position on water, 12
presentation of, 31, 58-60, 66, 88-91
range of patterns, 31-32
size of, 60, 67-68, 89, 98, 107, 108, 118
speed of, 60, 91
Spey patterns, 37, 162
styles in, 30
successful, 37
testing on short leader, 76
why salmon take, 40-41
why successful, 37
worn-out, 108
Fly boxes, 98-99
cost of, 99
Fly dressing, 149-174
all-hackle dry flies, 172-173
bodies, 158-163
British methods of, 150-151
butt, 157
case for materials, 149
dressings of favorite flies, 173-174
finishing, 170
hackles, 162-163
materials for, 44, 149, 150, 152, 171, 172
tag, 155-158
tail, 156-157
tools for, 149, 151, 152
wings, 162-170
Fly tying. See Fly dressing
Fog, 59, 93-94, 107
"Forest and Stream," 139
Fox Island River, 179
Francis, Newel, Indian guide, 15, 93-94
Free fishing, 2, 8
Fry, 130, 133, 143

G

Gaffing, 12-13, 103, 110
Gaffs, 99
Galiotte, Rivière, 182
Gambo River, 180
Gander River, 180
Gaspé boats, 15, 50, 64, 65, 80, 147
equipment of, 55
Gaspé County, Quebec, 137, 139
Gloucester County, New Brunswick, 137
Godbout River, 177
Goelet, Robert W., 141
Gold River, 179
Grand Cascapedia River, 20, 24, 30, 32, 39, 58, 64, 99, 116, 127, 128, 132, 137, 175-176
Grande River, 176
Grand Lake Stream, 45
Grand Pabos River, 176
Grandy's Brook, 180
Greased line fishing, 87-91, 112-113, 116-117. See also Arthur Wood method
casting, 88-91, 112, 116-117
flies, 87, 89
hooking, 113
invention by Arthur Wood, 87
leaders for, 112
preparations for, 87, 112
presentation of fly, 88-91
seasonal considerations, 89-91, 120-121
speed of fly, 91
Green Drake fly, 29, 30, 37, 38
Green, George, guide, 77
Greenwell's Glory fly, 44, 153
Grey or Little River, 180
Grilse, 118-121, 127, 134, 136
Grilse fishing, 119-120, 127
tackle for, 118-119
Griswold, Frank Gray, 33, 81, 130
Griswold Gray fly, 29, 33, 36, 98
dressing of, 174
Grizzly King fly, 45
Guides, 69, 147-148
care of tackle by, 14
duties and prerogatives of, 11-14, 18, 55-56
knowledge of pool, 14
position in boat, 55
requisites for, 11-12
selection of, 11-18

H

Hail, 93
Hair flies, 44-45
method of fishing, 45
Hale, 163
Hallock, Charles, 139
Hanson Pool, St. John River, New Brunswick, 37
Harry's River, 180
Hartland Pool, St. John, New Brunswick, 4, 30
Hart's Island Pool, St. John River, 74
Hatching, artificial, 130, 134, 138, 139, 146-147

Hewitt, Edward R., "Secrets of the Salmon," 79
Highlander fly, 29
Highland River, 180
High water, 118
Hooking salmon, 12, 60, 75, 88, 100-101, 102, 104, 113, 116
Hooks, 19, 39-40, 109
  Dee irons, 19
  double, 40
  dry fly, 39
  eyed, 34
  Hardy's Oval Wire, 39
  Rational, 39
  size of, 30, 63
  with gut loop, 34
Howard, Austie, guide, 67-68
Howard, Manzer, guide, 23, 43, 70, 105, 147
Howard, Murray, guide, 60, 86
Howe, Major, 18
Hughes, Reginald, 71
Hutton, J. Arthur, 132-133

I

Improving salmon water, 141-143
Insects, natural, 85-86

J

Jacquet River, 137
Jam Pool, Kedgwick River, 57
Jefferson, Joe, 18
"Jigging" grilse, 119
"Jigging" salmon, 111
"Jim," 97, 99-121
Jock Scott fly, 25, 29, 36, 98, 104, 109, 118, 127, 150, 151, 154, 156, 157, 161, 165, 167, 169
  dressing of, 174
  invention of, 29
Jumping salmon, 73-74, 102, 126, 144
Jupiter River, 182

K

Kedgwick River, 38, 41, 57, 60, 63, 77, 125, 126, 134, 140, 178
Kelson, 32, 152, 153, 163, 172
  "exaggeration and modification" method, 63
  flies, 32, 42-43
  "Salmon Fly, The," 42, 152, 153
  theory of river's color, 38
  "Tips," 42
Kelt, 128
  ratio of return, 125, 132-133
  "slink," 128
  value of, 131
  "well-mended," 132-133
Kelt fishing, 131
  unsportsmanlike, 133
Kenamu River, 181
Killick, 11, 15, 56
Killing, 12
Knapp, Claude, 35, 37, 38, 62-63, 77, 128, 154
Knapp, Joseph P., 60, 61, 177
Knots, 40
  Blood, 40
  Cairnton, 40
  figure-eight, 12, 40
  Turle, 40
  water, 40

L

Labrador, salmon rivers of, 180
La Branche, George, 34, 79-81, 87
  "Salmon and the Dry Fly," 79
Lady Amherst fly, 39
Lady Caroline fly, 29
Lahave River, 179
L'Huile, Rivière, 182
Lake Melville, 181
La Loutre, Rivière, 182
Landing salmon, 101, 103, 110
La Poile River, 180
Laval River, 176
Leader box, 98-99
  cost of, 99
Leader case, 98-99
  cost of, 99
Leaders, 22-23, 98, 108
  box for, 98-99
  case for, 98-99
  cost of, 98
  dry fly, 81, 98, 112, 114-115
  for greased line fishing, 112
  level, 22
  tapered, 23
  testing, 22-23
Leased water, cost of, 7
  kinds of, 3, 139-140
Leasing salmon water, 2-9

INDEX

Leonard, Hiram, 20, 23
Lightly dressed flies, 35, 42-43, 71, 109
Lightning, 94
Lines, 24, 98
  backing, 24, 98
  care of, 14, 22
  cost of, 24, 98
  dry fly, 81
Little Barachois Brook, 180
Little Cascapedia River, 176
Little Codroy River, 180
Little Inky Boy fly, 32, 43, 162
Little Main Restigouche River, 37, 38, 62, 85, 127, 140
Little River, 180
Little Tobique River, 67
Liverpool River, 179
Log drives, 2
Lola, Nick, Indian guide, 15
"London Field, The," 35
"London Fishing Gazette," 32
Long Harbour River, 180
Low water, 65-66
  greased line fishing, 90
  tackle for, 171
Low-water flies, dressings of, 38, 171

M

McDonald River, 182
McKane River, 182
Mack, Jack, guide, 12, 53, 94
Madeleine River, 176
Maine, salmon rivers of, 181
Malbie River, 176
Manikuagan River, 177
March Brown fly, 44
Margaree River, 2, 5, 179
Mar Lodge fly, 29, 36, 98
Marston, 32
Matapedia River, 37, 38, 80, 175
Materials, for fly dressing, 44, 149, 150, 152, 171, 172
Meadows Pool, Kedgwick River, 60
Medway River, 123, 179
Melicete Indians, 15-16
  reservation of, 15, 93, 126
"Mending" casts, 49
Menzies, 131-132
Mershon, William B., 68, 175-176
Meunier, Henri, 182
Middle Barachois Brook, 180
Mingan River, 177
Miramichi Bay, 177-178
Miramichi River, 2, 12, 30, 31, 37, 41, 53, 130, 134, 177-178
Mitchell, Archibald, 80
Mitchell fly, 29
  dressing of, 174
Moccasins, 107
Moisie River, 177
Mole dry fly, 79, 98
Monell, Col. Ambrose, 79
Monell dry fly, 79, 98, 114
Montreal fly, 30
Moser River, 179
Moulton, Tom, Indian guide, 15-16
Mowat, Alex, 4, 127, 141
Mowat, Fred, 127-128
Mowat, John, 139, 141
Mowat, Max, 4, 127, 141
Mowat, W. A., 141
Mulligan River, 181
Murray, guide, 77
Musquodoboit River, 179

N

Nadeau, Henry, 175
Natashquan River, 20, 60-61, 177
Nets, 25-26
Netting, of salmon, 119, 137-138
New Brunswick, salmon rivers of, 177-178
Newfoundland, salmon rivers of, 179-180
Nicholson fly, 31, 151
Night Hawk fly, 29, 30, 36, 67, 98, 100, 102, 118, 153
  dressing of, 173-174
Nipisiguit Grey fly, 29, 31, 37, 38
Nipisiguit River, 2, 31, 37, 57, 66, 137, 178
Northcote, Lord, 18
"North Country Angler, The," 172
North River, 180
Northwest River, 181
Nova Scotia, salmon rivers of, 178-179
Nymph fishing, 35

O

Ocean feeding of salmon, 136
Octave, guide, 69-70
Olomane River, 177
Otter River, 182

P

Pabineau Falls, Nipisiguit River, 2, 31, 57

Paradise River, 181
Parmacheene Belle fly, 157
Parr, 125, 126-127, 133, 136, 143
  tagging, 127
Patapedia River, 140, 178
"Patent," the, 44-45
Penobscot River, 181
Pink Lady fly, 34
  dry fly, 79, 98
Plaster Rock, Tobique River, 126
Playing salmon, 12, 75-77, 80, 101, 103, 114, 119, 121
  elevation of rod while, 26, 101, 103
  "jigging" salmon, 111
  "minute to pound" in, 13
  sulking fish, 13-14
  with single-hand rod, 109
Poaching, 144-146
Pools, 73
  approaching, 11, 56, 99
  for dry fly fishing, 83-84
  ideal, 3-4
  improving, 142-143
  names of, 3
  position of fish in, 57, 64, 83-84, 142
  resting, 57, 65-66
  "rocking," 57-58
  seasonal considerations, 3
  "sore spots" in, 58
Popham fly, 151, 161, 162
Potato River, 182
Predators, 130, 143-144
Private water, 1-2
  inexpensive, 7
  leasing, 2-9
  securing accommodations upon, 6-8, 97-98
Professor fly, 30, 157
Protection, of salmon water, 143-146
  cost of, 140, 141
Pryce-Tannatt, 39, 154, 163, 172
  "How to Dress Salmon Flies," 154, 163, 172
  rational hooks, 39

Q

Quebec, salmon rivers of, 175-177

R

Rain, 93, 118
Reels, 20-21, 24
  cost of, 24, 98
  Tobique, 21, 24, 98
Renous River, 178
Restigouche County, New Brunswick, 137
Restigouche Riparian Association, 127, 141
Restigouche River, 4, 5, 8, 12, 20, 23, 24, 32, 33, 35, 38, 43, 57, 63-65, 80, 94, 99, 109, 124, 125, 127, 132, 133, 134, 146, 147, 175, 178, 181
  history of, 137-141
  Little Main. See Little Main Restigouche River
Restigouche Salmon Club, 5, 140
Richards, Wesley, 151
Riley Brook, Tobique River, 67
Rising water, 66-67, 114
"Riverside information," 3
Robinson's River, 180
Rock Pool, Grand Cascapedia River, 64
Rods, 19-20, 23, 24, 107
  bamboo, 20
  care of, 14, 23
  cost of, 24, 98
  dry fly, 79-81, 111-112
  elevation of while playing, 26, 101, 103
  finish of, 23
  fittings of, 23
  for greased line fishing, 89-90
  for grilse fishing, 25, 118-119
  Leonard, 20
  made by Indians, 16
  new, care of, 23
  Payne, 23, 98
  single-hand, 109
  Thomas, 20
Rogan, Michael, 172
Rogers, Col. Archibald, 21, 32, 35, 38, 63, 109
Rogers, Col. Edmund P., 44
Rube Wood fly, 30, 41

S

Saguenay River, 176
St. George River, 180
St. Jean River, 177
St. John River, New Brunswick, 30, 37, 38, 39, 41, 71, 73, 74, 93, 126, 177
St. John River, Quebec, 176
St. Mary River, Nova Scotia, 179
St. Mary's River, Labrador, 181
St. Mary's River, Nova Scotia, 123
Ste. Anne des Monts River, 33, 176

INDEX

Ste. Marguerite River, 176
Ste. Marguerite River, 177
Ste. Marie, Rivière, 182
Salmon, adapted to native river, 129
  alevin. See Alevin
  and dry fly, 117
  artificial hatching of. See Hatching, artificial
  beaching, 111
  behavior in pools, 3-4
  condition of, early in season, 134
    late in season, 127, 134
  cruising, 85-86, 108
  effect of concussion upon, 72
  effects of weather upon, 126
  enter rivers to spawn, 123
  foul-hooked, 77
  fry. See Fry
  grilse. See Grilse
  habits in fresh water, 41
  hooked, 75-76
  increase in weight of, 132, 136
  incubation period of eggs, 125
  "jigging," 111
  jumping, 73-74, 102, 126, 144
  kelt. See Kelt
  length of life of, 130, 135
  life history of, 123-136
  loss of weight by, 134
  manner of rising to fly, 41, 61-62, 74-75, 101, 102, 108, 115
  number of eggs deposited, 125
  number of returns to river, 125
  number which return, 130
  obstacles to reaching spawning ground, 124
  ocean feeding of, 123
  ocean travel of, 123-124
  packing and shipping, 7-8
  parr. See Parr
  percentages of loss, 130
  position above rapids, 69-70
  position in pools, 57, 64, 83-84, 142
  predatory enemies of, 130, 143-144
  productivity of spawn, 125
  ratio of return, 134
  reaction to pollution, 143
  remaining in river for winter, 128
  return to native river, 123
  return to sea, 124-125
  river life of, 135-136
  running up river, 104
  runs of, 104, 106, 118, 126, 134, 139
  sleeping, 57
  smoked, 14
  smolt. See Smolt
  spawning process, 124
  spawning season, 124
  spearing, 16-17
  speed of travel of, 125-126
  split tails, 120-121
  spring, 134
  stages in life of, 133
  sulking, 13-14
  summer, 134
  vision of, 66, 68
  waste in life of, 131
  why take fly, 40-41
"Salmon and the Dry Fly," La Branche, 87
Salmon fishing trip, 97-121
  expenses of, 97
  planning, 97-99
  preparations for, 97-99
  seasonal considerations, 97, 121
  tackle, 98-99
Salmon flies. See Flies
"Salmon Fly, The," Kelson, 42, 152, 153
Salmon fly dressing. See Fly dressing
Salmon River, 179
Salmon River, Anticosti Island, 182
Salmon rivers, of Anticosti Island, 182
  of Labrador, 180
  of Maine, 181
  of New Brunswick, 177-178
  of Newfoundland, 179-180
  of Nova Scotia, 178-179
  of Quebec, 175-177
Salmon water, accommodations upon, 6-8, 97-98
  advance in price of, 8
  club membership, 1-2
  cost of protecting, 140, 141
  early leasing of, 2
  for dry fly fishing, 5, 80, 83-86, 110
  free fishing, 2
  improving, 141-143
  leasing, 2-9
  over-fished, 73
  poaching, 144-146
  pollution of, 143
  private, 1-9
  protecting, 143-146
  rental prices of, 139-141
  stocking, 138, 139, 146-147

wardening, 144-146
Sandwich Bay, 180
Scale reading, 134-136
Schlotman, J. B., 176
Scores, fishing, 121, 176
Scott, Jock, 29
Scott, Lord, 29
Scows, 65
"Secrets of the Salmon," Hewitt, 79
Serpentine River, 126, 134
Serpentine River, Newfoundland, 179
"Setting in," 99
Shaw, Fred, 70
Silver Betty fly, 45
Silver Blue fly, 36, 89, 98, 162
dressing of, 173
Silver Bob fly, 45
Silver Doctor fly, 29, 33, 167
Silver Grey fly, 25, 29, 36, 58, 98, 119, 127, 150, 160, 162, 167
dressing of, 174
Silver Wilkinson fly, 29, 37
Skiff Lake Club, 17
Smolt, 125, 133, 143
Southeast River, 180
Spruce Brook, 179
Stewart, John, 18
Stocking salmon water, 138, 139, 146-147
Sumner, Dr. C. R., 176
Sunday rule, 59-60

T

Tabusintac River, 178
Tackle, 19-27, 98-99
adequate outfit, 25
complete outfit, 24, 98-99
cost of, 98, 99
flies. See Flies
gaffs. See Gaffs
leaders. See Leaders
light-weight, fad for, 20
preparing for fishing, 99
reels. See Reels
rods. See Rods
"Tailing" salmon, 112-113
Tangier River, 179
Teagle Bee fly, 45
Teagle, Walter C., 44
Temperature of water, 95
Terra Nova River, 180
Thermometers, 94-95
Thomas, Fred, 20, 21
Thompson, Col. Lewis, 35, 44, 63
Thunder, 59, 94, 106
Thunder and Lightning fly, 29, 32, 36, 98
dressing of, 174
"Tips," Kelson, 42
Tobique River, 5, 13, 15, 18, 20, 23, 30, 32, 33, 37, 38, 67, 73, 74, 93, 125, 126, 127, 134, 145, 177, 181
Tomah Joe fly, 157
Tom's Brook Pool, Restigouche River, 4, 8, 30, 57, 65, 125
Tools, for fly dressing, 149, 151, 152
Torrey, H. N., 176
Torrish fly, 37
Towing, 64-65
Trinity River, 177
Tusket River, 179
Tying flies. See Fly dressing

U

Upper Humber River, 179
Upsalquitch River, 178

V

Vanderbeck, Lindsey, guide, 69
Vaureal River, 182

W

Waders, 99
cost of, 99
Wainright Lodge, Tobique River, 13
Wainright Pool, 13
Wallace River, 179
Wardening, 144-146
Washicautal River, 177
Waters, Jimmy, guide, 13
Weather, 59, 93-95
almanacs, 108
barometers, 94-95, 107-108
cold, 106-107
effect upon fishing, 93-95
effect upon salmon, 126
fishing calendars, 94-95
fog, 59, 93-94, 107
hail, 93
ideal conditions, 95
rain, 93, 118
temperature of water, 95
thermometers, 94-95
thunder, 106

thunder and lightning, 94
West Sheet Harbour River, 179
Wet fly fishing, 55-77, 99-111
Wharton, Edith, 31
White Bear River, 180, 181
White Miller fly, 41
Williams, George G., 181
Wood, Arthur, 87, 89, 90
method. See Arthur Wood method. See also Greased line fishing
Wyers, Jack, 4, 5, 30, 66, 67

Y

York River, 176